Contents

H50 150 072 2

Please renew/return this item by the last date shown.

So that your telephone call is charged at local rate, please call the numbers as set out below:

7/12 999

	From Area codes 01923 or 0208:	From the rest of Herts:
Renewals:	01923 471373	01438 737373
Enquiries:	01923 471333	01438 737333
Minicom:	01923 471599	01438 737599

155.
904
MON

Hertfordshire
COUNTY COUNCIL
Community Information

- 3 APR 2004

2 4 MAY 2003

2 9 JUL 2004

0 5 MAR 2005

2 0 JUN 2003
- 3 JUL 2003

3 0 SEP 2002

← 6 NOV 2002   2 1 AUG 2003

0 3 MAY 2005

24 MAY 2005

27 JUN 2005

2 5 FEB 2003   1 3 OCT 2003

1 0 DEC 2003

Mon 5th Jan
26th Jan

- 9 JAN 2006

1 6 APR 2003

13 MAY 2009

16 JUL 2010

- 6 AUG 2010 -

L32a

L32

YOU AND STRESS

BOB MONTGOMERY, BA, PhD, MAPsS
and **LYNETTE EVANS,** BBSc, MPsych.

PENGUIN BOOKS

PENGUIN BOOKS

Published by the Penguin Group
Penguin Books Australia Ltd, Ringwood, Victoria, Australia
Penguin Books Ltd, 27 Wrights Lane, London W8 5TZ, England
Penguin Books USA Inc., 375 Hudson Street, New York, New York 10014, USA
Penguin Books Canada Ltd, 10 Alcorn Avenue, Toronto, Ontario, Canada M4V 3B2
Penguin Books (NZ) Ltd, 182-190 Wairau Road, Auckland 10, New Zealand

Penguin Books Ltd, Registered Offices: Harmondsworth, Middlesex, England

First published in Australia by Thomas Nelson 1984
Viking O'Neil edition 1989
Published in Penguin Books 1995

10 9 8 7 6 5 4 3 2 1

Copyright © Bob Montgomery and Lynette Evans, 1984
Printed in Australia by Australian Print Group, Maryborough, Victoria

National Library of Australia
Cataloguing-in-Publication data
Montgomery, Bob, 1943–
  You and stress

ISBN 0 14 025046 8 (pbk.).

1. Stress (Psychology). 2. Self-care, Health. I. Evans, Lynette. II. Title.

155.9042

INTRODUCTION

Stress is a very broad notion. Its possible ill effects are many, both physical and psychological, so any worthwhile guide to managing stress effectively must inevitably become a guide to living successfully. From our clinical experience of helping individuals with stress problems, and our consulting experience conducting stress-management courses for groups in business and industry, we have identified the living skills whose absence or weakness seem to be the most common cause of stress problems. This book sets out, in as concrete and practical a manner as possible, how you can acquire or strengthen the living skills appropriate to you to help you manage the stress in your life more effectively.

Stress is not the sudden scourge of the late twentieth century. It is not even necessarily bad for you. Stress is an inevitable and desirable part of being alive. The only people completely free of stress are dead ones – that is one way of managing stress, but we don't recommend it. The trick is to manage the inevitable stress in your life so that it works for you, and not against you.

Self-help books seem to be like guinea pigs: every time you turn around there are more of them. Their rate of proliferation is only exceeded by the number of extravagant promises made in each one. Sadly, careful reviews of these books most often show little or no evidence to support their claims or to warrant their purchase. (In some areas, such as sexual difficulties, some people have had their problems made worse by trying to apply some of the self-help advice around.) You may already have had a discouraging experience of trying out the advice in one of these books.

Before you decide that there must be something wrong with you, consider the alternative explanation: the authors didn't really know how to tell you what would be genuinely helpful.

Our stress-management programme, as outlined in this book, is based on our clinical and consulting experience, and on current experimental clinical research. We are confident of the effectiveness of this approach, if applied appropriately and correctly. Our programme is not a panacea. It requires persistence to carry it through and it may mean personal discomfort as you face up to problems you have been avoiding. Getting support from family, friends or a professional therapist can help you maintain the effort and cope with the discomfort.

Self-help has two major advantages. First, and most obviously, it's cheaper! If you are able to apply the programme in this book successfully, all it will have cost is the price of the book. It will also cost you persistent effort and occasional discomfort, but that is not as bad as the costs arising from not doing something about your problem.

Second and more subtle, but very important, the gains you make from your own efforts are readily seen as just that: all your own work. Seeing yourself cope better is the best way of increasing your self-esteem. This is a key ingredient of successful stress-management. When you are faced with new problems in the future, your increased confidence in yourself should help you tackle them successfully, too. You won't be tempted, as some therapy clients are, to see new problems as indicating you need another dose of therapy.

Successful self-help means doing two things. First, you must identify your problem correctly, including its extent and any complications, so that you obtain the appropriate self-help manual. Second, you must follow the self-help programme correctly and fully so that you get the maximum benefit from it. Failures in self-help usually result from mistakes in one or both of these two areas.

For example, you may decide your problem is insomnia and that you will solve it by working through a self-help insomnia-management programme (there is quite a good one, mentioned later). What you haven't recognised is that your difficulty in going to sleep is really the result of the tension you have built up during the day and your habit of reviewing that day's problems when you go to bed. Unless you learn how to reduce your daily tension, stop worrying unnecessarily and cope more effectively with your daily problems, a simple insomnia-management programme is not likely to give you any lasting help with your sleeping difficulty.

Or, suppose you have decided that you have a stress problem which you intend to solve by working through this book. But when you get to Chapter 3, which discusses recreation and exercise, you decide that you have never been very 'sporty' so you will skip the advice in that chapter. Later, when you are still over-involved in your job and not very fit, you may wonder why the programme doesn't seem to be helping you.

In Chapter 1 and at some other points in the book, we have set out some practical steps to help you identify the level, causes and effects of your stress. Go through these steps carefully to identify which parts of the programme are relevant to you. If you are in doubt about including any part, try it to see if it helps. You will lose less by doing a few unnecessary exercises than you will if you leave out a step that would have been helpful to you.

Throughout, we have described practical steps to help you manage the stress in your life more effectively. Follow these steps as closely and fully as possible. What seems to you to be a small change in the programme could make a big difference to how it works.

If you have a lot of trouble with either of these tasks – assessing your stress problems or following the programme – or if you have tried self-help as well as you can but it doesn't seem to be working, don't despair. That probably just means that self-help isn't for you.

IS THIS BOOK FOR YOU?

This book is for anyone who wants to learn to manage stress more effectively. That could mean that you already think you are having a problem with stress, and you want some advice on how to solve it. This does not necessarily mean you are a high-powered executive with a jet-age job. As you will see later, stress problems are more likely amongst people with many demands but little autonomy, like middle-level management, or boring and monotonous jobs, like many work-face employees and housewives.

But we believe this manual will be just as helpful, if not more so, for people who don't necessarily see themselves as having a real stress 'problem' but who believe they could be getting more out of life. Modern psychology strongly rejects the old-fashioned view that you are either 'ill' – with visible signs, symptoms or problems – or 'healthy' – with no visible signs, symptoms or problems. Health professionals nowadays regard health, including both physical and psychological well-being, as a continuum. You can range from being very ill, through to not living or feeling anywhere near as well as you could, up to being very fit and living very successfully and enjoyably.

Curing illness and solving problems are the traditional aims of clinical practice. But it is just as important, and usually much more cost-effective, to prevent illness and problems and to promote higher levels of health and well-being. Problem prevention and health promotion deserve much more priority than they are currently given in Australia, although there are hopeful signs that this is changing.

We believe this manual is well-suited to people who want to prevent stress from becoming a problem for them, and who would like to increase their success and enjoyment from life, as well as to those who think they already have a stress problem.

SOME LIMITATIONS

We have not been able to cover in this book all the problems which can cause or contribute to stress. For example, chronic pain can naturally cause stress, and your stress levels may exacerbate your experience of pain. We do not offer any advice on pain-management because this has already been done very well. There are sensible and effective steps you can take to manage pain, and Dr Connie Peck has set them out very clearly in her manual, *Chronic Pain*, published as a paperback by Fontana.

A major source and result of personal stress is often a distressed marriage. Indeed, some research has found that, for senior executives, their marriages are more likely to be serious causes of stress than are their jobs! Of course, this can be the result of over-devotion to their jobs, accompanied by neglect of their relationships. The practical implication is that they will gain most by working on improving their relationships. The same applies to many housewives. If you decide your relationship is a part of your stress problem, we recommend our self-help manual *Living and Loving Together*, also published by Viking O'Neil. In that book, we have also included advice on how to make better relationships with your children, if they have become stressful for you.

(We have outlined in Chapter 9 of this book, since it is not covered by the other, some steps for starting relationships. A lack of social or intimate relationships, and the resulting loneliness, are often a part of a person's stress problems.)

There is one final major limitation of this programme we want to spell out clearly. A central assumption underlying traditional psychotherapy was the belief that the cause, and therefore the solution, of a person's problems lay within the person, or as it is often put, 'It's all in your head'.

Even if we extend that to include the rest of your body, as we do in Chapters 1, 2 and 3, it's still not true. Stress is an interaction between you and your environment. Following our programme, you can strengthen your skills for coping with the stress your environment puts on you, and you can increase your ability to change your environment.

But single-handedly you cannot change the world. If you decide that a major part of your stress problem is a failing marriage, and your spouse refuses to accept that or do anything constructive about it, you have two choices. Quit the relationship as constructively as possible (we have explained how to do this in *Living and Loving Together*), or choose to put up with it.

Similarly, you may decide that your job is your major source of stress. You might improve it by becoming more assertive (see Chapter 4), by communicating better (see Chapter 5), or doing some problem-solving (see Chapter 6). But unless you are able to convince those you work with to undertake the wholesale redesign of work outlined in Chapter 10, all your efforts may only serve to lessen the impact of an intrinsically stressful work situation. Again, you have two choices.

We do not believe leaving your spouse is a trivial step and a decision to quit your job may be difficult when jobs are scarce. But if you choose to stay in a stress-inducing situation, however good your reasons may be, you must recognise that you may be choosing to survive, not thrive.

Properly designed and applied clinical psychology offers solutions for many common human problems, but it is not a universal magic wand. The stress experienced by people reflects the operation of social, political, economic and even climatic factors, as well as psychological ones. You may decide that part of the solution to your stress problem lies as much in taking political or social action, as in trying to change yourself. Good luck to you: you are starting to practise community psychology, which we see as the logical extension of clinical psychology.

There are plenty of common problems that are complicated by individual circumstances. That doesn't mean they can't be solved, just that they need professional analysis and assistance. If you decide this applies to you, we strongly recommend you see a properly qualified clinical psychologist.

GETTING PROFESSIONAL HELP

As a rule of thumb, getting professional help means a registered psychologist with a post-graduate qualification in clinical psychology or membership of the Clinical Board of the Australian Psychological Society. Beware of imitations, of which there are plenty. Only a minority of psychologists in Australia is clinically qualified. Providing you approach a psychologist politely and unaggressively, we know of no reason why he or she should not be willing to outline for you his or her qualifications, training and basic approach.

We recommend a psychologist rather than a psychiatrist, family doctor, social worker or some other sort of counsellor, because most of these people have not been trained in our sort of approach in general, or stress-management in particular. That doesn't mean that there aren't some who don't have such training or who can't provide very effective help with stress-management. It just means we can't give you any simple rule for identifying them. Our usual advice is that if, after you have had several consultations with your professional helper of whatever kind, you don't feel you have been helped much, change helpers. It should not take too long for you to see some progress if a professional is going to be helpful. We are not all equally helpful to all people, and you are perfectly entitled to shop around.

We think we have covered, directly or indirectly, most common expressions and complications of too much stress. However you may feel you have some individual variation not discussed in this book. You could be quite right, and you should do something about it. If you cannot or don't want to find an appropriate self-help manual for your particular problem, see a clinical psychologist and sort it out. Unusual and sometimes bizarre behaviours, like hallucinations and delusions, can be symptoms of too much stress for too long. The odd behaviours seem to act as safety valves, permitting the release of tension. They may also provide a plausible excuse for opting out of a stressful life situation and sometimes gain a person sympathetic support which they otherwise couldn't get. We are not suggesting all psychotic-like behaviour results simply from stress. If a person's behaviour has become very disorganised and incoherent, he or she will almost certainly need the help of a properly trained professional.

HE / SHE / US

About half of the population is female. They are not automatically invited into male-dominated clubs or professions but for the sake of brevity, they have been made honorary linguistic males. The logic of this convention in our language escapes us. Throughout this book, unless it is clearly silly to do so, for 'he' you can read 'she', for 'hers' you can read 'his', and so on. After all, what we are really talking about is you and all of us.

1
GETTING STARTED

STRESS: WHAT IT IS AND WHAT IT DOES

What is stress? If the number of times stress is mentioned in the media was a genuine indication of how widely it is understood, then this book would be redundant. If the number of gadgets, gimmicks, drugs and courses being hawked around as answers to stress was a genuine indication of how easy it is to manage stress, then this book would be a waste of a few good trees.

Media attention notwithstanding, we believe that stress is neither well understood nor effectively managed by most people. Yet, as you will see, it is a part of **everyone's** life and a source of difficulty for many. Why? Because, without it, you would be dead. Thirst is a kind of stress. So is hunger. If we did not notice and respond to these very basic stresses, we really would die.

Essentially, stress refers to the application of some force or pressure to something. We need some force in our lives to get us moving, whether it is simply hunger or thirst, or a more complex human desire to know, to understand or to create.

If you apply too much pressure or force to something, it will bend. If the force is too great, you may get a permanent distortion or the object may break. So with people. This crucial role of stress is shown clearly in the graph on page 10. This graph shows the relationship between your level of arousal, ranging from low at the left to high at the right, and your performance and well-being, ranging from low at the bottom to high at the top. A number of studies have found this same relationship applies to both performance and

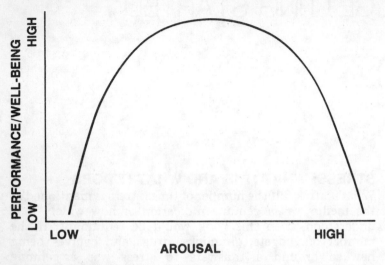

THE KAMIN CURVE

well-being, both physical and psychological. You can see that it is therefore a very important relationship.

At very low levels of arousal, you are under-stimulated and under-motivated. You need more stimulation. Both your quality of performance and well-being are low. Good examples of this situation are people in monotonous, boring, repetitive jobs, with little control over what they do or how they do it, such as production-line workers or some housewives. People in these situations will show all of the usual signs of too much stress, although they may try to cope with it by avoiding or mucking up the work, or by smoking, eating or drinking too much, and they may be patronisingly told they have the 'housewife's syndrome'.

At very high levels of arousal, you are over-stimulated and typically subject to conflicting motivations and demands. You are in the position of trying to tolerate an excess of stimulation. Once again, both your performance and well-being are declining. Good examples of this situation are people who have busy jobs which make too many, often competing demands on them but who have little real control over what they do or how they do it. This is typically the case of middle-level management, including foremen and women, supervisors and people in similar roles. Often it occurs as a result of over-commitment, resulting from a basic inability to refuse unreasonable requests.

People in this state of over-arousal show all the usual signs of too much stress: fatigue, anxiety, tension and sometimes physical symptoms. They may try to cope with it through health-reducing behaviours. Smoking, eating or drinking too much and excessive use of other drugs, prescribed or not, are the indirect attacks by stress on your physical health. Later, we'll describe the direct ones.

Effective-stress management is aimed at helping you get the stress in your life under your control, as much as is possible, so that you can stay effectively at the middle of this graph, and use the stress in your life to perform and feel at your best.

You may find your stress involves both under-arousal and over-arousal. For example, your job may be boring and monotonous, while at home your spouse and children expect you to do all the housework and look after all their domestic needs. You may need to aim to beef up some parts of your life by increasing rewarding or enjoyable activities and cut back on some of the unrewarding, unpleasant or boring activities.

Some people flip-flop between the two. For example, emergency workers, such as the police, fire and ambulance officers, or qualified people put in charge of a process which has been automated often face long periods of under-demand, punctuated by unpredictable bursts of over-demand. Again, a mixed approach to stress-management is indicated.

So, if some stress is good for you, but too much isn't, how do you tell which is which?

THE GOODIES AND THE BADDIES
Manageable levels of stress, for reasonable durations, mobilise your resources, and get you going on tackling the tasks and problems in your life. This is the situation around the middle of the graph on page 10, and is accompanied by positive emotions, such as enjoyment, satisfaction, excitement and even zest. To distinguish this beneficial stress, Hans Selye, one of the pioneers in this field, called it

eustress, borrowing the Greek prefix, 'eu-', meaning good.

An overload of stress from a situation of under- or over-arousal going on for too long produces first unpleasant feelings, and then physical damage and fatigue, and ultimately even death. Not surprisingly, Selye called this level **dystress**, using the Greek prefix, 'dys-', meaning bad. We think Selye's distinction was a valuable one. It recognises the inevitability and desirability of having some stress in your life, while guarding against its possible ill-effects.

Already you can see that the simple term, 'stress', masks something more complicated. How much more complicated? Lots. Don't be deterred by that; the better you understand your stress, the better your chances of managing it effectively.

STRESS IS AN INTERACTIVE PROCESS

The confusion begins with the way the one word, 'stress', is used to refer to at least two different sets of phenomena, that is, both to the forces being applied to you and to the effects of those forces.

Sometimes we use 'stress' to refer to the **sources** of stress in our lives, to what are technically known as **stressors**. These are situations which are potentially or actually harmful, unpleasant or which demand some response from us.

So you will hear people talk about someone being 'under a lot of stress' when they see his life as placing too many demands on him. He may have large debts and a complicated and demanding job, a near relative has died, while his children are having trouble after moving to a new school.

At other times we use 'stress' to refer to the **effects** of stress in our lives, including the thoughts, physiological changes, emotions and behaviours that we experience in response to a stressor. So people talk about someone 'suffering a lot of stress' when they see her showing many of the signs and symptoms of dystress. She may be fatigued and crabby all of the time, often with a cold or the flu.

In other words, stress is a **process**. Another prominent worker in the field, Charles Spielberger, has defined stress as an interaction between the coping skills of the person, on the one hand, and the demands of her environment, on the other. We shall spell out this interactive process in some detail, for a good understanding of the stress process will help you realise why simple gimmicks don't reduce dystress and help you plan your own stress-management programme tailored to meet your individual needs.

THE FIVE-FACTOR MODEL OF STRESS

We find it useful to pick out five major components in the stress process in humans. They are shown in the diagram on the next page, together with the interactions between them. Don't be put off by an initial impression of complexity. We'll stroll through the process, one factor at a time, and you will see it makes good sense.

FACTOR 1   STRESSORS

Logically, the stress process begins with the sources of stress, the stressors, although, since stress is an on-going process, you will always be already experiencing stress at some level as a result of other stressors, when a new stressor enters your life.

Common kinds of stressors, or situations which are potentially or actually harmful, unpleasant or demanding, include insults, assaults, frustrations and demands, or a lack of them. For example, you may be insulted by your spouse when he loses his temper; or you may be threatened with assault by a drunk at a party; or your plans to fix your car may be frustrated by the dealer not having the spare parts you need; or your boss may ask you to do several jobs all at the same time; or your job may be very boring and repetitive with little chance for you to use your skills or creativity. All of these are stressors.

Recent European research has identified uncertainty and a lack of control as major stressors for humans, confirming the suggestions of previous American research with animals. Again, it's a question of degree as to whether they produce eustress or dystress.

If you feel very uncertain about your future or if important events in your life seem to be unpredictable, you are quite likely to experience some dystress. For example, if

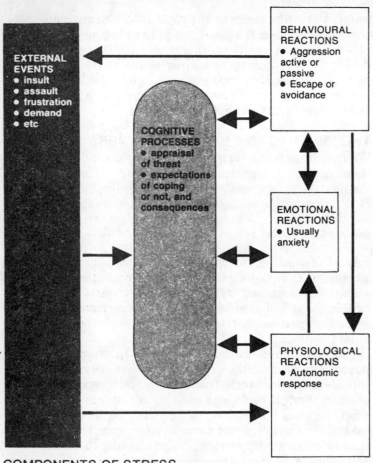

COMPONENTS OF STRESS

the future of your job is shaky, or if the 'right' way to do part of your job changes in unexpected ways, you will probably suffer some dystress.

If you feel you have little or no influence over important parts of your life, you are again likely to experience dystress. For example, you may know that you do your job very well and that this is appreciated by your boss, but you fear she may still sack you because her company is going broke. Or you may have a secure job, but no opportunity or encouragement to suggest ways in which it could be done better. Each day you have to put up with doing the job in an inefficient and wasteful way, even though your experience tells you there is a better way.

These related elements of uncertainty and a lack of control account for much of the stress experienced by workers in typical Australian jobs, which are generally designed on very old-fashioned principles. In Chapter 10, we describe a more modern approach to designing jobs, one which usually results in decreased dystress and increased eustress for the workers, and increased productivity for all.

As we said, it's a question of degree. Too much certainty or control can lead to the dystress of monotony and boredom. People with too predictable and unstimulating lives often seek out extra arousal. This is a common motivation for taking part in risky sports, going to horror movies, or queueing to ride the new roller coaster that does complete loops. But participants in these activities choose to take part, and they try to retain final control. It feels very different if you choose to put yourself into such a situation than it does if someone else has forced that situation on you.

Skiing fast down a steep slope can be very exciting, as long as you feel in control. Lose control, and it can feel very unpleasant, even terrifying. If the movie gets too frightening, you can always close your eyes, or even walk out.

The belief that you are in control is a major determinant of whether or not any event gives you eustress or dystress. We will explain this further under the next factor, but first there is another way that your mind can contribute stressors to your life.

So far, the stressors we have considered have all been 'real' events, in that they are actually happening to you at the time of your stress experience. Humans can also experience imaginary events. Indeed, so powerful is human imagination that imagined events can be just as arousing as 'real' ones, even though they are only 'really' occurring in your mind at the time. Many people increase their dystress by dwelling on past unpleasant experiences or failures, or by imagining future ones. The latter practice is a real trap:

practise failing in your mind and, when the 'real' event comes along, you will be very good at failing.

If your imagination can work against you like this, it can also be made to work for you. Recent research into the practical application of imagination has been getting some exciting results which are already being used to train champion athletes and sportspeople. We will explain how you can use your imagination to manage your stress more effectively.

At the end of this chapter, there is a way of measuring how many stressors life is currently sending your way compared with the rest of the population. Your score makes some interesting predictions about your physical health, as we explain a little later.

FACTOR 2   THOUGHTS

The second factor in the stress process is your thoughts. This includes what you say to yourself (your 'self-talk'), your beliefs, your expectations, your attitudes and so on. They are involved in stress in three ways.

First, a situation only becomes a stressor for you because you see it as one. You have to think that this event may be unpleasant or harmful to you or that it requires some response from you in order for it to act as a stressor for you. Some people increase their dystress by exaggerating the threats and demands in their lives.

Second, once you have decided a situation is a stressor, you will have expectations about whether or not you can cope with it. These expectations depend mostly on your previous experiences with similar stressors, but they can also be influenced by the example of others coping with the same stressor, by encouragement and instruction from someone who has previously handled that situation, and by your present stress level.

Some people increase their dystress by always underrating their ability to manage problems, even ones they have handled before, and by making little or no use of successful examples, or the encouragement and instruction available from others who are successful. This book is intended to provide you with some examples, encouragement and instruction, as a therapist does. Providing the personal experiences of coping successfully will be up to you, as it is in therapy.

If you are already in some dystress, then not surprisingly you are inclined to see another major stressor as the straw that will break the camel's back. Effective stress-management is one of the best preparations for the problems life occasionally throws at all of us.

Third, if you don't expect to be able to cope with this stressor, you will have expectations of the bad consequences of not coping. These should depend mostly on your previous experience of similar events, but some people increase their dystress by exaggerating how bad it will be if they fail to cope with a stressor, or by accepting other people's exaggerations.

Let's look at a simple example of how your thoughts influence your stress levels. Suppose you and a friend have gone to the beach. He is an experienced and accomplished surfer, but you grew up inland. You can swim quite well, but you have never been to the beach before.

He looks at the sea, and thinks, 'Oh, boy, the surf's up. It's going to be a great day!' Result: eustress.

You look at the sea, and think, 'Gosh, the waves are so big! I wonder if there are any of those rips or undercurrents I've read about? How can I see if a shark is coming?' Result: dystress.

He walks down towards the water, and thinks, 'There are some good waves there for riding. I'm going to have fun.' Result: eustress.

You follow him rather reluctantly, thinking to yourself, 'I've never ridden a wave in my life, and it took me years just to learn to swim. I bet I'll get knocked over by the first wave.' Result: your dystress increases.

He has now dived in and is swimming out for his first ride, thoroughly enjoying the eustress of tackling a task with some mastery and self-confidence.

You have ventured in up to your ankles, and have begun to imagine being dumped by a wave and looking foolish to your friend, or staying on the beach and looking foolish to your friend, or forcing yourself into the water and being eaten by a shark. Result: dystress, whichever way you go.

We know it's an over-simple example, but it will do to

illustrate the role of your thoughts in your stress. Notice that you first see the sea as a threat, placing new demands on you, and then you expect not to be able to cope with those demands, and then you are imagining the various possible horrible outcomes of the situation.

You will also have noticed that some of your thoughts are realistic: if you have never been in the sea before, you should begin with reasonable caution, finding out the appropriate skills, gradually going a bit further. But much of your thinking is unrealistic: you are exaggerating the difference between swimming in the sea and in still water; you are underrating your established capacity to swim; and you are exaggerating how badly things will go for you. Statistically, your chances of being bitten by a shark are about the same as your chances of being hit by lightning.

'But,' you are shouting, 'wouldn't it be dreadful if that remote possibility actually occurred and I *was* hit by lightning or bitten by a shark!' Yes, it would. But we have never seen a lightning bolt deflected or a shark deterred by someone worrying about them.

You also haven't made much use of the example of successful surfing being provided by your friend, but then he isn't providing you with much encouragement or instruction to help you change how you are looking at the situation.

Unrealistic and exaggerated thinking plays a major role in stress, and we will spend some time showing you how to train yourself to think more realistically. At the end of this chapter, we have provided a way for you to measure your tendency to think unrealistically. It is called the automatic thoughts questionnaire, and you are asked to rate how often you have thoughts which are characteristic of someone with a stress problem. You won't be able to compare your score on this test with trends in the general population, because those figures aren't available. The value of this test is as a measure of progress. Making your thinking more realistic is a central part of effective stress-management, and if you are making headway in this part of your programme, it will show up as lower scores on this test. You might like to take it now, and then, say, every two weeks, to check your progress in thinking more realistically.

FACTOR 3   PHYSIOLOGICAL RESPONSES

Your body reacts to a stressor with a roughly constant set of physiological changes called the general adaptation syndrome (or GAS). A syndrome is a set of biological or psychological events which tend to occur together, and this one is called the adaptation syndrome because it represents your body's attempts to adapt to the demand situation created by the stressor.

The GAS can go through three stages, depending on how long the stressor continues. It will be useful to outline these stages in some detail because some of the physiological changes in them account for the direct attack of stress on your physical health.

The first stage of the GAS is called the **alarm reaction**, the body's initial response to a stressor. Typically this involves increases in your heart rate, in your blood pressure, in the blood flow to and tension in your voluntary muscles, in your perspiration and in the depth and frequency of your breathing. At the same time there are reductions in what you can call your vegetative functions, like digestion. What your body is doing is preparing itself for a vigorous physical response by making energy available to the systems that would make such a response, while taking energy away from other systems. For most of the history of our species this has been adaptive, because you would usually have dealt with your stressor by fighting or fleeing. If your immediate stressor was a sabre-toothed tiger eyeing you off for lunch, then you would have to belt it over the head with a convenient rock, run like hell — or become lunch, which is not very adaptive at all. So the alarm reaction was preparing you for one or the other of those two vigorous physical responses, fight or flee.

The trouble for us is that in the last part of the 20th century your immediate stressor is more likely to be an over-demanding boss, an under-demanding job or an angry spouse, and a vigorous physical response is unlikely to be adaptive, at least in the long run. Hitting your boss over the head may ventilate your frustration, but would probably also cost you your job.

Nowadays what is more frequently called for is a

constructive and thoughtful response which may involve little vigour at all but your body will still be preparing itself for a vigorous response.

If your initial reaction to the stressor has not dealt with it satisfactorily, and it continues to press you, the GAS will proceed into its second phase, the **resistance stage**. This is when your body tries to maintain the higher rate of running begun in the alarm reaction. The physiological process underlying this is called homeostasis. The word may look strange but the process isn't: it is the tendency of living organisms to keep themselves in a more or less constant internal state, appropriate to their immediate environment and needs.

An example of homeostasis that will be familiar to you is your body temperature. The safe internal temperature for warm-blooded animals like us lies within a very narrow range, and your body has a number of homeostatic mechanisms, like sweating and shivering, to keep it within that range.

Since your stressor hasn't gone away, your body will try to maintain the energy supply needed to cope with it. This is fine as long as the stressor is one which is successfully handled with a vigorous physical response. As we have already pointed out, this isn't the case for many modern stressors, and there's the problem.

For most of human existence our stressors were usually dealt with, or dealt with us, fairly quickly. We didn't spend too much time in the resistance stage. Many of our modern stressors result from evolutionarily very recent events, such as industrialisation, urbanisation, automation and other technological innovation, and the social changes accompanying these events. These modern stressors are often not dealt with quickly; some may become a constant part of your lifestyle. The result is that many of us are spending a great deal of time in the resistance stage, a biological experience that was only 'meant' to occur more briefly.

It appears that this repeated and prolonged exposure to physiological changes that were originally more transitory is doing the direct physical damage of stress. For example, one of the physiological changes in the resistance stage is the release of hormones. Since hormones are chemicals released into the blood stream by special glands, to be transported around the body by the blood so that they can have their intended effect on a particular target organ or organs, they can have unwanted side effects, especially if their 'dose level' is abnormal. Most people have heard of cholesterol and its apparent role in heart and blood vessel disease. For a long time people have been advised to avoid foods with high cholesterol levels so as not to increase their own levels. It now appears that eating high cholesterol foods does **not** significantly affect your own levels. Cholesterol is a hormone released under stress. It now seems quite likely that high cholesterol levels, with their accompanying higher risk of heart and blood vessel disease, reflect too much dystress rather than your diet.

We began this discussion by stating that the GAS is a roughly constant set of events. This is because we now know that it shows some important variations, depending on the nature of your stressors, particularly in the kinds of hormones released during Stage 2.

One of the most interesting discoveries is summarised in the diagram. This shows that stress arising from uncertainty and a lack of control leads to a series of hormonal changes which ultimately directly interfere with the body's cells involved in your immunity, your resistance to infection. That's right. Good old-fashioned psychological stress directly reduces your immunity to physical illness. Even more recent research at the Australian National University has found that another result of these hormonal changes is to increase the risk of blood clots and hardening of the arteries. The same effect occurs after smoking tobacco, which is itself, of course, often triggered by stress.

It is now clear that stress is involved in **all** physical diseases and disorders, as either a trigger or a consequence. That sweeping conclusion, which you may at first feel inclined to scoff at, isn't ours. It was arrived at by the American Psychological and Psychiatric Associations when they undertook their recent, third major revision of their diagnostic manual. This is the handbook for practising clinical psychologists and psychiatrists, with descriptions of the various psychological problems to help the clinician

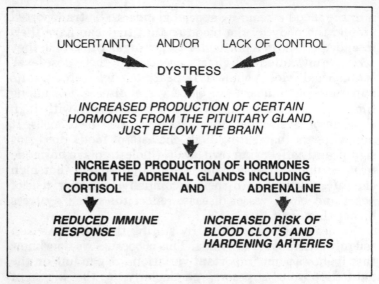

UNCERTAINTY AND/OR LACK OF CONTROL

DYSTRESS

*INCREASED PRODUCTION OF CERTAIN
HORMONES FROM THE PITUITARY GLAND,
JUST BELOW THE BRAIN*

**INCREASED PRODUCTION OF HORMONES
FROM THE ADRENAL GLANDS INCLUDING
CORTISOL   AND   ADRENALINE**

***REDUCED IMMUNE
RESPONSE***   ***INCREASED RISK OF
BLOOD CLOTS AND
HARDENING ARTERIES***

STRESS LEADS TO THE LOWERING OF THE IMMUNE
RESPONSE AND INCREASED HEALTH RISKS

identify a particular patient's problem. In the first edition
there was a group of problems called psychosomatic
disorders. In the second edition these were renamed
psychophysiological disorders, but the basic idea was the
same: it was a disorder in which you could see physical
damage in the patient — an ulcer in the gut, or a rash on
the skin, or whatever — but this damage did not result
from infection or injury, but from stress.

In the new edition this category of problems has been
dropped altogether, not because they don't exist, but
because they can no longer be meaningfully distinguished
from other physical diseases and disorders. If you wanted to
keep the old definition of a psychosomatic problem, then
you would have to list all physical diseases and disorders,
because stress is involved in them all.

We are exposed to infectious diseases much more often
than we get them. What makes a bout of infectious illness
more likely, especially the common ones like colds and flu, is
high dystress and its resultant lowered immunity. This is
stress acting as a trigger to physical illness.

Suppose you broke your leg, in a genuine accident, not even as a result of poor attention induced by a stressfully boring job. Your response to that broken leg would include some stress, and the level of that stress and how well you manage it would influence how well and how quickly your leg mended. This is stress acting as a consequence in physical illness.

The practical implication is that, when a physician is treating a patient for a physical illness, she should estimate how much stress was involved in that illness for that patient and, if indicated, offer stress-management as well as the more traditional medical treatment. Unfortunately this sound recommendation is only slowly seeping through the Australian medical profession.

The practical implication is also that, if you want to prevent physical illness (and its results of absenteeism and lost productivity) and promote physical health, then it is essential that you teach effective stress-management. And unfortunately this idea is only slowly seeping through Australian education and industry.

What happens if you still haven't got rid of your stressors? However adaptive the resistance stage may have been, you will realise that it is very energy-consuming. It's like driving your car around all day in first gear with your foot flat to the boards: lots of push, probably more than you need, and guzzling up the petrol fast. So not surprisingly the third phase of the GAS is the **exhaustion stage**. This means that your body's resources are running out and collapse is becoming imminent. This stage may first be marked by a recurrence of some of the alarm reaction, but now these signals seem to be saying to you, 'Look, pal, either we slow down or we're going to fall in a heap!' If you ignore those warning signs and allow your dystress to continue, then you will indeed collapse, and this is probably what often gets called a 'nervous breakdown'. If the stress were still to continue, it can even lead to death, although this is fortunately averted in most cases by the preceding collapse and the help that finally brings.

So you can see how our biological history and make-up have rendered us vulnerable to stress. We can't change them much, although in Chapters 2 and 3 we'll be making some relevant suggestions, so it becomes obviously important for our health's sake to learn to manage stress effectively.

FACTOR 4   FEELINGS

The fourth factor in your stress process is your feelings, your emotional responses to the stressor. As we foreshadowed earlier, your feelings under stress can be good or bad, like stress itself.

Eustress is typically accompanied by positive feelings: happiness, satisfaction, enjoyment, exhilaration. Dystress is typically accompanied by negative feelings: unhappiness, dissatisfaction, misery, depression, fear, anxiety, anger and so on. Most of the interest in stress tends to focus on dystress, and similarly more attention is paid to the accompanying bad feelings. You might even think that feeling bad is the central component of stress, and be surprised to find feelings are only the fourth of our five factors. The order is deliberate and it represents a theory of human emotions that is probably new to you.

If you listen to people talking about their feelings in daily conversation, you quickly get an impression that most people believe their feelings are controlled by events outside them or their control. For example, they may say, 'My boss makes me frustrated', or 'Fishing makes me relaxed'.

In fact, a growing body of careful research now supports the theory that it is not the outside event that determines how you feel, but how you **think** about that event. Of course, you will recognise that we have drawn on this theory in our discussion of Factor 2, your thoughts, in the stress process.

This close relationship between your thoughts and your feelings is not peculiar to stress. It applies to all aspects of your life. Some people find this hard to accept at first, especially when we ask them to try to identify their self-talk in a dystressing situation.

'But I'm not thinking anything', they will assert, 'I'm just feeling dreadful!' And they could be right. Sometimes people are surprised to find out how much self-talk is going on in their heads, when they finally pay systematic attention to it. But sometimes, no matter how hard they try to listen to their thoughts in a particular dystressing situation, there don't seem to be any.

Try to remember what it was like when you were learning to drive a car or to do some similarly complicated task. Remember how you used to talk yourself through the task? 'OK, now push this pedal down, now move that lever up there. What's next? Ah, check the mirror . . .' and so on. While you are learning, you talk to yourself 'out loud' inside your head. However, once you master driving (or whatever), your conscious self-talk disappears. You can talk to a companion in the car or listen to a radio, and your driving seems to occur 'automatically' in response to changes in the traffic situation.

In the same way, if you practise your emotional response to a particular situation many times, eventually your conscious self-talk in that situation may disappear, and you appear to respond to it 'automatically'. But your self-talk was the path for learning that emotional response, and in Chapter 2 we explain how it is the path to changing your emotional response.

There is a biological explanation for why thoughts precede feelings. Feelings are essentially a mixture of changes in your body which are interpreted and experienced in your mind. The final location of human emotional experience is definitely between your ears, but what's happening between your ears is influenced by what's happening in the rest of your body. The bodily components of your emotions, such as changes in your heart rate and blood pressure and so on, are called autonomic responses because they are controlled by a part of your nervous system which seems to function autonomously, without voluntary control. The GAS is an example of a well-known set of autonomic responses.

The nerve pathways that carry information from your sense organs, like your eyes, to the autonomic part of your nervous system are remarkably slow. It takes about three seconds for them to transmit information about a new stressor, so it takes that long before the bodily component of your emotions can begin, and therefore your mind's experience of them.

In the meantime, the rest of your brain, which gets its information via some very fast nerve pathways, has had about three seconds to think about the new stressor. In simple terms, you are built to think before you feel, even if you aren't always aware of doing that, and even if you now seem to find it difficult to do in dystressing situations. We'll work on that.

Our culture deals very badly with bad feelings. From birth onwards, we are taught that there is something dreadfully wrong with feeling bad. You start to cry, and someone gives you a cuddle and says, 'There, there, don't cry'. You begin to get angry, and someone pats you on the head and says, 'Now, you shouldn't get angry about that'. The repeated message is that you shouldn't feel bad, and if you do there is something wrong. Unfortunately, this message is rarely accompanied by any really helpful advice on how to cope with bad feelings, so instead we fumble about looking for ways to reduce our bad feelings. It's at this point that many of us are introduced to over-eating, over-drinking, smoking and other drugs, both social and pharmaceutical. Or we may discover the short-term pay-off of dodging our stressors, but more of that in the next factor.

The trouble with these short-term ways of reducing our bad feelings is that many of them are health-reducing, and none of them really tackles the stressors. In the long run relying on them usually increases your dystress. In Chapter 2 we have outlined a procedure for coping with bad feelings rather more effectively.

In the self-assessment section at the end of this chapter, we have included a scale for measuring your emotional dystress, both right now and in general, and for comparing your emotional dystress level with those in the general population. Although this test seems to focus on anxiety, we find it a very good measure of stress in general, and we recommend you use it to get an idea of your stress level.

FACTOR 5   BEHAVIOURS

Your behavioural choices in response to a stressor remain basically what they have always been, fight or flee. Fighting includes a variety of aggressive responses, while fleeing boils down to either escaping from or avoiding your stressors.

Both approaches can be successful or unsuccessful stress-management.

Don't confuse aggression with violence, which is only one form of it. From our point of view, aggression can include approaching your stressors with a realistic frame of mind and a constructive plan of action, in other words, facing up to them and handling them as well as you can. Many of the living skills described in this book are intended to help you do this.

But aggression can include violence, actual or threatened, physical or emotional. In Chapter 4 we spend some time defining aggression of the violent kind, and contrasting it with assertion, which we see as a generally more successful way of behaving. You can get the illusion that your violent aggression works, because you can scare some of the people some of the time, so you appear to have got your way. What they do when your back is turned may be another matter. Often your aggression will only provoke a similarly aggressive or defensive response, so no one gets anything good from the situation. Even on those occasions when your aggression seems to have worked, it usually involves your feeling very angry and hostile. Was it worth it?

Aggression can also be passive. This usually means sulking, withdrawing from the conversation, ignoring the other person or not doing something you said you would. Some people proudly tell us they never fight. But when they describe some of their dystressing situations, it is clear just how aggressive their silences are. We think assertion and communication work better, perhaps leading to some problem solving.

Escape or avoidance can mean quite literally absenting yourself from the dystressing situation, and this too may sometimes be a sensible choice. We are struck by the number of people who stay in dystressing situations for a variety of unrealistic reasons, and then wonder why they feel dystressed. You may find you benefit from doing some honest cost-benefit analyses: what does it really cost me to keep this particular situation in my life versus what benefits do I get from it?

But, as we foreshadowed in the discussion on feelings, many people do start dodging their stressors, as a short-term way of reducing their feelings. Telling the bank manager you are going to be late with your next mortgage payment **will** probably be embarrassing for you, and you **do** avoid that immediate embarrassment by putting off calling him. But what happens to your stress level when he calls you to point out that you have defaulted on your loan? We have often observed that many of the problems people consult us about result largely from choosing a short-term but ineffective way of reducing their bad feelings. Solving many of those problems involves facing up to short-term bad feelings for the sake of working out a genuine long-term solution. Many of the living skills described in this book are intended to help you do this, too.

The unsuccessful responses you might have to a stressor are legion, and we cannot suggest self-assessment for all of them. Let us focus broadly on two areas.

We have suggested a common but maladaptive response to stress is violent aggression, meaning actual or threatened, emotional or physical attacks on others. You can get a reasonable idea of whether this is a problem for you by completing the test in the last section of this chapter called Novaco's dimensions of anger schedule. The higher your scores are, the more likely that anger is a problem for you.

The second area where you might like to do an honest if uncomfortable self-assessment is to do with those other common techniques for reducing bad feelings, smoking, over-drinking and over-eating.

Do you smoke? There is very clear evidence that any smoking is health-reducing. The only healthy level of smoking is zero.

Do you drink alcohol, or caffeine (in coffee or tea)? On an average day, how many of each? A generous safe daily limit is four cups of either, and fewer wouldn't hurt.

Are you overweight? You can compare yourself with the standard height-weight tables but probably the easiest test is to stand naked in front of a mirror and look at yourself. If you look overweight, you probably are.

Quitting smoking, sensible drinking and eating, and weight loss and management are all parts of healthy lifestyling. Like working on your marriage, this really needs a book of its own. If you think you are smoking, over-drinking or over-eating to reduce bad feelings or cope with stress, then **first** complete this programme fully, and **then** work through a health improvement programme. By reducing your dystress first, you will give your healthy lifestyle plan its best chance of working. If doing two programmes seems a lot to you, remember that you are literally working for your life.

AND THEIR INTERACTIONS

You will remember that we said each of the five factors can interact with and influence each of the others. The arrows in the diagram on page 14 are not a road map to a Turkish bazaar, but are meant to show these various interactions.

If you are already feeling angry, you are more likely to see some new event as a further provocation.

If you are feeling comfortable and confident, you are more likely to think you can cope with some new demand.

If you are physically run down and fatigued, you don't feel all that good, and you are likely to see any new demand as more than you can cope with.

If you see yourself handling a situation well, you feel more confident and expect to be able to continue handling it.

If you see yourself making a mess of something, you feel disappointed and discouraged, you start to feel tense, you think you look stupid, you begin to worry more about what other people think of you than about the task, you make some more mistakes, and uuuuupp goes your dystress level.

The diagram looks static, because that's the only way we can draw it in a book. Imagine it as a giant pinball machine: shoot in a stressor, which bounces off some thoughts, physiology, and so on, finally popping out as a behavioural score. Both views are inadequate, because stress is an ongoing process, with each factor influencing each of the others, as long as you are alive. It does not switch on (or off) when you drop in a coin (or pull out the plug). It is a continuous interaction between five factors in your life.

For just this reason, if you are going to manage your stress effectively, it is essential that you make the broadest possible assessment of all five factors as they occur in your life, and plan a stress-management strategy that involves all five factors. Do much less, and you can expect much less.

YOUR PERSONAL STRESS ASSESSMENT

Using the five-factor model of stress as a guide, now do your own analysis of the stress factors in your life. Take your time because it will help you to decide which parts of the programme are most relevant for you. The programme we have set out is a 'standard' programme: not all parts are necessary for all people. Doing written answers to the following self-assessment will help you design your own programme.

FACTOR 1 STRESSORS

Are there particular people or situations that frequently cause you dystress? If so, list them. Is your work over-demanding or under-demanding, or sometimes both? In what ways should, and could, your job improve? Do you spend a lot of time thinking over the problems in your life?

As we mentioned earlier, there is a standard way of measuring the number of stressors in your life, the survey of recent events. If you haven't already completed it, do so now.

The designers of this scale, Holmes and Rahe, found that your score is a good predictor of your future physical health. If you score 300 or more life change units (LCUs), you have a much higher probability of being seriously physically ill in the near future. If you score between 200 and 300 LCUs, you are in a grey area, while if you score less than 200 LCUs, you are much less likely to be seriously physically ill in the near future. As we discussed before, this research shows how clearly your psychological and physical well-being influence each other.

A couple of cautions about interpreting your score: if you scored high, this does not necessarily mean you **must** get ill soon. The relationship found by Holmes and Rahe is a general trend which shows up in a population; it does not rigidly apply to every individual in that population.

Your score shows how many 'standard' stressors you are coping with, not how much stress you are experiencing as a

THE HOLMES-RAHE SURVEY OF RECENT EXPERIENCES

Read each of the events listed below, and circle the number next to any event which has occurred in your life recently. There are no right or wrong answers. The aim is just to help identify which of these events you have experienced lately. A recent event is one which you think is still affecting you.

Life events	Life change units (LCU's)
Death of spouse	100
Divorce	73
Marital separation	65
Jail term	63
Death of close family member	63
Personal injury or illness	53
Marriage	50
Fired at work	47
Marital reconciliation	45
Retirement	45
Change in health of family member	44
Pregnancy	40
Sex difficulties	39
Gain of new family member	39
Business readjustment	39
Change of financial state	38
Death of close friend	37
Change to different line of work	36
Change in number of arguments with spouse	35
Mortgage over $30,000	31
Foreclosure of mortgage or loan	30
Change in responsibilities at work	29
Son or daughter leaving home	29
Trouble with in-laws	29
Outstanding personal achievement	28
Partner begins or stops work	26
Begin or end school	26
Change in living conditions	25
Revision of personal habits	24
Trouble with boss	23
Change in work hours or conditions	20
Change in residence	20
Change in schools	20
Change in recreation	19
Change in church activities	19
Change in social activities	18
Mortgage or loan less than $30,000	17

Change in sleeping habits	16
Change in number of family get-togethers	15
Change in eating habits	15
Vacation	13
Christmas	12
Minor violations of the law	11

Now add up the numbers you have circled, to obtain your total life change units score.

result. (This is better indicated by the Anxiety Inventory on page 35.) If you have good coping skills, or if you strengthen them by working through this programme, you may carry a high load of stressors quite well.

Conversely, a low score does not necessarily mean you have few stressors in your life, only that you have few of the common stressors listed in the Table. You may still be carrying your own, quite high, individual load of stressors that they have not listed. So answer our questions before the Table carefully, too.

FACTOR 2 THOUGHTS
Do you think you lack confidence or self-esteem? Do you think you are very shy? Are you a 'perfectionist'? Do you often expect things to turn out badly? Are you pessimistic about your future? Do you worry a lot about how other people think of you? Again, you can use a standard measure of how your thoughts are contributing to your stress, the automatic thoughts questionnaire.

As we said earlier, you can't compare yourself with the general population on the automatic thoughts question-naire, but you can compare yourself with you, as you work through the programme. We have **never** seen anyone for stress-management who didn't need to increase the realism of her thinking. Testing yourself on the questionnaire every two or three weeks, looking for a lower score each time, will help you monitor your progress on this vital living skill.

FACTOR 3 PHYSIOLOGICAL RESPONSES
Do you feel physically tense much of the time? Do you think you are fit and in good condition, or run down and in poor

THE AUTOMATIC THOUGHTS QUESTIONNAIRE

Listed below are a variety of thoughts that pop into people's heads. Please read each thought and indicate how frequently, if at all, the thought occurred to you *over the last week*. Pleae read each item carefully and rate it on a scale 1 to 5 where 1 = NOT AT ALL, 2 = SOMETIMES, 3 = MODERATELY OFTEN, 4 = OFTEN, 5 = ALL THE TIME.

I feel like I'm up against the world. ☐
I'm no good. ☐
Why can't I ever succeed? ☐
No one understands me. ☐
I've let people down. ☐
I don't think I can go on. ☐
I wish I were a better person. ☐
I'm so weak. ☐
My life's not going the way I want it to. ☐
I'm so disappointed in myself. ☐
Nothing feels good anymore. ☐
I can't stand this anymore. ☐
I can't get started. ☐
What's wrong with me? ☐
I wish I were somewhere else. ☐
I can't get things together. ☐
I hate myself. ☐
I'm worthless. ☐
Wish I could just disappear. ☐
What's the matter with me? ☐
I'm a loser. ☐
My life is a mess. ☐
I'm a failure. ☐
I'll never make it. ☐
I feel so helpless. ☐
Something has to change. ☐
There must be something wrong with me. ☐
My future is bleak. ☐
It's just not worth it. ☐
I can't finish anything. ☐

Now add up the numbers to obtain your total automatic thoughts score.

---

condition? Do you exercise regularly? Do you feel tired or fatigued often? Do you have trouble sleeping?

We are not suggesting any elaborate self-assessment of

your physical health and fitness, because generally most people have a reasonably accurate idea of where they stand, depending largely on whether or not they have been doing anything about it.

If you are unsure about your present physical condition, go and get it checked by a doctor, preferably thoroughly. Since we will be recommending a moderate exercise programme in Chapter 3, if you haven't exercised much for a long time, or if you know you have a heart condition, or if you are forty years or older, it is highly desirable you have a thorough physical check-up before you get to Chapter 3. Show the doctor the exercise programme in Chapter 3 so that he knows what you plan to do.

FACTOR 4   FEELINGS

Do you think you are generally aware of your feelings, or would you have difficulty saying how you feel in a particular situation? Do you think you bottle up your feelings and try to hide them from other people? Do you often feel very bad? Do you feel bad for much of the time? Do you cry more than you used to? Are you unable to cry now, even when you feel like it? Are you using any drugs, social or prescribed, to cope with bad feelings?

This time the standard measure of this stress factor is the state-trait anxiety inventory. If you haven't already done it, do so now.

Compare your scores with the population levels, as set out in the table. How do you rate? Anything over 50 per cent says your stress level is higher than it should be. Given the abundant evidence that ours is an over-stressed society, even 50 per cent, the 'average', is too high in our opinion.

If you score much less than that (and you are sure you answered honestly), good for you. You don't seem to have too much of a stress problem now. If you still feel troubled, it may mean that this is the wrong self-help programme for you, and you may need some professional help deciding exactly what your problem is. If you don't feel troubled, you might like to see if there are useful skills in the programme to keep you that way.

THE SPIELBERGER STATE-TRAIT ANXIETY INVENTORY

State anxiety self-evaluation scale

Read each statement and then circle the number that indicates how you feel *right now*, that is, *at this moment*. There are no right or wrong answers. Do not spend too much time on any one statement, but give the answer which seems to describe your present feelings best. Add up the eight numbers you have circled to obtain your score.

	Not at all	Somewhat	Moderately	Very much
I feel calm.	4	3	2	1
I am tense.	1	2	3	4
I feel upset.	1	2	3	4
I feel frightened.	1	2	3	4
I feel nervous.	1	2	3	4
I am relaxed.	4	3	2	1
I am worried.	1	2	3	4
I feel confused.	1	2	3	4

Trait anxiety self-evaluation scale

Read each statement and then circle the appropriate number that indicates how you *generally* feel. There are no right or wrong answers. Do not spend too much time on any one statement, but give the answer which seems to describe how you *generally* feel. Add up the eight numbers you have circled to obtain your score.

	Almost never	Sometimes	Often	Almost always
I feel nervous and restless.	1	2	3	4
I feel satisfied with myself.	4	3	2	1
I feel that difficulties are piling up so that I cannot overcome them.	1	2	3	4
I feel like a failure.	1	2	3	4
I have disturbing thoughts.	1	2	3	4
I lack self-confidence.	1	2	3	4
I feel secure.	4	3	2	1
I worry too much over something that really does not matter.	1	2	3	4

You can compare your score with the general population in this table. For example, if your score is on or above 50 per cent, you are more stressed than 50 per cent of men or women; if your score is on or above 75 per cent, you are more stressed than 75 per cent of men or women. A man with a state anxiety score of, say, 18 is experiencing more emotional dystress now than 75 per cent of men. A woman with a trait anxiety score of, say, 22 generally experiences more dystress than 95 per cent of women.

Percentage ranks for state and trait anxiety scores

Per cent	State anxiety		Trait anxiety	
	Males	Females	Males	Females
95	21	25	23	25
75	17	17	18	20
50	14	15	15	16
25	12	12	13	13
5	10	10	10	10

FACTOR 5   BEHAVIOURS

Do you lose your temper often? Do you attack other people, verbally or physically, often? Do you attack objects often? Do you sulk much? Do you walk out on arguments or ignore people who disagree with you? Do you go along with other people and bottle up your feelings or opinions, even when you feel strongly about something? Completing the dimensions of anger questionnaire on page 37 will give you a reasonable idea whether anger is a problem for you.

Do the significant people in your life not understand you? Do you have trouble understanding the significant people in your life? Do you have lots of misunderstandings with people who are important to you?

Do you mull over and over problems, without ever really solving them? Do you have trouble making your mind up? Do you think you are indecisive? Do you think you often act impulsively and later regret your decision?

Are there problems or situations in your life that you know you ought to face up to, but that you usually escape from or avoid? Are you reasonably able to go where you want and do what you would like (assuming you can afford to) or are you aware of holding yourself back and restricting your life?

To assess how much your lifestyle and characteristic behaviours may be making you vulnerable to dystress, you should now complete the Miller-Smith lifestyle inventory.

NOVACO'S DIMENSIONS OF ANGER REACTIONS

Do your best to judge as accurately as you can the degree to which the following statements describe your feelings and behaviour, that is, rate the degree to which each statement applies to you on a scale 0 to 8, where 0 = NOT AT ALL, 1 = VERY LITTLE, 2 = A LITTLE, 3 = SOME, NOT MUCH, 4 = MODERATELY SO, 5 = FAIRLY MUCH, 6 = MUCH, 7 = VERY MUCH, 8 = EXACTLY SO.

1   I often find myself getting angry at people or situations. ☐

2   When I do get angry, I get really mad. ☐

3   When I get angry, I stay angry. ☐

4   When I get angry at someone, I want to hit or clobber that person. ☐

5   My anger interferes with my ability to get my work done. ☐

6   My anger prevents me from getting along with people as well as I should like to. ☐

7   My anger has had a bad effect on my health. ☐

Now add up the numbers to obtain your total anger score. High scores on questions 1, 2 or 3 suggest you will benefit from Chapter 2. A high score on question 4 indicates you will benefit from Chapter 4. A high score on question 6 suggests you will benefit from Chapter 5. A high score on question 7 suggests you will benefit from Chapter 3 and possibly a healthy lifestyle programme.

THE MILLER-SMITH LIFESTYLE ASSESSMENT INVENTORY

Stress often results from some factors in your lifestyle, and in turn can influence you into an unhealthy lifestyle. The aim of this inventory is to help you systematically to assess your current lifestyle to see if there are factors in it which may be increasing your vulnerability to stress, and which could be suitable targets for change.

Read each item carefully, and then give it a rating from 1 to 5, depending on how often that item applies to you now, where 1 = ALMOST ALWAYS, 2 = OFTEN, 3 = SOMETIMES, 4 = OCCASIONALLY, 5 = ALMOST NEVER. There are no right or wrong answers. The more accurately you answer, the better you will identify ways you can manage your stress better.

1   I eat at least one hot, balanced meal a day. ☐

2   I get seven to eight hours sleep at least four nights a week. ☐

3   I give and receive affection regularly. ☐

4 I have at least one relative within 50 kilometres on whom I can rely. ☐

5 I exercise to the point of perspiration at least twice a week. ☐

6 I smoke less than half a pack of cigarettes a day. (Non-smokers score 1.) ☐

7 I take fewer than five alcoholic drinks a week. (Non-drinkers score 1.) ☐

8 I am the appropriate weight for my height. ☐

9 I have an income adequate to meet basic expenses. ☐

10 I get strength from my religious beliefs, *or* I feel comfortable with my view of the universe and my place in it. ☐

11 I regularly attend club or social activities. ☐

12 I have a network of friends and acquaintances. ☐

13 I have one or more friends to confide in about personal matters. ☐

14 I am in good health (including eyesight, hearing, teeth). ☐

15 I am able to speak openly about my feelings when angry or worried. ☐

16 I have regular conversations with the people I live with about domestic problems, e.g. chores, money and daily living issues. ☐

17 I do something for fun at least once a week. ☐

18 I am able to organise my time effectively. ☐

19 I drink fewer than three cups of coffee (or tea or cola drinks) a day. ☐

20 I take quiet time for myself during the day. ☐

TOTAL ☐

To get your score on this test, add up the figures you have given. First, you can obtain a general indication of how much your lifestyle is making you vulnerable to dystress, according to this scale:

Score	Indicates
Less than 50	Low vulnerability
50 to 70	Vulnerable to dystress
70 to 95	Seriously vulnerable
More than 95	Extremely vulnerable

Probably more useful, however, is to use each of the items to identify possible goals for your stress-management programme. A score of 3, 4, or 5 on an item suggests you should look carefully at that part of your lifestyle to see if you should be making some changes to reduce your dystress vulnerability. The implications of some of the items will be clear, but let's spell them out, especially how they relate to other parts of this manual. A high score on the numbered items listed suggests the following:

1 Check your nutrition habits.
2 Sleeping problem? See Chapter 7.
3 Problems in your relationship? See our book, *Living and Loving Together*, published by Nelson. Lack of close relationships? See Chapter 9.
4 Poor family relationships? Would more communication (see Chapter 5) help?
5 Lack of exercise? See Chapter 3.
6 Smoking too much? Reduce your dystress levels before you try to quit.
7 Drinking to cope with bad feelings? See Chapter 2.
8 Eating to cope with bad feelings? See Chapter 2.
9 Not managing your finances well? See Chapter 6.
10 Uncertain about your personal identity and where you fit into the world? See Chapter 2.
11 Lack of social activities? See Chapter 9.
12 Lack of friendships? See Chapter 9.
13 Lack of intimate friendships? See Chapter 9.
14 Do you need a medical or dental check-up? Should you be following your doctor or dentist's advice more? Check the Luxury Myth at the end of Chapter 2.
15 Do you lack assertion? Are you often angry or aggressive? See Chapter 4.
16 Is there a lack of communication at home? See Chapter 5. Are you living alone and lonely? See Chapter 9.
17 Lack of recreation? See Chapter 3.
18 Lack of time-management skills? See Chapter 6.
19 Drinking tea, coffee or coke to pick you up? See Chapters 2 and 3.
20 Lack of solitude? See Chapter 3.

A thoughtful review of your answers to this inventory will help you pinpoint just which parts of the programme are most relevant for you, so take your time over it.

MONITORING YOUR STRESS LEVEL

A very useful way of identifying important factors in your stress process is called self-monitoring. This involves you doing some careful self-observation and recording the information that will help you identify targets for your stress-management programme.

We recommend you use a small, spiral-backed notebook for this, as they are easily carried and used. Whenever you feel your dystress level is rising, or whenever you have any strong or prolonged bad feelings, record the following information:

1   details of the situation including where you were, what you were doing and with whom
2   what you were thinking about the situation
3   how you felt physically, e.g. relaxed and comfortable or tense
4   how you felt emotionally
5   what you did, and how it turned out.

For example, one entry in your stress log might look like this:

1   Situation: at home in the morning, rushing to get ready to go to work, while the wife and kids have breakfast.
2   Self-talk: 'I'm going to be late again; the boss will be sarcastic about it again. Why the hell can't Mary put my shirts in the right place? Those bloody kids are so noisy!'
3   Physical feelings: getting tenser by the minute; my daily headache is starting already.
4   Emotional feelings: worried, frustrated, fed up.
5   Behaviour: snapped at Mary about my shirts, screamed at the kids, then went off to work feeling guilty about that.

Or it may look like this:

1   Situation: at home by myself after my husband has gone to work and the kids have gone to school, looking at the household chores waiting to be done.
2   Self-talk: 'I only tidied up yesterday! Why am I everybody's slave? John leaves his things all over the place, and the kids are even worse. God, I can't even keep a house clean; what's wrong with me?'
3   Physical feelings: washed out and exhausted, even though it's only 10 in the morning. (I wonder if those sleeping pills are helping. Maybe I should take more?)
4   Emotional feelings: depressed and worthless.
5   Behaviour: sit around staring at the housework, practising my self-talk as above. Feel so bad I decide to cheer myself up with some chocolate cake. (I wonder if I'm getting overweight because it runs in my family?)

These two examples may seem extreme to you, although we have seen plenty of people with lives like these. The point is that you can see how careful monitoring of their dystress will help these people identify their personally relevant goals for change in their stress-management programmes.

We recommend you start self-monitoring now, and keep it up as long as it is helpful.

2
TOTAL RELAXATION

Relaxation is one of the 'popular' approaches to stress-management, and many of the courses or gadgets being sold as cure-alls for stress are variations of relaxation, such as yoga, meditation, biofeedback, hypnosis and so on. The trouble is that these approaches consist largely or entirely of physical relaxation, or how to relax your muscles, yet you experience dystress, especially its emotions, mostly in your mind. There is a muscular tension component of dystress for many people on many occasions, but not always, and even if there is this bodily component, it is secondary to the mental component, as we explained in Chapter 1. We see many people who say they try to relax physically, or may be well able to do so, but it isn't any help because their minds are racing and hassled.

The bottom line on this situation is a thorough survey of research on relaxation, conducted by Dr Neville King of the Phillip Institute of Technology, of no less than 197 research reports and related articles. There seems to be no convincing scientific evidence for the efficacy of relaxation-training, probably because such training does nothing about what is causing the person's tension in the first place.

Many people **believe** that relaxation-training is helpful. Those who are selling it to you have an obvious vested interest in believing so, or at least in getting you to believe it, while some of those who have experienced it believe relaxation-training was helpful because 'it made them feel good **at the time**' (our emphasis).

And there's the rub. As so many people say to us, 'I feel wonderful at my yoga (or whatever) class, but once I go back to work (or home, or wherever), I feel tense again.' Or, 'I can relax my muscles fine, but when I do, all that happens is I worry more.' A clear example of this is the form of insomnia where a person will tell us that he can relax quite well in bed, but he can't sleep because he is worrying too much (more about this in Chapter 7).

If you go back to the model of stress on page 14, it will be apparent why physical relaxation alone is unlikely to be enough to help anyone with a stress problem. It is able to influence only one of the five factors in the stress process, your physiological reactions, and it leaves the others untouched. Indeed, if the other four factors are important in your stress process, they may overcome any relaxation-training and prevent you from even relaxing.

This possibility has now been confirmed in recent research in Canberra where some 478 people received physical relaxation-training. As many as 82 per cent of these people did **not** achieve a general relaxation response. While 60 per cent of them were reducing one component of their stress, usually muscle tension, another component was actually increasing and cancelling out any gains. The startling conclusion of this research was that the more these people practised their relaxation, the higher were their tension levels!

We have spent some time on this issue because we know you will continue to be bombarded with suggestions that physical relaxation is the answer to your stress problem. Since it looks easy and doesn't have the stigma of implying there is 'something wrong inside your head', it will appeal to many people. Well, if you try it and find it isn't enough, or if you have already had this disappointment, don't blame yourself. By now you should realise why it is unlikely to be enough for many dystressed people, including you. (Of course, if you try it and it is enough, good luck to you. Keep practising your relaxation and give this book to a friend who needs it.)

The key to getting help from relaxation lies in Neville King's second conclusion: the lack of evidence in favour of relaxation-training probably reflects its lack of impact on the causes of the person's tension. He recommended 'a multi-faceted stress-management programme', like this one. He didn't add that last bit; we did.

We believe that effective relaxation has two major components, one of which is simply ignored or glossed over in most popular relaxation-training programmes. In addition to physical relaxation, which seems to have a useful contribution to make, you need mental relaxation in order to achieve what we have called total relaxation.

Some of the relaxation procedures, such as yoga and Zen meditation, imported here from other cultures do include or even emphasise mental techniques in their original forms. The trouble is that most popular Western versions of them don't do justice to the mental component, or depend on the user holding a philosophical or religious view of the universe that is novel or alien to most of us. Most people in our community need specific instruction in mental as well as physical relaxation, if they are to relax effectively.

In the light of our theory of human emotions outlined in Chapter 1 you will not be surprised that we begin with mental relaxation, because of the primary role that we see for thoughts in our emotions in general and stress in particular. Once you begin to relax your mind, we will make some suggestions about relaxing your body.

PART I: MENTAL RELAXATION

We spent some time, under Factors 2 (your thoughts) and 4 (your feelings) of the stress model in Chapter 1, outlining our theory of human emotions. The idea that how you think about something largely determines how you will feel about it, and how strong those feelings will be, has an important implication that is the basis of our approach to mental relaxation. If you are ever feeling very bad, for very long, that will largely result from how you are thinking, and if those feelings are unreasonably strong or long-lasting, it will be because your thinking is unreasonable. The way to make your feelings more reasonable is to make your thinking more reasonable.

Here are six steps for **feeling better by thinking straighter**: the first three you do on the spot, to help you cope with your bad feelings there and then; the last three you do later, when you have time to review the situation, to prepare yourself to cope better in the future.

STEP 1   GET IN TOUCH WITH YOUR FEELINGS

Your feelings are the signalling system that tells you when it is time to do some mental relaxation. Whenever you have a very strong or prolonged bad feeling, then it may be time to start this exercise. There is nothing wrong with bad feelings, as such. You ought to feel bad when the circumstances warrant it. For example, if you have your heart set on something and you miss out, you should feel disappointed. If a close friend is cruel to you, you should feel hurt. When you try something important to you for the first time, it is reasonable to have some anxiety.

We are not out to make you a robot with no feelings; even if that were possible, it wouldn't be desirable. A human being that couldn't feel bad probably wouldn't be able to feel good, either. Khalil Gibran explains this rather more poetically in his story, *The Prophet* (published by Heinemann), if you would like to explore it further.

Our target in mental relaxation is exaggerated bad feelings. So, whenever you are feeling worse about something than you would like to or than you think is reasonable, or if it is apparent to you that your bad feelings are unreasonably interfering with your life, it's time for some mental relaxation.

Getting in touch with your feelings can be trickier than it looks. One of the two popular ways of dealing with bad feelings, especially if you are male, is to try to deny them. This can mean trying to kid yourself – 'I shouldn't feel bad about that!' – or trying to kid others – 'Oh, no, that doesn't worry me!' – when in fact you **are** feeling bad.

If you have spent some years practising denying bad feelings, you may now have to spend some time practising getting in touch with them again. Monitoring your stress levels will help you begin mental relaxation by identifying the situations which increase your dystress. If you have not already begun this self-monitoring, as outlined at the end of Chapter 1, start now.

When you are recording your feelings, make sure they are feelings, that is, emotional experiences (e.g. sad, happy, anxious, excited, hurt, angry) and not thoughts (e.g. 'I felt as if he was attacking me', or 'I felt that she didn't understand me'). You will need your thoughts, but first you need your feelings. One way of denying feelings is to talk **about** them, instead of just accepting them.

If you have trouble identifying your feelings, start simply and work up. At first, you might only recognise you are feeling 'good' or 'bad'. That's enough to begin mental relaxation, your target being any excessive bad feelings.

Later you can improve your bad feeling recognition by asking yourself, 'What kind of bad feeling?' Looking down a bad feelings list like that on page 46 may help you answer this question. Try to identify both the **nature** and **intensity** of your bad feeling correctly.

Example Here is an example of mental relaxation. Suppose that, in your self-monitoring, you have identified a dystressing situation at work, where your boss often gives you a lot of work late in the day and expects you to finish it before you go, even though he doesn't ask if you mind or offer to pay you overtime. Although you feel bad about this, you are too scared of losing your job to speak up, so you stay back to do the work.

Doing **Step 1**, you identify your feelings in the situation as being anger and anxiety.

STEP 2   ACCEPT THAT YOU CAN COPE WITH BAD FEELINGS

One of the most frequent remarks we hear from people beginning stress management is the forlorn complaint, 'I just can't cope'. The trouble is their expectations of coping are unrealistic, and typically involve the impossible goal of not feeling bad about something that any normal person would feel bad about.

'Cope' properly means just to manage, to get by. In this step we want you to begin accepting that you can cope with bad feelings. That is, you will survive them: there are no terminal cases of bad feelings.

How many times in your life have you felt anxious? Or angry? Or hurt? Or any other bad feeling? Let us draw to your attention the obvious fact that you have survived those bad feelings. We don't deny that they were genuinely unpleasant at the time, but that's **all** they were. And, unless the event was very recent, or you are working very hard at keeping the feelings alive, they are gone now.

BAD FEELINGS

Angry	Frightened	Crabby
Frustrated	Tense	Irritated
Furious	Uncertain	Down
Upset	Disturbed	Depressed
Hurt	Nervous	Sullen
Disappointed	Anxious	Embarrassed
Hopeless	Restless	Bitter
Regret	Dissatisfied	Envious
Mad	Up-tight	Jealous
Unhappy	Hassled	Exasperated
Sad	Guilty	Disgust
Worried	Annoyed	Gloomy
Confused	Fearful	

As we discussed in Chapter 1, our culture makes a bogeyman out of bad feelings, and cons us into thinking we must avoid them at all costs because we cannot possibly survive them. Hogwash. You have already felt bad countless times, and you will again in the future. You may make life more difficult for yourself by choosing one of the unsuccessful ways of reducing your bad feelings, but you will still survive the feeling itself. We are encouraging you to accept the basic truth that you can cope with bad **feelings**. This does not necessarily mean you will cope, in the sense of manage successfully, with the **situation** leading to the bad feelings. To cope with the situation, you will probably have to **do** something constructive (more about that later).

To help you cope with bad feelings, here is a piece of self-talk you can use to enhance your coping in any dystressing situation. As soon as you become aware of feeling very bad, you should deliberately make yourself think through a coping self-statement such as this:

'I expect to feel (*bad*) (*in this situation*) but I can cope with feeling (*bad*). So I won't deny my feelings, but I won't exaggerate them, either. Is there something constructive I can do to improve the situation? If there is, I'll plan it now, and do it. If there isn't, I'm not going to make myself feel worse than is reasonable. Now, what will I do instead?'

No one has an empty mind, least of all in a dystressing

situation. If you leave your mind unoccupied, the thoughts that come marching through will be your most habitual ones. If they make you feel worse than you need, then leaving your mind unoccupied is a short invitation to feeling dystressed.

So instead keep your mind busy, but realistically and constructively, with a coping self-statement such as the one above. Rehearsing it a number of times can help to lower your bad feeling level immediately, especially if you follow through with some constructive steps to improve the situation. It will work best if you say it to yourself with conviction, not just a mechanical recital, so let's examine its parts so that they have meaning for you.

'I expect to feel (*bad*) (*in this situation*), but I can cope with feeling (*bad*).' We have explained these ideas already: normal people are entitled to normal bad feelings when the circumstances warrant them, and no one ever died of feeling bad. Use this general purpose statement in any situation by substituting your feelings where we have (*bad*), and the details of your situation where we have (*in this situation*).

'So I won't deny my feelings . . .' This is the first of the two common traps in dealing with bad feelings. Fooled by the nonsense our culture teaches about how dreadful it is to feel bad, many people will try to deny quite understandable bad feelings. As soon as they become aware of feeling bad, they think something like, 'I shouldn't feel bad about something like this. It's silly and illogical for me to feel bad!' They then feel extra bad about being so 'silly' and 'illogical'. All they have achieved is a doubling of their bad feelings. Not very helpful. Bad feelings that are denied don't go away; they generally get worse because your denial adds more bad feelings to them.

You can draw an important distinction between 'logical' feelings and 'understandable' ones. Imagine one day you are riding in a lift when its cable snaps and it falls a couple of metres before the brakes stop it. After a short delay, you are released from the lift and leave, rattled but unhurt. The next time you rode in a lift it would be quite understandable if you felt anxious. In a sense, your anxiety would be illogical, because the chance of a similar accident occurring would be remote and you weren't hurt anyway. But your anxiety would be **understandable**.

You can use the mental relaxation procedure to make your feelings more logical. That's fine; there's no point feeling bad when you don't need to. But if you try to deny understandable feelings, however illogical they may be, you will only make yourself feel worse. So in a coping self-statement, you are giving yourself permission to have normal bad feelings and you can afford to do this because you know you can cope with them.

'. . . but I won't exaggerate my feelings, either.' This is the second common trap in managing bad feelings. It usually consists of continually repeating your original self-talk about the situation, making yourself feel worse with each repetition. This also serves to prolong the bad feelings unnecessarily.

Another variation of the same technique is to repeat the same self-talk to someone else, if you can find someone silly enough to put up with it. Unfortunately, some people confuse this encouragement of your bad feelings with being 'supportive'.

Frankly, we wonder why people do this to themselves. The original feelings were bad enough; why exaggerate and prolong them? Our best guess is that many people don't believe they can do anything else about the situation (a belief we will shortly encourage you to question) and the most common example they have seen of how to tackle bad situations has been to whinge, to themselves or someone else.

'Is there something constructive I can do to improve the situation? If there is, I'll plan it now, and do it.' Humans behave in two domains: in your head you think, imagine and feel; in the outside world you act. Both streams of your behaviour are important, both influence each other, and usually you need to change both to achieve significant and lasting improvement.

In this section of the programme, we are focusing on how you change your thoughts, your imagination and your feelings. We believe this is an essential set of coping skills. In much of the rest of the programme, we focus on how you change your actions. In most dystressing situations you will need to draw on both sets of skills.

At this point in the coping self-statement, you are reminding yourself of this, the need to change both your thoughts **and** your actions, to achieve maximum effectiveness. For the moment, that may mean you will say to yourself, 'Yes, I know I should do something constructive, but I don't know **what** or **how**.'

The what will typically be making an assertive response, or practising communication, or trying to solve a problem, and how to do all these is described in the rest of this book. If you feel impatient, having talked yourself into doing something constructive, but having to postpone it until you get further on in the programme, take it easy! You cannot master the entire programme instantly. Right now, concentrate on mastering mental relaxation. It will underpin every change in action you finally decide to make.

Notice that you are telling yourself to **plan** your action, and then carry it out. Yes, this is slow, especially at first. Yes, you may well feel awkward while you think about the best way to respond to a stressor, but as you know by now you can cope with feeling awkward.

A considered response usually has a better chance of being successful than a hasty one. Even just seeing yourself slow down and take time to respond effectively to stressors can improve your feelings and your self-esteem. We will emphasise in later chapters the value of planning how to respond to a stressor and rehearsing it in your imagination.

'If there isn't anything I can do to improve the situation, I'm not going to make myself feel worse than is reasonable. Now, what will I do instead?' Some stressors, such as government decisions, world recessions, droughts, death of a friend, or the final refusal of your spouse to work on improving your marriage are genuinely completely out of your influence. In such cases your goal is simply not to overreact. In each case, you are entitled to reasonable bad feelings and accepting these is important, such as working through your grief reaction to the death of someone close.

But it is equally valuable to avoid exaggerating or prolonging your bad feelings. Making yourself feel rotten about such an event won't change the event; it just makes you feel rotten.

People usually exaggerate their bad feelings by dwelling on and rehearsing their negative thoughts about the situation, either in self-talk or talking to others. The practical way to stop these unnecessary repetitions is to find some task or activity that will occupy your mind, pleasantly or constructively. Take the question, 'What will I do instead?' as your next task. Instead of sitting around rehearsing negative thoughts, find yourself something to do that meets one of those criteria: pleasant or constructive occupation of your mind.

If your feelings have sunk really low, taking some active steps can be difficult. You may have to settle for just standing up and walking around the room, and then out into the garden or street, and then actually tackling some more complicated task. If you build up behaviour changes gradually, you are more likely to keep succeeding, and that will encourage you to keep trying. But, however small your beginning, move! Do something! Don't let yourself sit there and slip back into negative self-talk and wallow in bad feelings.

Continuing our example After becoming aware that you are feeling bad about your boss's actions, you would work out and practise a coping self-statement:

'I expect to feel angry when the boss keeps me back unreasonably, but I can cope with feeling angry. So I won't deny my understandable anger, but I won't exaggerate it, either. Is there something constructive I can do? Yes, I should assert myself. Now, how do I do that?' (And you begin planning your assertive response, as shown in Chapter 4.)

NOW, HOW DO YOU FEEL?

By the time you get to the end of Step 2 of the mental relaxation procedure – which means you are consciously rehearsing a coping self-statement and you are planning and taking some constructive action, either to improve the situation or occupy your mind – your bad feelings should be declining.

They usually won't go away and often shouldn't; but they will get less, which makes it easier for you to act constructively. If they don't seem to be getting any less at all, it could mean that you have not done some of the steps properly, so go back and try them again.

Sometimes people have difficulty with mental relaxation because they have developed some very persistent and intrusive negative self-talk, such as telling themselves persistently that they can't cope. These intrusive thoughts seem repeatedly to pop into their minds, causing more and more dystress. Although these people do try to apply the steps above to their intrusive thoughts, the intrusive thoughts just keep coming back.

If this happens to you, try the additional technique of **thought-stopping**. Despite what you may have come to believe, you **do** have considerable control over your mental content. You may not be able to stop a very well-rehearsed thought from beginning, but you do have a choice as to whether or not you continue it.

The first time your intrusive thought occurs today, deal with it by going through the standard mental relaxation steps. Any other time it occurs today, use your thought-stopping procedure instead of allowing the intrusive thought to continue.

To train yourself in thought-stopping, you must set aside some time and find yourself somewhere private to practise. First, rehearse the intrusive thought deliberately. (Notice that to do this you are proving that in fact you do control it.) When you have it clearly in your mind and it is affecting your feelings as it usually does, jump up and shout at yourself to stop. Say to yourself firmly, 'I know what that self-talk is all about and I have already dealt with it realistically once today. It isn't worth any more of my time, and I don't have to rehearse it. What will I do right now that will occupy my mind pleasantly or constructively?' A key to the success of stopping intrusive thoughts is to find an answer to that last question and to concentrate deliberately on your new task. You may have to repeat thought-stopping again soon – perhaps many times at first, if you have learned some very intrusive thoughts. Stick at it.

When you are doing thought-stopping in public try wearing a rubber band round your wrist, and instead of jumping up, twang it against your skin. It stings a little to remind you to stop that thought.

Another way to prove to yourself that you have control over intrusive thoughts, if they are very troublesome to you, is to **timetable** them. Suppose that you estimate that you currently have intrusive thoughts 20 per cent of the time. On average, that represents 12 minutes in every hour. So tell yourself that on the hour, every hour, you will stop what you are doing and deliberately practise your intrusive thoughts for 12 minutes. If they begin at any other time, use your thought-stopping technique, telling yourself that you won't allow such thoughts except when they are timetabled.

Once such a timetable is established, gradually reduce the amount of time you allow for deliberately practising your intrusive thoughts, until eventually they are no longer interfering with your life. Sometimes people surprise themselves by how quickly they do this, once they have conclusively proven to themselves that they do in fact control their own thoughts.

STEP 3   REWARD YOUR SUCCESSES

When you apply the coping strategy, and see yourself coping better, and when you plan and take some constructive action, reward yourself! This is a very important step, for several reasons.

The most important reward you give yourself for coping better will be a pat on the back, saying to yourself something like, 'Hey! I really handled that much better. Last week I felt dreadful when that happened; this time I felt a bit bad, but that's reasonable and I can cope with that. I'm really getting on top of things.'

Sometimes you may set yourself a concrete goal, like losing some weight or quitting smoking or whatever. Then you may help yourself achieve that goal by offering yourself a tangible reward, such as a holiday, or some new clothes or records or books. We'll talk about contracting as a motivational aid later.

But your most frequent and important reward ought to be your self-congratulations. What you are doing is practising a reality-based, positive self-esteem.

It is reality-based because you only get to Step 3 by working through Steps 1 and 2; you only reward yourself when you actually see yourself trying to cope better. You are not kidding yourself about 'being the greatest' when you know that isn't true. Because it is reality-based, this self-talk carries more clout for you. Your positive picture of yourself will produce good feelings. Some of the dystressed people we see claim to have forgotten what good feelings are like. By this stage in mental relaxation, you have earned some, so give them to yourself.

And it is **self**-esteem, you holding yourself in high esteem, not relying on the approval of others. It is nice to get approval from others, and disappointing or hurtful when you don't - no argument. But it is **not** essential. It **is** essential that you think well of yourself if you are going to run your life successfully.

There is a fanciful notion going around, called 'trial-and-error' learning. The truth is that people don't learn how to be successful by making mistakes. You may learn that what you did was wrong, but that doesn't tell you what would be right. Suffer enough errors, mistakes and failures and you get discouraged and give up.

Success, on the other hand, makes you feel good and encourages you to keep going. People actually learn to be successful by succeeding. This does not mean you have to get it right first time, whatever it may be. For complex problems, that's unlikely. What it does mean is that you have to have a realistic and changing notion of what success is.

If you look at where you are now, and where you would like to be, in an important area of your life, the gap may be quite large. Then you are likely to say, 'That's too much, I could never get there!' And not try at all. Or if you do try to jump the whole gap at once, and predictably fail, then you will get discouraged and quit.

Successful change programmes rest on breaking large changes down into small steps, and taking them one at a time. Then you have a good chance of succeeding at each step, which encourages you to keep trying and go on to the next one. In other words, your definition of a success is a realistic goal which changes as you progress through the problem.

We will return to this essential technique of breaking large problems down into smaller ones, to be taken one at a time, as we describe various procedures for problem-solving later. The point now is that setting yourself realistic goals gives you a good chance of being able to reward yourself often. And by now you should see how important rewarding yourself is.

Continuing our example If you had rehearsed your coping self-statement, you should find your anger has reduced to a reasonable level, which makes it easier to plan and make an assertive approach to your boss about his unreasonable treatment of you. Good for you! Give yourself a pat on the back:

'That was good. I was fuming for hours last time that happened. This time I feel a bit angry, but that's OK, and I did tell him assertively how I felt. I feel great about how I'm changing myself!'

STEP 4   TRY TO IDENTIFY YOUR SELF-TALK
Later, when the troublesome situation is over and you have time by yourself to think about it, try to remember what your original self-talk was. Listen to your thoughts about the situations you identify as involving excessive bad feelings for you. This can be harder after the event; if you didn't pay much attention to them at the time, you may have trouble remembering your thoughts now. Your self-monitoring should have prompted you to record your self-talk as soon as possible after you have decided a situation was dystressing for you.

If you find you have many thoughts in a dystressing situation, you are looking for the ones obviously linked to your bad feelings recorded at Step 1. Sometimes people who report a lot of self-talk are in fact practising only two or three thoughts, over and over again, with slight changes in the words each time. If you are doing this, try to summarise your self-talk into the two or three basic thoughts.

If you don't seem to have any thoughts at all, that could mean that you haven't noticed them yet, or they have become 'automatic' and you no longer 'say' them inside your head. Check which of these applies by waiting for the situation to occur again, and then make a special effort to listen to your thoughts. You may be surprised to find there is some obviously relevant self-talk, which you should record as soon as possible.

Or you may find, no matter how hard you try, that you just cannot identify any self-talk that seems to be associated with your bad feelings. That would probably mean that you have over-learned your emotional response to this particular situation, and the self-talk you used to learn it has now disappeared, as we explained in Chapter 1.

That's too bad, because you won't be able to do Step 5 this time, but you **can** do the rest of mental relaxation. Just go straight to Step 6, anytime you have tried to do Step 4, but can't identify your self-talk.

One more important variation to Step 4: so far, we have talked about self-talk as consisting of thoughts, words you say to yourself inside your head. Self-talk can also be pictures, mental movies that you run inside your head. These are called fantasies (when you're awake, or dreams when you're asleep), and as we explained before they can be very powerful influences on how we feel and act.

Humans do a lot of their thinking in images rather than words or other symbols. So when you check your self-talk, look for fantasies as well, imagined experiences from the past or the future. You can record them by describing their content because, when you fantasise, you are essentially saying, 'This is how I think (or wish) things were (or will be).' You are just thinking in pictures instead of words.

Continuing our example For Step 4, you recorded

'Gee, he's a pig. He doesn't care what else I might have on this evening. What right has he got to expect me to work unpaid overtime? I should tell him where he gets off.'

Then I imagined myself telling my boss he was being unfair, and him getting very angry and abusive, and finally telling me to quit if I don't like the job.

STEP 5 TEST YOUR SELF-TALK

Suppose you developed a habit of pulling your left earlobe whenever you were sitting around chatting to people. Because it was a habit, you would find you were largely unaware of doing it. Habits become 'automatic' and largely unconscious.

If someone drew it to your attention by saying, 'You know, you fiddle with your ear a lot', you would suddenly be aware of it, perhaps very aware. But most of the time you were doing it, you wouldn't pay much attention to your habit.

You can also develop habits of self-talk. You can practise a certain content or style of self-talk so much that it becomes habitual. Because these thoughts or fantasies are so habitual for you, you don't really pay much attention to them any more. You accept them into your mind uncritically, as though they were naturally true and accurate, when in fact they could be exaggerated, biased or completely wrong.

Because you have accepted unrealistic thoughts as true ones, you will then have exaggerated bad feelings. What you are doing at Step 5 is stopping that uncritical acceptance of your self-talk, and instead you are saying: 'Hold it! How reasonable is my view of this event?'

To do this, take each of your thoughts or fantasies as though it was a small theory about the situation, and not necessarily an accurate picture, and then test it by asking yourself:

'What is the real world evidence about this point?'
'How realistic and reasonable am I being about this?'

This questioning of the assumptions you have made about a dystressing situation is important in helping you approach it more realistically, but it can be difficult to do at first. After all, if it was immediately apparent to you that your self-talk was unrealistic, you wouldn't go on with it, would you? Or would you?

To help you do this step, we list the common thinking errors that people make. (These are taken from research by Dr Aaron Beck, a leading American researcher in the field of depression, see Chapter 8.) To test how realistic or reasonable your self-talk is, look at it critically to see if you

COMMON MISTAKES IN THINKING

Overgeneralising

This involves drawing a general conclusion on the basis of only one incident. You are telling yourself that, if something was true in one case, it will apply to any case that is remotely similar. In fact life is rarely that simple.

Black and white thinking

This means to see things as being only one extreme or the other, such as telling yourself a friendship must be very good, otherwise it is very bad. In the real world there are many shades of grey.

'Who needs evidence?'

This mistake involves drawing a conclusion without any real evidence to support it, or in the face of contradictory evidence. For example, saying no one likes you when you could not possibly have asked everybody, or even do have some friends. Ask yourself, 'What is the real world evidence to support my conclusions in this self-talk?'

Looking at the world through deep blue glasses

This means focussing on what is wrong and blowing it up out of all proportion — your mistakes, your failures, your problems — and ignoring or belittling anything that's right — your successes, good times and achievements. Looking at the world through rose-coloured glasses can be misleading too. Stop distorting the world in either direction.

Imagining the worst

This is a special case of exaggeration or looking through the world through deep blue glasses, but it is so common that it deserves a mention of its own: imagining the worst means assuming the worst possible outcome for any event, usually so exaggerated that it's really improbable, if not impossible.

Taking things personally

This means blaming yourself for everything wrong, even when you may only be partly or not at all responsible, like blaming only yourself for problems in your marriage (we'll bet your spouse contributes to them too). If you really run the whole universe, please tell us how.

Taking things personally can also mean assuming that everybody notices every mistake you make, that you are the centre of everybody's (disapproving) attention. You will usually find most people are too busy worrying about their own problems even to notice yours.

are making any of these common mistakes. Remember you think in images as well as words.

Continuing our example For Step 5, you decide that your thinking mistakes were:

    1   Black and white thinking ('He is unfair in this respect, but he's not a bad boss or person in other ways.')

    2   Lack of evidence ('I don't know that he doesn't care about my feelings because I've never told him how I feel.')

    3   Imagining the worst ('I don't know how he will react if I stick up for myself; expecting the worst only makes me anxious and submissive.')

STEP 6   TEACH YOURSELF TO THINK RATIONALLY

The first three steps of mental relaxation you can think of as firefighting. They are a systematic way of coping with any dystressing situation on the spot. With persistent practice, you will be able to do them in your head, whenever you need to.

Your longer term goal is to need those steps less and less often, because you are gradually overreacting to your stressors less and less often. This means you are teaching yourself to look at the world more realistically.

Humans are not born thinking. Thinking, as we usually mean it, develops throughout childhood and can continue to do so in adulthood. You are **taught** how to think. You may not have seen it as learning because your parents did not stand there with a blackboard and chalk. But they systematically taught you how to think. They set you the example of their own thinking, when they talked out loud. They encouraged thoughts in you – 'Good boy, good girl!' – and discouraged others – 'How could you think like that!' After them, your brothers and sisters, playmates and friends, teachers and other adults influential in your life, books, movies, television, and many other forces in our society shaped your thinking. After all, that's only what you would expect. The problem, as we see it, is that our culture teaches you to think in irrational ways.

As far back as there is literature, there are observations

by philosophers, poets, playwrights, novelists and other students of human behaviour to the effect that some of the ideas current in their culture were basically illogical. The psychologist who has made the most influential statement of this point of view is Albert Ellis, who heads his own Institute for Advanced Study in Rational Psychotherapy in New York and who has written a large number of self-help and professional books. (We describe him as most influential because, in the last survey on the question, more psychotherapists practised his form of therapy, rational emotive therapy, than any other. In other words, more practising psychotherapists find his approach helpful than they do any other approach.)

Ellis proposes that all psychological problems arise from irrational thinking. Solving all psychological problems involves changing your thinking to be more rational. He also uses other procedures, like those described later but he sees the rational thinking component as the most important and essential.

He argues that we have all wound up sharing, to a greater or lesser degree, a common set of irrational beliefs about ourselves and the world. This shared irrational view of things results from our being exposed to similar influences at home, in school and in the community. Ellis summarised this view in ten popular irrational beliefs which we list in plainer English than he uses.

To train yourself to think more rationally, use this list of irrational beliefs when you review a dystressing situation afterwards. Look down the list and see which of the irrational beliefs you were buying into when you overreacted to the dystressing situation. You may be helped in this task by looking at your original self-talk as you have identified it at Step 4.

You may pick one or more irrational beliefs as being applicable to your overreaction to any situation, and you may find different ones apply to different situations. Don't dismiss the irrational beliefs as never applying to you because they are so extreme. It's easy to see they are silly, spelled out in black and white. The question you should ask yourself is **not**, 'Which of these do I believe?' but rather, 'Which of these beliefs influenced me to overreact this time,

TEN POPULAR IRRATIONAL BELIEFS

Irrational Belief 1
I must be loved or liked and approved of by every person in my life.

Irrational Belief 2
I must be completely competent, make no mistakes, and achieve all the time, if I am to be considered worthwhile.

Irrational Belief 3
Some people are bad, wicked or evil, and they should be punished for this.

Irrational Belief 4
It is dreadful, nearly the end of the world, when things aren't how I want them to be.

Irrational Belief 5
My bad feelings are caused by things outside my control, so I can't do anything about it.

Irrational Belief 6
If something might be dangerous, unpleasant or frightening, I should worry about it a lot.

Irrational Belief 7
It is easier to put off something difficult or unpleasant than it is to face up to it.

Irrational Belief 8
I need to depend on someone stronger than myself.

Irrational Belief 9
My problem(s) was (were) caused by some event(s) in my past, so that's why I have my problem(s) now.

Irrational Belief 10
I should be very upset by other people's problems and difficulties.

even if I can see it is silly when it's written out?'

Once you have identified the irrational beliefs underlying your overreaction to a particular situation, spend a couple of minutes rehearsing the alternative rational ideas. The numbers match: if this time you were reacting as though irrational beliefs 6 and 7 were true, you would spend time rehearsing rational ideas 6 and 7.

Just read the appropriate rational ideas to yourself a few times. They are written in general terms; try to fit them to your dystressing situation but be careful not to change their central ideas.

Some people find this step, or even all of them, awkward and artificial. 'Fancy reading my thoughts off a piece of paper! This is so contrived and unnatural!' We don't see this step as any more artificial than reading your thoughts off a parent, or a teacher, or a book, or any of the other places where you learned how to think.

The big difference we see is that this time you are learning to think rationally and realistically, and that is going to help you feel better and act more effectively.

Concluding our example When you review the situation later, you decide that you have been buying into irrational belief no. 3 (telling yourself what a bad person your boss is), irrational belief no. 5 (putting all of the blame for the situation and your feelings onto your boss), irrational belief no. 6 (imagining your boss overreacting angrily) and irrational belief no. 7 (if you put off asserting yourself with your boss).

You then spend a few minutes reading over rational ideas 3, 5, 6 and 7, trying to see how you can apply them to this situation. The next time it occurs, you can expect to look at it more rationally, feel better, and handle it more effectively (although the last outcome depends on your also working through Chapter 4).

PREPARING FOR FUTURE STRESSORS

So far, we have described the application of mental relaxation in, and after, a dystressing situation which has already happened to you. The signal to begin mental relaxation was when you became aware of intense or prolonged bad feelings.

You can also use the mental relaxation procedure to prepare yourself for future stressors. If there is a situation coming up that you expect to find dystressing, work through all six steps of mental relaxation beforehand. Imagine how you would feel, what your self-talk would be, and then apply the rest of the procedure.

TEN RATIONAL IDEAS

Rational Idea 1
I want to be loved or liked and approved of by some of the people in my life. I will feel disappointed or lonely when that doesn't happen, but I can cope with those feelings, and I can take constructive steps to make and keep better relationships.

Rational Idea 2
I want to do some things well, most of the time. Like everybody, I will occasionally fail or make a mistake. Then I will feel bad, but I can cope with that, and I can take constructive steps to do better next time.

Rational Idea 3
It is sad that most of us do some bad things from time to time, and some people do a lot of bad things. But making myself very upset won't change that.

Rational Idea 4
It is disappointing when things aren't how I would like them to be, but I can cope with that. Usually I can take constructive steps to make things more as I would like them to be, but, if I can't, it doesn't help me to exaggerate my disappointment.

Rational Idea 5
My problem(s) may be influenced by factors outside my control, but my thoughts and actions also influence my problem(s), and they *are* under my control.

Rational Idea 6
Worrying about something that might go wrong won't stop it from happening, it just makes me unhappy now! I can take constructive steps to prepare for possible problems, and that's as much as anyone can do. So I won't dwell on the future now.

Rational Idea 7
Facing difficult situations will make me feel bad at the time, but I can cope with that. Putting off problems doesn't make them any easier, it just gives me longer to worry about them.

Rational Idea 8
It's good to get support from others when I want it, but the only person I really *need* to rely on is myself.

Rational Idea 9
My problem(s) may have started in some past events, but what keeps it (them) going *now* are my thoughts and actions, and they are under my control.

Rational Idea 10
It is sad to see other people in trouble, but I don't help them by making mvself miserable. I can cope with feeling sad, and sometimes I can take constructive steps to help them.

Get yourself a small card, like a recipe or file card, and write on one side a coping self-statement, and on the other side the appropriate rational ideas, to fit the coming situation. Carry the card around with you, and read it to yourself several times a day. By the time you actually step into that situation, you will find it easier to use realistic self-talk, so you will feel better and act more effectively.

A BRIEF REVIEW
Phew! That was a long and detailed description of a procedure which, with practice, you will do very quickly in your head and, with more practice of Step 6, you won't need to do as much.

To help you begin applying mental relaxation to your own dystressing situations, we will now provide a very brief review of the whole procedure. You might want to write this on a small card, too, to carry with you.

Mental relaxation
On the spot:
Step 1 Get in touch with my feelings.
Step 2 Practise my coping self-statement.
Step 3 Give myself a pat on the back.
Later:
Step 4 Try to identify my original self-talk.
Step 5 Test my self-talk.
Step 6 Which irrational beliefs did I buy into that time? Practise the matching rational ideas.

PRACTISE!
We have repeatedly found that most people do not have too

much difficulty with mental relaxation. It may have struck you as complicated or technical the first time through but, with practice, you will find the steps are really not hard.

The hard bit, for most people, is the need to do it again and again and again. You are going to change years-old thinking habits, and that takes **persistence**. We have often found that the people who say mental relaxation has been no help to them either have not followed the procedure fully and properly, or have tried it a couple of times, and then given up.

Mental relaxation is one of the most rewarding procedures to introduce to someone because you know that, if she applies it carefully and persistently, she will first solve most of the problems in her life, but long after that she will be still making her life better and better. So start now, and stick to it.

PART II: PHYSICAL RELAXATION

As we said at the beginning of this chapter, some people have a physical tension component in their dystress. Some people are very aware of this, and will complain of feeling tense most of the time. Some people are unfortunate enough to suffer from tension headaches. And some people are prevented from sleeping by their physical tension. All of these people will benefit from learning to relax physically.

Even if you don't feel physically tense much of the time, don't dismiss the possible benefit to you of physical relaxation. Being able quickly to relax yourself physically in your dystressing situations can help you to feel in control and strengthen your belief in your ability to cope. And just relaxing feels good: people usually enjoy their relaxation-training. It's good to feel comfortable, without any drugs.

We made the point that physical relaxation, while not the panacea it is often touted as, and possibly even harmful if applied by itself, does have a contribution to make to stress management. So don't be in a hurry to throw the baby out with the bathwater. Don't rely **only** on physical relaxation to manage your stress. But do try it properly to see what contribution it can make to your programme.

RELAXATION IS BRAIN EXERCISE

Relaxation can be deceptive. It can look as if you aren't doing much at all. In fact, for dystressed people, it involves considerable mental effort. You will use your mind to relax your body. Even those relaxation procedures which aim at an 'empty' mind take some mental effort to get there.

In other words, relaxation is a very practical skill. Like other practical skills, to master it you need to **learn** and **practise** it.

LEARNING TO RELAX PHYSICALLY

This is one skill that is very hard to learn from a book. Just as you begin to relax, you have to sit up and turn the page! So you need a relaxation teacher you can listen to, while you do it. This can be a live teacher, or a recorded one.

Live relaxation teachers are usually easy to find in a town of any size. Yoga classes, meditation courses, relaxation courses at community health centres or in adult education classes are all suitable to try, and some doctors and psychologists offer individual physical relaxation training. If you try one of these resources and it doesn't suit you, skip it and try something else.

Advantages of a live relaxation teacher are the commitment you make if you join a course, the group support of others trying to master the same skill, the low cost of most group programmes, and there is some evidence that a live relaxation-induction works better than a recorded one, assuming the teacher is competent. Disadvantages are the inconvenience of having to travel to the class and keep a certain time free, discomfort if you don't like groups, and there are no quality controls on the teachers, some of whom try to go well beyond their limited training.

A recorded relaxation 'teacher' can be one you buy, or one you make. There are plenty of commercially available relaxation cassettes, with the same variability of quality as live relaxation teachers, so don't rush into buying one. Listen to it first and decide whether it sounds helpful to you.

We unashamedly recommend ours: Dr Bob Montgomery's *Total Relaxation*, explaining mental relaxation on

Side 1 and physical relaxation on Side 2 (published by Effective Communications, distributed by Pitman Publishing). We have been getting good feedback from users who find repeating Side 1 helps them to master mental relaxation, while Side 2 gets them very physically relaxed.

If you feel confident of your ability to instruct yourself, make your own relaxation cassette. You do not need elaborate equipment, because you are only recording your voice, not hifi. What you do need is a good script to follow, in putting down your own relaxation instructions. Two good resources are *The Relaxation Book* by Gerald Rosen, and *Learn To Relax* by C. Eugene Walker (both published by Prentice-Hall). Using either one, work out your relaxation routine, and then record it slowly and calmly. Making your own tape, you can experiment with it until you get it right.

Advantages of using a recorded 'teacher' are the convenience of being able to practise whenever it suits you, the privacy of doing it alone if you prefer, and the low cost since you only pay for the tape once. If it is made by a competent relaxation teacher it can approach the effectiveness of a live lesson. Disadvantages are the need for you to motivate yourself to practise regularly, and its insensitivity to feedback from you about an appropriate pace.

PRACTISING RELAXATION

We have made the point that relaxation is a practical skill which you strengthen through regular practice. If you are attending a relaxation course of some kind, your teacher should be advising you how often and how long to practise. On our cassette, we recommend three half-hour practice sessions a week.

We advise you to have those practices at any time other than in bed just before you go to sleep. If you are having trouble going to sleep, you could well find relaxation training helps (see Chapter 7). But the aim of our physical relaxation programme is that you should be able to relax physically while staying mentally alert. So if you are having a tense day at work, stop for a couple of minutes, repeat your self-instruction, 'Relax, relax', shed your excess tension and get on with the job. If you are using our cassette or your own, then practise at least three times a week, while you are alert. Then feel free to use it to help you sleep as well, if you want to.

INSTANT RELAXATION: THE QUIETING RESPONSE

The quieting response is a brief coping skill, developed by Dr Charles F. Stroebel and his colleagues, for use as an instant response to a stressor. It combines elements of both mental and physical relaxation, and has the advantages of being very brief. It takes about six seconds, and so it can be used on the spot with minimal interruption to the flow of your activities.

You may find that a quieting response is enough to cope with minor stressors, or at least that it gives you breathing space to prepare a coping self-statement and plan a constructive response to a larger stressor. Here is how to use it.

As soon as you notice an increase in your stress level (for example, increased muscle tension, especially in your face; change in your breathing; anxiety, annoyance, or other dystress):

Smile inwardly (that is, imagine yourself smiling, especially with your eyes),
Think: 'Alert mind, calm body';
Inhale an easy, natural breath;
While exhaling, relax your muscles (first your face, then shoulders, then feel a wave of relaxation and warmth flow down to your toes).

If you are then able to resume your normal activities, do so. Give yourself a pat on the back for coping. If the quieting response isn't enough, go on with the full mental relaxation procedure, by thinking a coping self-statement and backing it up with constructive action.

Dr Stroebel believes that if you practise the quieting response regularly, it should become a quieting reflex, automatically triggered by increases in your stress level. We think this is more likely to occur if you combine it with mental relaxation, but it is certainly a useful, quick coping skill.

EXPLODING THE LUXURY MYTH

'What a great idea,' you say. 'This total relaxation looks like just what I need. I must do some . . . later.' After all, there's work to be done, and the lawn needs mowing, and the kids want help with their homework, and you know they all can't get by without your personal aid and supervision. And you **owe** it to them; that's your role as a manager/worker/parent/citizen/etc. Beware: you have swallowed the luxury myth, hook, line and thumbscrews.

The luxury myth is the belief that any time (or effort or money) spent on you is a luxury and it therefore can only occur after you have spent all the time (or effort or money) necessary to fulfil everyone else's wants. This luxury myth is a very pervasive one in our society. We are often presented with the idea that it is noble and desirable to deny our own needs so as to meet the needs of others. Sacrifice is a short-cut to sainthood. Have you ever noticed how all the saints are dead? We aren't surprised, if that's how they really ran their lives.

Imagine you owned a delivery truck, and you ran it according to the luxury myth. On the road, engine running, 24 hours a day, seven days a week. No time for service, no time for repairs. Gotta keep those deliveries going because all of those people are relying on you to deliver as much as possible as quickly as possible.

When your engine blew up and your wheels fell off through a lack of commonsense maintenance you could hardly complain. When you looked at the bill for repairs, the cost of time lost off your delivery run, or perhaps the price of a new truck, you would have to accept that you had not been running your truck in a cost-effective way and you had finally let down all those people relying on you.

The time (and effort and money) you will have to spend maintaining yourself, through total relaxation and the other skills in this book, is a cost-effective investment you make in yourself. You **owe** it to anyone who relies on you, to give your needs genuine priority. That may mean you meet some of their wants a little more slowly, but it also means you are likely to be able to continue doing that for some time.

Making time available to practise and use your mental and physical relaxation skills is **not** indulging in luxury; it is **essential** self-repair.

PROMISES, PROMISES

'Yes,' you say, 'I can see the foolishness of the luxury myth and I renounce it immediately forever . . . but I still have trouble remembering to practise my physical relaxation. I know it's good for me, but I seem to forget or keep finding other things to do.'

You need a contract. Not with a hit-man to shoot you if you don't practise, although we have seen a few stubborn cases who needed that sort of incentive, but with yourself. Contracting with yourself is a useful motivational aid to help people do something they know is in their own interests, but expect to have trouble sticking to.

You may find contracting helps you to stick to your relaxation practice, or later to your exercise programme, or to any of the procedures described in this book that require regular practice. We will show you how to contract with yourself for relaxation practice, but you can write yourself a contract for any behavioural goal.

Get a large piece of paper or cardboard and write on it:

My relaxation contract

I promise myself that each week I will practise relaxing physically at least three times, for at least half an hour each time.

Each week that I keep this contract, I will reward myself with X (e.g. a favourite activity or food or drink, a record or book, or cash).

Each week that I don't keep this contract, I will penalise myself with Y (e.g. missing out on a favourite activity, doing a disliked chore, loss of cash).

When I have kept this contract for three months, my grand reward will be Z (e.g. a new suit, a holiday, a special outing).

I recognise that this contract is a promise I make myself to achieve something I want but expect to find difficult. If I cheat on this contract I only cheat myself.

Signed . . . .   Date . . . .

Pin your contract up somewhere where you will see it often. Much of its value is as a prompt to you. Next to it, pin up a tally sheet on which you will record your relaxation practices. Rule up columns headed, 'Week beginning (next Monday's date, and so on)'. In each column, put the dates for a practice, so that you can see at a glance how you are going on your contract.

At the end of each week, apply your reward or penalty to yourself as soon as possible. You can accept **real** excuses from yourself for not being able to complete a week's assignment, but bear in mind the last paragraph of your contract.

In the examples of rewards and penalties, we have suggested cash. Open a special purpose account, into which you pay your cash reward when you earn it. When you earn a penalty, pay the money to a charity that you dislike. If you have a cheque account, you can make another good visual prompt for yourself by writing out a cheque to that charity for your penalty amount, signing but not dating the cheque. Pin the cheque up next to your contract and tally sheet, where it also acts as a reminder. Any week you fail to keep your contract, date the cheque and post it off. Write out a new one and pin it up. The amount for your reward and penalty should be enough to be an incentive to you, but practical, so you do apply it.

It is not unusual to need to revise a contract. You may have set your behavioural goal too high or too low, or your reward or penalty too big or too small. If you are working towards a large behaviour change, you may gradually increase the standard you set in your contract.

Remember that a contract is only a motivational aid to help you to change some part of your behaviour, so feel free to modify it to make it as helpful as possible. And feel free to throw it away when you no longer need it.

But don't be put off contracting by its apparent artificiality. Common objections to contracting are that it is 'bribery' or just shows that you 'lack willpower'. Bribery means trying to get someone to do something 'wicked, evil or corrupt', while willpower is just another word for motivation, which results from **both** internal and external factors.

Sadly, many of the factors in our society are actively anti-health and irrational. They support self-defeating and dystress-inducing behaviour. Contracting is just a way of making a part of your environment support health-promoting and rational behaviour.

TAKE A CONSOLIDATION BREAK

We have already covered a lot of ground and set out some important techniques. If you are just reading through the book to get an overview of the programme before starting, or you want to read ahead to see what's coming up, fine. Go ahead.

But if you are working through the programme and trying to implement it now, we advise you to stop here to take some time to establish and consolidate your total relaxation skills. We encourage people coming to us for stress management to allow two or three weeks between appointments, so that they have enough time to try out the new skills introduced in each session.

If you are putting yourself through the programme, allow at least a similar time so that you can concentrate on your relaxation skills. If you try to change too much at once, you will wind up confused and distracted, and be unlikely to make real progress.

As we said in the introduction, the skills described in this book should become living skills for you, a permanent part of your lifestyle. You can afford to take your time to achieve such lasting change.

At any point in the programme where you feel you need it, give yourself a consolidation break, but especially after each new major topic. Use the break to focus on strengthening your new skills, and revise and refresh earlier ones.

3

TUNING UP YOUR BODY: RECREATION AND EXERCISE

You will remember from Chapter 1 that stress burns up a lot of energy. Even if you spend most of your day sitting at a desk – or perhaps because you do – you can end the day feeling utterly fatigued and washed out if you are suffering a lot of dystress.

Tiredness generally comes from working hard. It can even feel good because it is associated with achievement, and is 'cured' by a good night's sleep. Fatigue is more likely to arise from dystress, which may arise from having too little to do as well as too much; it rarely feels good and it usually isn't removed by sleep. Some people even find they are too fatigued to sleep properly (see Chapter 7).

If your car is out of tune, it burns up unnecessary fuel, and it runs roughly, which increases its wear and tear. It does not run efficiently or economically, and it is more likely to break down eventually.

Similarly, if your body is 'out of tune', meaning unfit, it will not run efficiently, and its struggle to keep up with your stress load will also lead to increased wear and tear. You become more likely to 'break down' in the exhaustion stage of the General Adaptation Syndrome. To prevent this, your human tune-up programme will have two streams to it: recreation and exercise. As you will see, they are different, and they overlap less often than most people think.

If you are already thinking you don't have time for recreation, you need to go back and review the luxury myth. And if you are already thinking you don't like the pain and sweat of exercise, you had better read our debunking of the exercise myths below.

In Chapter 1 we explained how the old divisions between

mind and body, and between psychological well-being and physical health, have been shown to be false. Your psychology and your biology are in perpetual interaction; ignore your biological well-being at your psychological peril.

RECREATION AND WORK

According to our dictionary, recreation means any activity which relaxes, amuses or refreshes you. It is potentially a very broad range of activities, and its purposes relaxation, enjoyment and refreshment. Given those aims, you can see why recreation has an important contribution to make to any stress-management programme.

We believe that recreation also ought to serve two other purposes. They may at first appear contradictory, but they aren't; they just show that you need different things at different times. In addition to the three aims above, recreation ought to help you meet your social needs, and your need for some time to yourself. We'll elaborate on these two goals later.

It's possible that your work gives you some enjoyment, and maybe even occasional relaxation and refreshment. But for many people, unfortunately, their work rarely provides these benefits.

We are talking about the work itself, not other activities that you may do at, or through, your workplace, such as sporting or social activities with your workmates. They are recreation and, if you are doing some, keep it up. By 'work' here, we mean the bit you're getting paid for (or should be, if your work is looking after a household). In Chapter 10 we discuss some of the reasons for most people's work offering them little of positive value other than wages, and we have some suggestions there for improving that situation. For now, we will assume that your work offers you, at best, insufficient relaxation, amusement or refreshment, and that you therefore need to plan your own recreation to meet these needs.

It's quite possible that you will need to make some deliberate plans and put some effort into making them happen. Some managers and workers do acknowledge that there are some basically dreadful jobs: hot, dirty, heavy, noisy, boring, repetitive, or whatever. But it is usually assumed that the workers in these jobs can make up for their negative effects in after-work activities, through recreation.

Some trade unions and professional associations make a big fuss about getting shorter working hours for their members, ostensibly so that they can have more time for recreation. And then their members use the extra time to work overtime! Some workplaces proudly point out the recreational facilities they provide for their staff. The current status symbol is a gymnasium full of shiny, impressive equipment. But have you ever noticed what proportion of the staff ever use these facilities on a regular basis?

The sad fact, as we discuss in Chapter 10, is that the worse your job is, the **less** likely you are to be using recreation that might otherwise compensate for the stress-inducing effects of your job. So, if you think you do have a job that's a source of dystress to you, that does not offer much relaxation, amusement or refreshment, then you will just have to accept your personal responsibility to look after yourself, by making sure you do have sufficient recreation in your life.

Andrew worked for the local council as a general labourer. The job he did was repetitive, slow and most of the time boring. Andrew was a reasonably intelligent person, although he had never done well at school, so he found the job pretty uninteresting. After a couple of months working, he began taking a sick day more and more often, like many of the guys working in this job. On his days off, he did nothing but just sat in front of the TV, usually went down to the pub in the afternoon and stayed there until 10 o'clock.

When he worked a full day, he spent the rest of the evening at the pub, sometimes not getting home until 8 or 9 o'clock and then sitting in front of the TV until after midnight. If he stayed late at the pub, he usually took a sick day the next day to recover from a hangover.

Andrew felt increasingly dissatisfied. He didn't like doing what he was doing but he saw no way out. He had to earn the money; his wife and baby daughter relied on him. But he felt like escaping from all the responsibility. His wife was nagging more and more and even though he cared a lot for his daughter he was spending less and less time with her and more and more time drinking alone, or at the pub.

His life seemed pointless.

A recipe for depression. Let's add a dash of recreation.

Andrew worked in the same job, he occasionally went to the pub with his friends but he was also very interested in archery.

He spent a great deal of his time at work, particularly when there was nothing much to do, thinking about how to improve his shots, his stance, etc. He would often be reading sales brochures about the latest gear for archers. He put a small amount of money aside each week so that he could buy any new equipment he needed. He would go to practice one night a week, then another night of the week he and his wife would attend the social evening which they both enjoyed. At weekends they usually took their daughter to the family outings that the archery club organised.

Andrew recognised that his job was boring and sometimes it was hard to drag himself off to work but he usually looked forward to spending a bit of time reading or thinking about archery.

Andrew would often compete in local competitions and afterwards, regardless of whether he won or not, he and his wife would spend the evenings alone together celebrating at one of their favourite eating places.

Andrew's wife was also involved in a tennis club, which provided them with more opportunities for meeting people socially. When Andrew went to the pub, his wife usually went out with girlfriends from tennis.

In all Andrew enjoyed his life.

There is another reason why recreation needs to be taken more seriously than it often has been, a reason that is going to be urgently important to us all as a nation. If you define a job as working full-time for pay, then Australia has already passed the point where we have enough jobs for all the people who want them. A high unemployment rate, especially amongst school leavers, seems to have become a permanent feature of our society; we notice that no political party now promises to end unemployment. Of course the economy will pick up again, and governments and private business will create new jobs, but the processes of automation and computerisation inevitably mean that the supply of jobs will continue to shrink.

We leave it to the economists and politicians to tackle issues such as job-sharing and permanent part-time work, but whatever answers they come up with, one thing is clear. Increasing numbers of people will have increasing amounts of so-called leisure time, time for recreation. If we are not to create Roman circuses out of football or horse-racing, and perhaps go the way of the Roman empire, we must do two things: teach people how to have healthy recreation, and teach them to value it.

That's going to be a big job for the nation; right now, it's important that you do both of these things for yourself: develop healthy recreation as a **part** of your lifestyle, and recognise how valuable it is for you. (Incidentally we have found that developing recreation and leisure skills is one very good way for the unemployed to find jobs more easily.)

Developing these skills will eventually be vital to you as an individual in any case, because in all probability you will eventually retire from your paid job. It's a sad paradox that many people say how much they are looking forward to doing nothing after they retire, but find they have nothing to do after retiring.

It's no mistake that Holmes and Rahe include vacations in their survey of recent experiences (see page 31) to assess how much stress life is putting on you at present. For many people, a vacation is a source of stress because they simply don't know what to do with themselves, and they devalue recreational activities.

Developing good recreational habits will serve you well now as part of your stress-management programme, and it will serve you well in the future, to ensure that you have a long and happy retirement.

HOW TO DEVELOP GOOD RECREATIONAL HABITS

STEP 1   ASSESS YOUR PRESENT RECREATIONS

You need to know first how much recreation you are already having, and whether it meets the various aims of recreation.

So you will need an accurate record of how much recreation you do, what kinds of activities are involved, and with whom you do them.

Practical exercise: Record your present recreations. Use a small spiral-backed notebook or a diary, and keep an accurate record of your present recreations, day by day. You need a reasonably representative picture, so you will probably need to keep this record for at least a week, and maybe longer if you have some regular activities which occur fortnightly, or monthly, or whatever.

Record what you do, how long you spend on it, with whom you are sharing that activity and the pleasure you get from that activity.

STEP 2   REVIEW YOUR PRESENT RECREATIONS

When you think you have a reasonably complete picture of your present recreations, review them. We know that for some people, this won't take long because they do little or no recreation! If that's you, at least you have lots of room for improvement.

But some people will have recorded a number of recreations, and may be unsure about whether it's enough. Be guided in your review by the stated aims of recreation. Do your present recreations provide you with enough

relaxation?
amusement?
refreshment?
exercise?
social relationships?
solitude?

Some of these are clear: relaxation we have already explained in the previous chapter; exercise we will explain later in this chapter, and you will need to read that information to review your exercise properly. Let us explain now about the social and solitude aims of recreation.

Most people benefit from having good relationships with others. Somewhere there may be a genuine hermit or two, but they are rare. For most of us, successful relationships are an important resource, and lacking them, or having unsuccessful relationships, are usually sources of dystress.

RECORD WHAT YOU DO EACH HOUR DURING THE WEEK AND GIVE THE ACTIVITY A 'P' IF YOU FOUND IT PLEASURABLE

	Mon.	Tues.	Wed.	Thur.	Fri.	Sat.	Sun.
7–10	Got up, breakfast	Got up, late	Got up, breakfast	Got up, breakfast	Got up, breakfast	Sleep in P	Sleep in P
10–11	Work	Work	Work P	Work	Work	Breakfast	Breakfast
11–12						Mow lawns	Read P
12–1	Lunch P	Lunch with friends P	Lunch	Lunch P	Lunch and drink P	Gardening P	Tidied house
1–2	Work	Work	Work	Work	Work	Lunch P	Cooked lunch P
2–3						Watched son play football P	Family for lunch
3–4							
4–5	Travelled home	Travelled home	Met a friend, had a drink P	Work	Shopping P		
5–6	Read paper P	Talked to wife P		Dinner out with wife P		Drinks at Club P	Cleaned up
6–7	Dinner P	Dinner P	Dinner P		Dinner out with wife and kids P		Watched TV
7–8	Watched TV	Watched TV	Watched TV	Read paper P		Dinner P	Watched TV P
8–12	TV, bed	TV, bed	TV, bed	Bed P	Bed	Read paper, bed	Bed

In our book, *Living and Loving Together*, also published by Viking O'Neil, we have given detailed advice on how to improve your relationship with your spouse, and some advice on improving your relationships with your children. In Chapter 9 of this book we give you advice on how to make and develop friendships.

In both of these discussions you will find that shared recreation is an important part of making and keeping successful relationships. By having a good time together, you refresh the other person's rewardingness for you (and vice versa), and you create new material for conversations.

We don't mean that you have to do everything good together, just some things. If your only dealings with a person are business-like or around work or chores, you may get on well and respect each other, but you are unlikely to develop a close and enjoyable relationship.

Of course, with many people, you want only a polite acquaintance, and that's fine. But with some people you will want a closer, more enjoyable relationship, and to achieve that shared recreation is vital.

Doing good things together as a couple, with your spouse or specially intimate friend, we call **coupling**. As we have explained in *Living and Loving Together*, a lack of coupling is the most common reason for Australian marriages failing so don't neglect this part of your recreation plans if you are in a couple relationship.

Familying, you will guess, is doing good things as a family, perhaps as a whole, sometimes just a few family members together. Just as coupling is vital for a successful couple relationship, sharing fun as a family is essential to good family relationships.

You should also be sharing some recreation with friends. In Chapter 9 we explain how recreation is the best pathway to making and developing friendships. Even if you are in a couple relationship like a marriage, you and it will benefit from your having some recreation independent of that relationship, recreation which you may well share with other friends. This allows each of the partners in your marriage or special relationship to maintain his individual interests and keep a set of personal friendships outside the partnership. It saves you from being over-dependent on your couple relationship and suffocating it, and at the same time can increase your commitment to it because it recognises your individuality.

Being alone when you don't want to be usually leads to loneliness, which is itself a common source of dystress (see Chapter 9); but being alone by choice, to take a break from other people and spend some time with your own thoughts and activities is **solitude**, and that also should play a part in your recreation plan. Just as most of us need some shared recreation and recreation with friends, so we need some time to be by ourselves. You may wish to use your solo recreation time for activities like relaxation, meditation, exercise, reading, listening to music, and so on. But one thing many people like solitude for is thinking. Typically this thinking includes reflecting, contemplating, evaluating, daydreaming, and working out what your current priorities are. For some time, you may need some solitude to work on and think about your stress-management programme.

If you haven't been finding time for yourself, you may wonder how you will manage. Some techniques people use include getting up an hour before everybody else, staying up after everybody has gone to bed, getting up during the night, and using coffee breaks, lunch-times and travelling time, especially if you drive alone.

You may need to make some special provision for a place and time to be alone, at home or at work. Discussing your wish for solitude may lead to other people identifying the same desire, and some arrangements being made like setting aside a room for solitude. Then it's up to you to use it.

Practical exercise: Review your present recreations. Using the guidelines above, are there gaps in your recreations? Is work or some other commitment taking up a disproportionate amount of your time? Does one activity, even if it is a recreation, hog your time to the exclusion of other recreational needs? Remember, a healthy life is a balanced one.

STEP 3   PLAN YOUR NEW RECREATIONS
If you have identified gaps or imbalances in your present recreation menu, you should now plan to fill the gaps and

correct the imbalances. Are you missing out on relaxation? Or exercise? Does one interest take up so much of your time that there isn't any left to share recreation with family or friends?

Stuck for ideas? If you haven't been doing much recreation, that's quite possible. You may find some ideas in newspapers, especially local papers and the entertainment sections of daily papers; in rural areas, try your local radio and television reports of local activities; also look at the programmes run by the Council for Adult Education, the various University Unions, the Colleges of Advanced Education and the Colleges of Tertiary and Further Education.

Come on, we can't do it for you. Do let your imagination go, and be willing to try something different. If you can identify activities you would like to try, but you are held back by being anxious about meeting new people, you will need to work on Chapter 9 as well.

Practical exercise: Plan your new activities. Draw up your personal plan for meeting all your recreational needs. If there are gaps you can't fill straight away, don't worry. Make a start on those you can.

STEP 4 TRY OUT YOUR NEW ACTIVITIES
Grit your teeth and give it a whirl. If you are troubled by shyness, follow the advice in Chapter 9. But do it.

Of course, it's possible you will try a new recreation and not like it. It isn't what you imagined it would be. Well, that's disappointing, but you can cope with being disappointed and at least you tried it. If you are sure it really isn't your cup of tea, give yourself a pat on the back for trying, drop it, and plan something else to take its place.

In all this expansion of activities, do follow our basic rule of thumb of gradual change, especially if you have been depressed. Trying to do too much too quickly can just set you up for failure which will only discourage you. Take small but steady steps and you have a much better chance of making a success of your new recreation plan.

Practical exercise: Implement your recreation plan. Feel free to amend it as you go; it's meant to make your life better. In any case,

HOW THE PERSON IN THE PREVIOUS EXAMPLE CHANGED HIS RECREATION

	Mon.	Tues.	Wed.	Thur.	Fri.	Sat.	Sun.
7–10	Early rise, walk with kids P	Early rise, read at breakfast P	Walk with kids, breakfast P	Breakfast P	Breakfast P	Sleep in P	Sleep in P
10–11	Work, coffee break	Work, went for walk	Work	Work	Work	Played with kids P	Game of golf with wife and friends P
11–12	Work	Work				Household chores	
12–1	Swam with friend, lunch P	Lunch with wife P	Swam with friend, lunch P	Walk, lunch with workmates P	Lunch at pub with workmates P	Picnic lunch with family at local football match (son playing) P	Lunch P
1–2	Work	Work	Work	Work	Work		
2–3	Work, afternoon tea P		Work, afternoon tea P	Work, afternoon tea P			
3–4	Work		Work	Work			
4–5	Met wife & kids, played tennis P	Went for a swim and sauna	Wore headphones on way home P	Drink after work P	Swim and sauna P		Relax at home P
5–6	Dinner P	Travelled with headphones P	Dinner P	Dinner P	Theatre and dinner with wife P	Listen to music P	Dinner P
6–7	Game of cards with friends P	Candlelight dinner with wife P	Pottery classes P	Played with kids P		Dinner P	Watched TV P
7–8				Watched TV P		Went to party with friends P	
8–12	Bed	Bed	Bed	Bed	Bed		Bed

you will probably need to revise it from time to time to cope with changes in your interests, capacities and relationships. Just be guided by the same principles you used above to draw up your recreation plan.

EXERCISE

Exercise is one special part of your recreation programme. It's possible that you will get sufficient exercise through some of your other recreations – we'll tell you how to check that later – but it serves such an important purpose and it is so often misunderstood that it deserves detailed consideration in its own right.

Your exercise programme will be that part of your recreation plan especially designed to improve and maintain your physical fitness. If you are run down and unfit, it won't take much of a load on you to push you into dystress. On the other hand, if you are reasonably fit, the same load will fall within your normal coping range of demand, and you will experience eustress. This isn't just a theoretical notion; if you haven't been fit for a while, you will really feel the positive gains from a sensible exercise programme, both physically and emotionally.

Exercise has at least two other major advantages, as well as making a key contribution to your stress-management programme; it will help prevent heart disease, and help to manage your weight. The exercise programme we will outline is based on aerobic exercise, which is the kind that strengthens your heart-lung system. This will help you prevent heart disease, now one of our major killers. And we now know that for most people with overweight problems, a sensible exercise programme is essential if they are going to lose excess weight, and then maintain a healthy weight. So you will win in at least three ways from an exercise programme.

Still not convinced? If the idea of exercise puts you right off, you are probably being influenced by one or more of the popular myths about exercise. Before we debunk them, let us explain our sources of information.

We are not exercise physiologists (although we have both studied human physiology), nor are we physical education instructors (although Lyn has worked as a gym instructor and Bob as a scuba diving instructor). In preparing this section of our programme, we have relied heavily on the research and ideas of Dr Laurence Morehouse who is professor of exercise physiology and director of the human performance laboratory at the University of California in Los Angeles. He wrote the section on exercise in the Encyclopaedia Britannica, as well as a number of textbooks in the field. His research was the basis of the physical training programme for NASA's astronauts on the lunar landing missions. We thought he knew what he was talking about and, most importantly, his approach to exercise for ordinary people is realistic.

THE MYTHS OF EXERCISE
Myth Number 1
'Exercise must be long, hard, demanding and unpleasant to be good for you.'
Every lunchtime we see joggers threading their way through the traffic, sweat pouring off them, wearing looks of noble

suffering. Most ordinary people shudder inwardly and feel glad that they are sloths. And the myth that exercise, like medicine, must be nasty to be good, is reinforced again.

In fact, those joggers running on roads and concrete footpaths run the risk of damaging their joints and tendons and, if there's much motor traffic around, over-dosing on carbon monoxide and lead. If they aren't already in very good condition, then they are subjecting themselves to a health-reducing and body-damaging overload. It wouldn't be so bad if they chose to damage only themselves like this, but by doing it in public they help to give exercise a bad name.

The facts are that you don't need long to achieve genuine benefit from exercise – three 10-minute workouts a week are sufficient – and healthy exercise involves moderate exertion – enough demand to get a training effect, but not so much as to be harmful or unpleasant.

Myth Number 2
'Don't drink while exercising.'
This is a bit like the myth that you shouldn't drink while eating, or you 'dilute' your digestive juices. Quaint ideas but no evidence to support them.

When your body is working, as in exercise, its cells produce waste products, which need to be removed. If you dehydrate yourself by abstaining from drinking while exercising, you have less fluid available to do the waste removal and you lose energy.

You also risk death, particularly if it is hot. There was a report recently on a jogger who literally cooked his brain and died because he didn't drink during a fun run.

Myth Number 3
'Take sugar (or glucose) before exercise, but avoid spicy, heavy or gassy foods.'
This one's back to front; if you want to avoid eating anything before exercise (or at any time), it's straight sugar (including glucose). Straight sugar, including sweets, may give a temporary lift, but can actually cause the body to withdraw its natural sugar reserves. Even if you get your lift, it will be followed by a thumping down.

As for those tasty, spicy, heavy, gassy foods that are supposed to be bad for you, Professor Morehouse's group found they made no difference at all to your performance or well-being.

Myth Number 4
'Avoid eating before swimming.'

Do you remember being told this as a child? 'You can't go in for a swim yet,' Mum would say, 'it's not an hour since lunch. You'll get cramp and drown.' And that was the theory: your blood was supposedly occupied around your gut in digesting lunch, and so was unavailable for exercise.

Well, your body knows better than Mum did; start exercising and it withdraws the blood from your gut and sends it to the muscles, where it's needed.

Myth Number 5
'Salt tablets prevent fatigue.'

If you took your glucose tablets before the game or race, chances are you were taking salt tablets afterwards, 'to replace the salt you had sweated out'. It's true that you lose salt when you sweat, but you have to do a lot of sweating before you lose a significant amount and taking a salt tablet to replace it is a real example of using a sledge hammer to crack a peanut.

The role of salt in causing high blood pressure, and therefore contributing to heart disease, is now well known. Unless you are sweating a great deal, you will replace your losses just by eating a balanced diet. If you think you need any supplement, sprinkle a little salt on your food.

Myth Number 6
'Extra protein makes you stronger.'

This myth is helped along by commercials depicting various athletes downing their protein supplements or scoffing their protein breakfast foods. The related myth is the idea that high protein foods help in weight loss.

The facts are that the body needs comparatively small amounts of protein, of which it has large reserves. Even when you are working hard, you don't need protein supplements. And as for weight loss, protein is a very rich

energy source. Eating lots of it will help you put on more fat.
Carbohydrate is a much better energy source.

Myth Number 7
'You should sweat a lot during exercise, but don't get cold afterwards.'

Some people will wear tracksuits and other heavy garments
to increase their sweating during exercise. Others might
wear lighter clothes while working out, but rush to put on
jumpers or tracksuits as soon as they are finished, 'to avoid
getting a chill'.

In fact, your body works and feels best within a fairly
narrow temperature range, and has its own systems for
staying within that range. If anything, it needs help to
achieve this goal, not hindrance.

Overheating yourself during exercise, or afterwards, only
increases the strain on the system, sometimes dangerously.
Dress lightly for exercise; let your body cool down
afterwards. In very hot weather or for very demanding
performances, you can even cool down beforehand with a
cold shower.

Myth Number 8
'Exercise is for getting big muscles, because that makes you stronger (so it's probably not a good idea for women who want to stay feminine).'

Again a belief promoted by using big-muscled men to
advertise gymnasiums, although it's been good to see a few
women creeping into the ads.

Exercise is for increasing fitness and health, or ours is, at
any rate. You will get some increase in muscle bulk, but not
that much. You can have large muscles without being very
strong, and large muscles can be a disadvantage because
they are extra weight to carry around.

Women have different hormones circulating in their
bodies to men, so they have characteristically different body
shapes, as you have probably noticed. Exercise doesn't
change that difference, it just tones up your body shape,
whichever sex you are. Many women models and movie stars
use exercise programmes to maintain their attractive body
shapes.

Myth Number 9
'I get enough exercise from my sport, or my job.'
Maybe, but usually not. As you will see below, to get a worthwhile training effect, exercise needs to be done often enough, for long enough, and hard enough. Many people will correctly recognise they meet one or two of these criteria already, but not all three, so they are not getting worthwhile exercise.

If you play two hard games of squash a week, with no other real exercise, you may play hard enough and long enough, but not often enough. Your body will lose so much condition between games that each game actually imposes a health-damaging overload. Three workouts a week is the acceptable minimum.

If you take the dog for a walk nearly every day, or your job keeps you moving a lot, you may work often and long enough, but probably not hard enough. To get a training effect, you need to subject yourself to an overload: large enough to improve your condition, small enough not to be damaging. This is usually a moderate level of exertion. Later we'll explain how to use your pulse rate to monitor this.

If you play some sport three times a week, including training or practice sessions, such as netball, you may find you are playing often enough, and when you've got the ball it's hard enough, but a careful look shows you aren't really active long enough. The nature of your game is that you spend a fair bit of time standing around, or in relatively mild activity. The acceptable minimum is ten minutes consistent workout although, as you will see, this is not all at top speed.

To sum that up, an acceptable exercise programme will consist of three 10-minute workouts a week, involving moderate exertion. You can certainly do more, if you like, providing you don't exceed your moderate exertion level, but you cannot do less if you want a genuine training effect.

BE GUIDED BY YOUR HEART
No, this is not advice to the lovelorn, but the means for achieving those desirable moderate levels of exertion. Your heart, you will know, is the muscular pump which

transports oxygen to the organs in your body and removes the waste products, via your blood. Your body's ability to transport oxygen and remove waste products determines its level of fitness, so your heart's condition is a key to your general level of fitness, and your heart rate reliably indicates how hard you are working.

Your heart rate, or pulse, is the best measure of how hard you are working, much better than distances or times run, swum or bicycled, or dial readings on an exercise bike, or similar external measures. If you are already fit, running two kilometres in 15 minutes may be easy for you; if you aren't fit, walking them in half an hour may knock you out! Your heart rate would accurately reflect how hard that task was for you, at your present level of fitness.

As your fitness improves, you will find that you need to do a bit more work to achieve the same heart rate. This makes sense; since you are getting fitter, moderate exertion for you should require more actual work. It's getting easier because you are getting fitter.

Another way of putting this is to say that your heart rate will tend to decrease as you get fitter. In fact, a low heart rate while you are at rest is a good indicator of physical fitness. Later, we will give you the details of desirable heart rates to aim for during your exercise, depending on your age and level of fitness.

BEFORE YOU START EXERCISING

If you haven't done much exercise for a long time, or if you are over forty, or you have any history of heart trouble, you should have a medical check-up before you start an exercise programme. Other warning signs include occasional pains in the chest, breathing difficulties, high blood pressure, heavy smoking, dizziness or faintness, influenza or stomach upsets.

None of these will necessarily stop you from exercising, and the last two are typically temporary. But you should recognise that exercise will put an extra load on your body, and you should be sure it can cope with that, now.

HOW TO TAKE YOUR PULSE

Your pulse is waves of pressure flowing through your blood,

caused by your heart beats. It is not the movement of the blood itself, which is much slower. It does indicate how fast your heart is beating, and that's what we'll use it for.

You can detect your pulse in any artery, but it's easiest where there is a bone behind the artery to push against. If you go to have a medical check-up, ask your doctor to show you some of the usual places for taking a pulse, and pick the one you find easiest. We'll describe how to take your pulse at the wrist, because most people prefer that. You will need a clock or watch that measures seconds. If using your watch, wear it on your wrist so that you can see it, when your palm is facing up.

Place your wrist into the palm of your other hand, so that your wrist lies in the 'V' between your thumb and forefinger, with both hands palms upwards, pointing away from you. Allow the fingers of your lower hand to curl up around your other wrist, towards your thumb and you will find that the

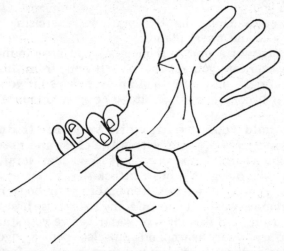

finger tips fit into the groove on the side of the wrist. This is where the radial artery lies over the bone, so gently pushing down with the pad of your middle finger should find your pulse.

Press firmly enough to get a clear pulse, but not too hard, or you will just block the artery. You may need to practise this for a while, if you aren't used to taking pulses.

When you are feeling a clear pulse, wait for a pulse to coincide with a clear time mark on your watch, such as one of the five-second marks. When it does, begin counting, from zero (then 1, 2, 3, etc.), until you have the number of beats that occur in six seconds. Multiply this number by ten, and you have your pulse rate.

It's important you start from zero, to get an accurate count. It's true that a longer count will give you a more accurate estimate of your resting pulse rate, but you need your pulse rate immediately after exercising, and that will drop quickly, especially when you are fit. So a short count works better here.

SOME GUIDELINES FOR EXERCISE

Try to work out on **alternate days**, such as Monday, Wednesday, then Friday, to achieve your three workouts a week. The longer the gap between workouts, the more condition you will lose.

Keep cool. Dress lightly; you are exercising your muscles, not your sweat glands.

Listen to your body. Remember you are aiming for moderate exertion; you get the most benefit from the first repetition or the first minute of an exercise, so if you find going on is becoming a strain, stop. You can do more next time.

Never hold your breath while you are straining. Doing so increases pressure within the chest and prevents blood from returning to your heart. You may faint as a result, or even bring on a heart attack.

Drink plenty of water. Remember your body needs water to remove waste. If you are going to exercise first thing in the morning, drink a glass of water before you start.

Warm up your heart and muscles before vigorous exercise. A sudden, high demand may be uncomfortable, even damaging. You only need about a minute to warm up from light to moderate activity. You'll see this is built into our programme.

Don't stand still after exercise. Walk around, or sit down, or again you may pass out. Exercise causes your blood vessels to open up, including those in your legs. They rely on the contractions of your leg muscles to pump the blood in them back to the heart. Exercise, then stand still, and blood will pool in these vessels, leaving your brain short. When you are taking your pulse immediately after an exercise to monitor your exertion level, walk around slowly, or sit down.

Take it easy. If you push yourself too hard, so that your exercise programme becomes unpleasant, you are just more likely to drop out, and then you haven't done yourself any good at all. Be guided by your pulse rate, in accordance with the next section.

YOUR TRAINING PULSE RATE

To get a training effect, an improvement in your fitness level, you must overload yourself a bit. If what you do is no overload, it will not improve your fitness, although it can maintain it, which we'll aim for later.

As we have emphasised, a healthy exercise programme involves a moderate overload – enough to get a training effect, but not enough to be unpleasant or harmful. The best way of ensuring this for yourself, is to be guided by your pulse rate.

The table lists the training pulse rates you should aim for, depending on your age, and what stage of your exercise programme you have reached. Look down the left-hand column and pick your age group. Now look across that row.

TRAINING PULSE RATE

Age	TPR1	TPR2	TPR3	TPR4
Under 30	120	140	150	150–160
30–44	110	130	140	140–150
45–60	100	120	130	130–140
Over 60	100	110	120	120–130

TPR1 is your training pulse rate for Stage 1 of your exercise programme, which will last eight weeks; TPR2 applies to Stage 2, which also takes eight weeks; and TPR3 to Stage 3, for another eight weeks. TPR4 is your training pulse rate for your fitness maintenance programme, after you have finished the first three stages to improve your fitness.

Check your pulse after the aerobic section of each

workout. If you are much below your current training pulse rate, you can work a bit harder next time. If you are much above, go a bit easier next time.

YOUR EXERCISE PROGRAMME

STAGE 1
The main aim of your first eight weeks is to build up muscle tissue. This is most important for those who haven't done much exercise for a while, since your muscles, and the blood vessels supplying them, will literally have shrunk. They can't do much work, as you may have sometimes noticed.

Now you are going to rebuild your muscles, and their blood supply, so that they are ready for the later stages of the programme. Each 10-minute workout is divided into three parts:

I   **One minute of limbering up.** This is to give you a warm-up, and to increase your flexibility. Spend about 15 seconds each on:
     1 High reaches: Reach as high as you can with one hand, directly over your head. Let your arm drop, and reach up with the other hand.

HIGH REACHES

2 Body twists: Extend your arms out sideways, and then twist your trunk as far around as it will go; then twist back the other way.

BODY TWISTS

3 Pull downs: Bend over, grasp your legs behind the knees, and pull your shoulders gently towards your knees; don't force yourself.

PULL DOWNS

4 Head turns: Turn your head to the left, over your shoulder, and put your left hand on the right side of your chin, and your right hand on the back of your head. Gently turn your head a little further than it will go by itself. Now the other way.

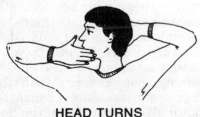

HEAD TURNS

II **Four minutes of muscle building.** Do alternate sets
of these two exercises:
    1 Expansion push-aways: Stand a little more than
your arms' reach from a wall; put your hands on the wall
level with your shoulders. Lean forward until your chest
is close to the wall, then push back to your starting

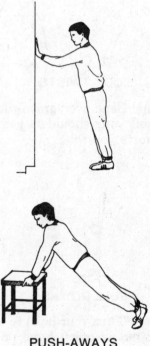

PUSH-AWAYS

position. If it's too hard, stand closer to the wall. A set of
these is 15 to 20. Check your pulse after the set.

Remember, you are aiming for moderate exertion. At
first, you can build up to 20 repetitions. Then you can
increase the difficulty by having your hands a bit lower,
say, on a chest of drawers. Eventually you will be doing
push-ups, with your hands and feet on the floor. If you
need something more difficult than that, you can
gradually raise your feet, onto a bench, for example.
    2 Expansion sit-backs: Sit on the floor with your

feet hooked under a piece of heavy furniture, to support you, and with your knees bent. Bring your chest as close to your knees as you can comfortably manage, and put your hands flat on your stomach, to feel the muscles. Lean back until you feel your stomach muscles are under a moderate load that you can maintain for 15 to 20 seconds. Then sit up again. This is one set. Check your pulse.

Gradually increase the load in this exercise, first by building up from 15 to 20 seconds per set, then by gradually leaning further back for each set. Once your back is nearly reaching the floor, move your hands from your stomach to folded on your chest, and finally behind your head.

You should be able to do two sets of each of these building exercises in your four minutes.

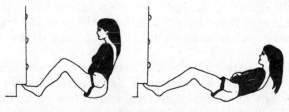

SIT-BACKS

III **Five minutes of aerobic activity.** Any activity that increases your heart and breathing rates will do. Try running on the spot, skipping, hopping, jogging (on grass, and never downhill), cycling, swimming or whatever. Keep up an easy, steady rhythm (do it to music!) and aim to reach your training pulse rate by the end of the second minute and then maintain it for three minutes. Keep moving while you check your pulse.

You will probably need to experiment with positions and speeds in your first few workouts to establish your moderate exertion levels. That's fine; over the rest of this eight weeks, gradually increase your load, as your fitness improves, to maintain moderate exertion.

STAGE 2

The main aim of this eight weeks is to build up your endurance, your capacity to sustain work over time. Now, each 10-minute workout will be divided into two sections.

I **Four minutes of muscle endurance training.** Do two sets each of these two exercises:

1 Endurance push-aways: These are the same push-aways as you did in Stage 1, but now do twice as many in each set and try to do them quickly. You will need to go back to an easier difficulty level than you finished Stage 1 on, and again gradually build up. So now a set is 40 to 50.

2 Endurance sit-backs: Start in the same sit-back position as before, then lean about a third of the way to the floor and hold that position for 10 to 15 seconds. Now lean further back, to halfway, and hold for 10 to 15 seconds. Finally move to three quarters of the way back and again try to hold for 10 to 15 seconds. If your stomach muscles start to quiver, the exertion is getting heavy: sit up or flop back. One sit-back is one set.

II **Six minutes of aerobic activity.** Now you are going to use interval training. This consists of alternating periods of intense exercise and active rest. The rest periods allow your body to deal with the waste produced during the intensive periods, and so avoid fatigue.

Start your chosen aerobic activity at your old rate, to reach TPR1, for 30 seconds; now speed up until you reach your TPR2. This will take some experimenting, at first.

After one minute, slow down, but not below your TPR1, for 30 seconds. Then just keep alternating between the two, for a total of six minutes. Don't exceed your TPR2.

STAGE 3

The main aim of this stage is to build up your muscle strength, the capacity to lift heavy loads for short durations. Again, there will be two sections to your workout, but strength-training does not take long, so you can spend more time on the aerobic section.

I   **Two minutes of muscle strengthening.**
     1 Strength push-aways: The same exercise as before, but now aiming for such a heavy load that you can't manage more than five in a set. Experiment with your feet position to achieve this level of load.
     2 Strength sit-backs: Same starting position as before, but now go to a position that you can hold for only five seconds. When you need to, you can increase the load in sit-backs, by extending your arms over your head, or by holding a weight on your chest.
     Do three alternating sets of these two exercises. Watch your pulse rate does not exceed your TPR3.

II   **Eight minutes of aerobic interval training.** This time your intervals will be alternating periods of 15 seconds. In the first interval, aim for your TPR2, then in the second interval, move up to your TPR3, then drop back to TPR2, and so on. It usually takes two to three minutes of these alternating intervals to reach TPR3. Check your pulse every two minutes and adjust your efforts accordingly. Don't exceed your TPR3.

STAGE 4

This is really the rest of your life. The aim of this stage is to maintain your now good level of fitness. You might achieve this by playing a sport at least three times a week, but do look at it critically to make sure it gives you all the workout you need.

Most of us will need to continue our three 10-minute workouts a week. Feel free to select amongst the exercises you have now been introduced to, to meet your needs and provide variety. Aim for your TPR4 when appropriate.

If you stop exercising for a while, as most people will from time to time, just put yourself back into the programme at an appropriate level. Aim for moderate exertion, and gradually build up your fitness again.

If you would like to stick to an exercise programme, but expect to find that difficult, contract with yourself, as we explained in Chapter 2 for relaxation practice. Contracting is a useful motivational aid.

BUT I'LL NEVER DO ALL THAT

Perhaps you won't. What appeals to us about this programme is that it places minimal demands on you if you are going to improve your fitness. It's an ordinary person's exercise programme.

But we accept that some people won't even want to do that much. If that's you, and contracting doesn't help you stick to an exercise programme or doesn't even appeal to you, we suggest you owe it to yourself at least to try to maintain your present level of fitness.

You can achieve the minimum of physical maintenance if you will meet five requirements each day. Here they are.

1 Turn and twist your body joints, nearly as far as they will go.

2 Stand for a total of two hours.

3 Lift something unusually heavy for five seconds.

4 Increase your heart rate to 120 beats per minute, for at least three minutes.

5 Burn up 300 calories in any physical activity. For example, as a rough guide you would need to

clean windows for 1½ hours
iron clothes for 1 hour 10 minutes
chop wood or push a wheelbarrow for 1 hour
make beds, mop floors or play golf for 55 minutes
shake carpets for 50 minutes
saw wood or play tennis for 45 minutes
shovel or cycle for 40 minutes
dig in the garden for 35 minutes
go jogging for 30 minutes
swim for 25 minutes

If you look for the opportunities, you'll find it's usually easy to meet these requirements in your normal daily activities. Some rules of thumb that will help

Don't lie down when you can sit.
Don't sit when you can stand.

Don't stand when you can move.
Beware of labour-saving devices; they may save
you labour, but cheat you out of life.

If you can meet these five requirements each day, you should maintain your present level of fitness and prevent unnecessary physical deterioration. If your activity level is much below this minimum, your body will be deteriorating and won't be much help to you in managing your stress.

CONSOLIDATION BREAK
Take time to implement your plans for adequate recreation, and to get your exercise programme started. These are activities that you will hopefully continue for ever, but take time now to get them started. Read ahead if you like, but don't try to change too much too quickly.

4

HOW TO BE MORE ASSERTIVE

According to our dictionary, to assert yourself is to stick up
for your rights. We think this definition needs some careful
refining, or you could easily make one of the most common
mistakes about assertion, and confuse it with aggression.

Many people and organisations have told us they don't
need to learn anything more about assertion because they've
got plenty of it, perhaps 'too much'. When we ask them to
give an example of too much assertion, they invariably
describe someone being aggressive.

ASSERTION VS AGGRESSION

Both assertion and aggression do involve sticking up for
your rights, but the similarity largely ends there. Some of
the differences will be hard to describe here, because they
involve non-verbal aspects of behaviour that are easier to see
than to read about, but we'll give it a try.

Aggression means sticking up for your rights and trying to
achieve your goals, regardless of how that affects others'
feelings or rights. It is this basic disregard for the rights of
other people that sets aggression apart from assertion in
terms of their respective aims. An aggressive person wants
to win at all costs. An assertive person wants to win, but not
at unreasonable cost to others.

Aggression and assertion usually look different, as a result
of their different aims, although sometimes the difference
can seem subtle. Aggression is usually noisier and harsher,
with lots of shouting and threatening. Even when it is more
manipulative than angry, aggression typically contains
abuse of or threats to the other person.

Assertion is usually quieter, although it can be quite firm, and you may be expressing considerable anger. In place of personal abuse, you may give the other person feedback about how her behaviour affects you, and in place of threats you may explain the probable real world consequences of her actions.

The choice to be assertive rather than aggressive represents a choice to respect the rights and feelings of others, even if that sometimes costs you a little. It should not cost you too much, or you are slipping into submissiveness, the other non-assertive behaviour, but we'll go into that shortly.

The choice for assertion rather than aggression is really a choice of values, of how you prefer to run your life. It has no special psychological standing, but comes from adopting the two beliefs underlying assertion. Our culture often praises aggression, especially in men and sports. Since you can scare some of the people some of the time, aggression will sometimes work. From research, we know that a behaviour that works some of the time can be very hard to change (look at playing poker machines). If you aren't too sure about the pros and cons of being aggressive, the following may help you choose your interpersonal style.

THE TWO FUNDAMENTAL ASSERTIVE BELIEFS

1 Assertion, rather than submission, manipulation or aggression, leads to more satisfying and successful interpersonal relationships and so enriches your life.

2 Everyone is entitled to act assertively, and to express his or her honest thoughts, feelings and beliefs.

DISTINGUISHING BETWEEN AGGRESSION AND ASSERTION

It is sometimes hard to distinguish between aggression and assertion. You can decide for yourself in two ways: by what you are saying to yourself and by your body language.

If your self-talk is very negative and aggressive, your body language is likely to be affected and you will behave in an aggressive way. Between 60 and 90 per cent of the meaning of a message is conveyed by **how** you say it, your non-verbal behaviour, and 10 to 40 per cent by **what** you say. Non-verbal behaviour is important in our response to other people. More often than not we will be responding to how they say something rather than just what they are saying. For example

The statement 'I feel fed up when you leave your books and papers lying all over the desk.'

Looking just at the words, this is a reasonably assertive statement. We need to look at the statement in the context of what the person is saying to himself and how he is behaving.

Aggressive self-talk: 'I will get back at him. He always leaves his stuff around. He drives me up the wall.'
Behaviour: Yells these words at the other person while hurling the books to the floor.

Instead an assertive response would be:
Assertive self-talk: 'I feel annoyed when this happens. I can let her know and then we can perhaps find a solution that suits both of us.'
Behaviour: Says the words in a frustrated but controlled manner, then asks if they could work out an alternative place for the books which suits both of them.

WHY ARE PEOPLE AGGRESSIVE?

BECAUSE THEY ARE SCARED.
This may seem an unlikely reason, at first, because aggressive people look as if they are scaring everybody else. But that, of course, is the aim of their game. Ever watched a frill-necked lizard when it's frightened? Or even the household dog when someone enters his territory? Lots of show and noise, but most of it is bluff.

Human behaviour is different from non-human in important ways, but still a common reason for people being aggressive is that they are scared, scared that they won't get what they want, or that something will be done that they don't want.

Aggression motivated by fear comes essentially from a

lack of self-confidence. It is because the person lacks faith in her own ability to stick up for herself that she goes for over-kill and is aggressive. You may find it surprising to think that some of the aggressive people you know are really showing their lack of self-confidence, but take a good look next time. Underneath every bully you will find a coward.

BECAUSE IT WORKS (SOMETIMES).

As we said, you can scare some of the people some of the time. If an aggressive person belongs to a hierarchical organisation, where everybody believes those higher up the ladder have more power, he may find his aggression seems to work a lot of the time. He may be able to make or imply lots of threats about other people's jobs. (See Chapter 10 for just how illusory this 'power' is.)

The fact that aggression can seem to work some, or even most, of the time encourages the aggressive person's belief in its usefulness. The fact that people may do the opposite as soon as his back is turned is explained away as being an example of other people's lack of trustworthiness or reliability, not recognised as the evidence it is for a failure in people-management skills.

Even when aggression appears to work, it usually involves two costs. First, there is an emotional cost to the aggressive person, especially if her aggression was an expression of anger. Have you ever 'won' an argument by being the person who got angriest, shouted loudest and made the biggest threats. How did you feel afterwards? You may have won, but we'll bet you felt angry and upset for some time after the argument. Was it really worth it?

Second, there is a heavy cost on your interpersonal relationships. Winning by being aggressive means winning by scaring others, by making them back down, often leaving them feeling threatened, frustrated or humiliated. Do you think they will like you, or even respect you, under those circumstances?

We have been surprised by how many people confuse fear and respect. 'Discipline teaches respect!' If by discipline you mean institutionalised aggression, then all it will teach is fear. There's an easy test of the difference: fear works only when you or the threat of you is around; respect works even when you aren't around. Which do you think you are gaining from others?

BECAUSE THEY ARE ANGRY.

Not all aggression is an expression of anger; it may just have become a person's habitual style of interacting with others because they think it works. But obviously a fair bit of aggression does stem from anger. Anger is like any of the other negative feelings considered in Chapter 2; when and how much you get angry will depend a lot on your self-talk about whatever is provoking you. For example, a common piece of self-talk that leads to unnecessary anger is to have too high expectations of yourself or others.

Unrealistically high expectations of how well or how much you or others will do, set you up to be frequently disappointed and frustrated. The clue that you may be doing this would be the presence of lots of criticism – of yourself or others – in your self-talk. The solution is set out in Chapter 2.

Like other negative feelings, anger is not necessarily a problem. Under some circumstances, it may be quite reasonable for you to feel angry. To decide if anger, or any other negative feeling, is a problem for you, consider how often, and how intensely you get angry, how long it lasts, and how you express your anger. If you think you are getting angry too often, or too much, or for too long, make a deliberate effort to use both the mental and physical relaxation skills described in Chapter 2 in the situations that usually make you angry.

If you think you are turning your anger in on yourself, bottling it up, or expressing it by being aggressive, then the suggestions in this chapter should help you to be more assertive instead.

ASSERTION VS SUBMISSION

You are unlikely to confuse submission with assertion, although it is sometimes confused with politeness. Essentially submission means not sticking up for your rights by failing to express honestly your feelings and thoughts on issues that are important to you, or by allowing other people to have their way at an unreasonable cost to you.

People usually feel very bad when they are being submissive: resentful towards the person they are submitting to, and angry with themselves for being submissive. Sometimes they let out these bad feelings at someone who has nothing to do with the original problem, such as shouting at your spouse or children or kicking the cat.

It is not unusual for people to go along being submissive much of the time, storing away more and more of these bad feelings, until they reach eruption point. Then they explode aggressively, often over something that is really trivial, then feel very guilty about doing that, and so go back to being submissive, and so on.

If being submissive is such a dead loss, why do people do it?

DISTINGUISHING BETWEEN ASSERTION AND SUBMISSION

The only way to discover if you are being submissive or assertive is to determine, once again, your self-talk, and body language. For example,

Situation: Someone pushes in before you in a queue waiting to be served in a shop.

Non-assertive self-talk: 'That's not fair. It was my turn next; she shouldn't have pushed in like that. I can't say anything though – I'd better not make a scene. Everyone would think I was silly.'

Behaviour: stomp feet, sigh, drum your fingers on the counter.

Choosing not to be assertive

Assertive self-talk: 'That person is certainly pushy. Oh well, I am in no tearing hurry. I'll let him be served without protesting, although if others continue to push in, I will calmly say that I was next.'

Behaviour: wait calmly to be served.

Choosing to be assertive

Assertive self-talk: 'I am in a hurry and that person has pushed in. I know I will feel uncertain standing up for my rights, but I can cope with those feelings. I will calmly let the shop assistant know that I was next.'

Behaviour: 'Would you excuse me; I believe it is my turn.'

WHY ARE PEOPLE SUBMISSIVE?

BECAUSE THEY ARE SCARED.
Just as aggression is often motivated by fear, in that case a fear of loss of power, so submission is also often motivated by fear of two kinds. Sometimes people are submissive because they fear losing the approval of others – 'They'll think I'm pushy if I say anything' – and sometimes because they fear the reaction of others – 'He'll do his block if I say anything.'

Both of these fears can be persuasive because they can both be realistic, at least on a superficial level. If you stand up for yourself, some people won't like it, especially if they are used to your being submissive. This raises an important point we should make clear now. Becoming assertive is not necessarily going to make you more popular, and isn't intended to. If people are accustomed to using you as a doormat or a convenience, some of them may well be upset when you start to assert yourself.

We hope that by now you will have learned that universal popularity is the impossible goal of Irrational Belief No. 1, and chasing impossible goals will only make you unhappy. If you need to, go back to Chapter 2 and review this irrational belief and its matching rational idea.

If someone offers you a friendship that depends on your being a doormat, we don't think it's much of a friendship. We believe genuine friends can always be assertive with each other, because assertion involves mutual respect.

It is embarrassing, awkward, and perhaps even frightening if the person you are assertively confronting does overreact, and responds aggressively. Still, as you learned in Chapter 2, you will survive all of those feelings, and later in this chapter we will describe some specific techniques to help you maintain your assertion in the face of someone else's aggression.

BECAUSE THEY THINK THEY SHOULD.
As we said above, people often confuse submission with politeness. Indeed, we are often systematically taught that submission is a 'proper' way of behaving, especially if we are women. The essential flavour of the traditional feminine

role is one of passivity. From an early age girls may still be taught to take second place to their brothers, in preparation for deferring to the needs and wishes of their husbands and their children. We have been struck by the number of young mothers who unquestionably see themselves as belonging at the bottom of the family totem pole.

If you think that one of the main reasons you find it difficult to assert yourself is that you have been overdosed on traditional ideas about being a proper, polite and therefore submissive woman, and you would like to challenge that part of your upbringing, we recommend the self-help manual, *The Assertive Woman*, by Stanlee Phelps and Nancy Austin (Impact Publishers).

You may sometimes think you are being helpful, when you accept a request from someone, even though you really don't want to, and when you think about it, you can see that the request is unreasonable. 'But,' you kid yourself, 'I can't turn them down. They need me.'

We are not suggesting you become a heartless brute, indifferent to the needs of others. But if you accept unreasonable requests, even if you help the other person in the short run, you do him a big disservice in the longer run. This is because you are giving him the illusion that he can make, and expect to have accepted, unreasonable requests.

You may be prepared to accept his unreasonable requests, but others probably won't. And some day you are quite likely to get fed up with them, and blow up aggressively. At that point, he would be quite entitled to ask, 'Why didn't you tell me before how you felt?'

BECAUSE THEY DON'T KNOW HOW TO BE ASSERTIVE.

Some people are not assertive because they simply don't know how to be. This ought not to be surprising; assertion can be complicated and, unless you've had the chance to learn it, there's again no reason to assume you will automatically know how to do it.

This may explain why you aren't very assertive, but it doesn't justify your staying that way. Submission, like aggression, costs you. First, it usually costs you self-esteem:

seeing yourself being manipulated or used and knowing you
are not sticking up for your reasonable rights, all just lower
your own opinion of yourself.

Second, submission usually costs you bad feelings. People
being submissive often feel hurt, angry, tense, devalued,
ashamed and so on. You can use your mental relaxation
skills from Chapter 2 to cope with such feelings, of course.
But when you reach the point in the coping statement of
asking yourself, 'Now, is there anything I can do to improve
this situation?', the answer is quite likely to be, 'Yes, I
should assert myself!'

Third, as we described above, being submissive also often
creates problems in your relationships. If you offer someone
a relationship based on your being submissive, you are really
offering them a phony relationship. You may be able to keep
up the pretence that you like being a doormat for a while,
but when you finally get fed up with that and bite back, you
should recognise that you have been encouraging the other
person to wipe her feet on you.

In this chapter we will outline the essentials of being
assertive but, as we said before, it is really a practical skill,
which can be hard to pick up from a written description.
You can tackle this difficulty in at least two ways. Look for
people around you who are good examples of assertion. If
they can do it, so can you. Or think about joining an
assertion group. But do shop around and be selective. Look
for one that will teach you responsible assertion. Now,
what's that?

ASSERTION

Assertion consists of standing up for your rights, and
expressing your thoughts, feelings and beliefs in direct,
honest and appropriate ways that respect the rights and
feelings of others.

Responsible assertion involves flexibility. It means
discriminating those situations where your rights are
genuinely threatened from those which just aren't how you
would prefer them. It means not going around with an
oversensitive chip on your shoulder, looking for someone on
whom you can unleash your assertive skills. And it includes
not using your assertive skills to overcome weaker people in

unfair ways. Responsible assertion involves your striking a balance between looking after your own rights, while respecting the rights of others. We will explain exactly how to go about this shortly.

Spending time trying to describe what assertion is, or is not, is fairly difficult because only by actually seeing examples of assertive, aggressive and non-assertive behaviour will it become clearer and clearer what is meant by assertion. One of the limitations of reading a book is that you can't actually see someone being assertive and, as we have said, non-verbal behaviour is an important part of being assertive. However we make use of the next best thing and that is a description of the differences, verbal and non-verbal, between aggressive, assertive and non-assertive behaviour.

Situation: A person whom you don't particularly like asks you for a lift home, when you had hoped to be by yourself to think something over.

Aggressive response
Self-talk: 'She always asks me for lifts home. I'm fed up with giving her lifts. I want to be alone today. I'm not putting myself out for her. I can't stand her anyway, having to put up with her all day at work is bad enough.'
Non-verbal behaviour: clenches fists, red in the face, speaks brusquely.
Verbal behaviour: 'No, I can't give you a lift, why don't you find someone else?'

Submissive response
Self-talk: 'There goes my time to think. I find him a real bore but I guess I had better give him a lift otherwise he'll think I'm mean. I'm a real sucker.'
Non-verbal behaviour: doesn't look at the other person, speaks in a muffled, uncertain tone of voice.
Verbal behaviour: 'Oh well, I suppose I could manage to give you a lift.'

Assertive response
Self-talk: 'I don't find her particularly good company and besides I wanted to think about something by myself. I will feel uncomfortable but I can calmly refuse her request.'

Non-verbal behaviour: looks directly at the other person, using a calm but firm voice.
Verbal behaviour: 'I'm sorry, but I'm afraid I can't give you a lift home tonight.'

Situation: Telling someone that you work for that you can't stay back and work overtime.

Aggressive response
Self-talk: 'He is always asking me to work late. I'm fed up with staying here until all hours. What do I get for it in return, nothing.'
Non-verbal behaviour: stares at person, angry tone of voice.
Verbal behaviour: 'No way, I'm not working. I'm fed up with being asked, leave me alone.'

Submissive response
Self-talk: 'Oh no, I didn't want to work tonight. My wife will be furious, but I can't refuse. They might sack me if I do. Anyway I don't feel like standing up to her. She's such a grouch.'
Non-verbal behaviour: looks at the ground, ummms and ahhhs, but reluctantly agrees.
Verbal behaviour: 'OK, I'll do it, I suppose.'

Assertive response
Self-talk: 'I will feel uncomfortable saying this but I can cope with that. It is important to me that I go home tonight. I will calmly state my point.'
Non-verbal behaviour: look directly at the person, speak in a calm voice.
Verbal behaviour: 'I am sorry but I am unable to work tonight. I have something important to attend to at home.'

The above examples have been chosen to give you some idea of simple assertive procedures which are easiest to use with strangers. Let's look at some more difficult examples when the person involved is a close friend or family member.

Situation: Your 15-year-old son wants to hitchhike down to the beach where he plans to stay with friends for the weekend.

Aggressive response
Thoughts: 'What a fool he is, hitchhiking. He is likely to get picked up by some drunk maniac and killed.'

Non-verbal behaviour: shouting.
Verbal behaviour: 'No way, sonny. I'm not going to let you go ahead with such a hair-brained scheme. You have to stay at home this weekend.'

Submissive response
Thoughts: 'What will happen to him? I don't want him to go. But if I say no, he may think that I'm just being mean.'
Non-verbal behaviour: whining tone of voice.
Verbal behaviour: 'Well, I don't know that that is such a good idea. Why don't you stay around here? You never spend time with your mother and father.'

Assertive response
Thoughts: 'I would be worried about him hitchhiking.'
Non-verbal response: firm but understanding tone of voice.
Verbal behaviour: 'It sounds like it would be a great weekend but I am worried about you hitchhiking. Could we come up with another way for you to get down to the beach?'

Situation: Your partner, in an angry voice, demands to know 'Where have you been and why are you so late?'

Aggressive response
Thoughts: 'There he goes again, always angry. It doesn't matter if he comes home late but if I'm a minute over time he gets furious. I'll show him.'
Non-verbal behaviour: shout.
Verbal behaviour: 'There you go again, always criticising me. If you're late, nothing said. I don't yell at you as you come in the door.'

Submissive response
Thoughts: 'Oh, she must be angry. I had better not say too much in case she gets worse.'
Non-verbal behaviour: speak in an uncertain voice.
Verbal behaviour: 'I was just talking to Jill for a little while after work.'

Assertive response
Thoughts: 'He sounds angry.'
Non-verbal behaviour: calm voice.
Verbal behaviour: 'You sound really angry. Is there something wrong?'

There are broadly six kinds of assertion, and you will select the kind appropriate to the situation facing you. You will find this selection makes more sense when you try to be assertive in some real situations. So, we'll describe the six kinds now, and you can refer back to this list when you are planning your assertive strategy for any situation.

THE SIX KINDS OF ASSERTION

1 BASIC ASSERTION
This means simply sticking up for your rights, and expressing your beliefs, feelings and opinions. It also includes making reasonable requests, and refusing unacceptable ones. This is all done with quiet confidence and as much firmness as the situation requires. Some examples:

'No, thanks, I don't want to go.'
'I think the Frogweed Party has a good foreign policy.'
'Would you please move your car so that I can get out.'
'I'm sorry, but I can't babysit for you tonight; I have something on myself.'

2 EMPATHIC ASSERTION
This is used when you are disagreeing with someone, to show that you respect her right to her opinion. You include a statement recognising the other person's opinion, but you still stick to yours. Some examples:

'Yes, I can see that's how you see it, but it's not how I see it.'
'I can understand that you would like your bill paid now, but I'm not willing to pay until the work is completed to my satisfaction.'
'I can see why you like his music, but it's a bit loud for me.'

3 ESCALATING ASSERTION
This is the way to handle a confrontation which becomes drawn out, so that you still stick up for your rights, but you don't unnecessarily squash the other person. It involves starting out with the minimum amount of assertion you think you need, only escalating to a stronger level if you really need to. For example:

Him: 'Would you like to buy a ticket in a raffle to support the orphans' home?'

You: 'No thanks.'

Him: 'I think it's a very worthy cause. Everybody else is buying tickets.'

You: 'I can appreciate that you see it as a worthwhile cause, but it's not one I want to support, thanks.'

Him: 'What are ya, some kind of cheapskate!'

You: 'I'm sure you're disappointed that I don't share your views, but your being rude isn't likely to convince me. Please go away and stop pestering me.'

4 CONFRONTATIVE ASSERTION

This is used when someone says one thing, but does something else. You objectively describe her words and her deeds, pointing out the contradiction. If you want to, you can add a reasonable request for change. Some examples:

'You said that you would fix my car first thing this morning, but you have left it sitting in the street. I would like you to start on it now, please.'

'You said you would be home on time tonight, but you are an hour late. I would prefer you came home when you said you would, or ring me if you are going to be late.'

Don't get into the trap of name calling or character assassination when you are confronting someone with the difference between their actions and words. For example:

'You are the stupidest, most forgetful, frustrating person I know. You agree to do things, then you just go off and forget about them.'

When you confront someone stick to the observable facts; do not add your own interpretations of the person's behaviour. A rule of thumb for making confrontative statements is that you should be able to **see** the other person's behaviour. For instance, you can't see laziness; you can interpret certain behaviour as being lazy, but you can't actually see it; you **can** see that someone hasn't completed a task that they had agreed to complete.

5 'I'-LANGUAGE ASSERTION

This is used when the other person's actions are affecting you or making you feel bad; again you can make a request for change if you want to. The basic formula is, 'When you do X, the effect on me is Y, and I feel Z. I would prefer you did Q instead.' You can leave out the feeling (Z) if you don't want to share that personal information. Some examples:

'When you use the phone in our office for personal calls, I can't get my work done and I feel angry. I would prefer you used this phone only for genuinely urgent calls, please.'

'When you don't fill up the truck at the end of the day, I have to do it in the morning, and that makes me late for deliveries. Would you please fill it each evening before you knock off?'

'When you keep telling me how to look after my baby, you are putting me down and I feel angry. I would prefer you let me look after him my way; I'll ask if I want any help.'

When you express feelings make sure you use 'I'-language. Only you can be responsible for how you feel; no one else is. Do not slip into 'You make me feel' statements; stick to 'I feel'. Be very specific about what aspect of the person's behaviour you find upsetting and under what circumstances. Do not make over-generalisations or character-assassination-type statements. For example:

'You always ignore me when I ask you to do something. Are you deaf or something?'

'You make me feel so angry when you always ignore me. It just shows what a hopeless woman you are.'

Instead

'When you do not respond when I ask you to do something, I feel annoyed.'

'When you do not greet me when I come home from work, I feel hurt. Could we do something about this situation?'

Many people we speak to in work settings find it hard to accept that talking about feelings is important. It is easy, however, to find examples where a breakdown in communication has occurred because the people involved have not spoken about their feelings. At the same time the people involved have often non-verbally expressed their feelings and this has caused further misinterpretations. You can always adjust the level of your feeling statement, depending on the situation, and the intimacy of the relationship.

6 PERSUASIVE ASSERTION

This is used to present your point of view most effectively to groups, like committees, boards and so on. The two keys are timing and tact.

Effective timing involves looking through the group's agenda, if there is one, and choosing the issues that are really important to you. Reserve your main contributions for those issues. When one of them comes up, wait until about a third to a half of the group have spoken before you say your piece.

Effective tact is an application of empathic assertion; try to reflect something you see as genuinely good in the views expressed by the previous speakers before you make your points. For example:

'I thought Charlie's idea for a new hall was a good one, and Fred is right that it needs to be considered carefully, so I would like to propose that we form a small working party to look at alternative plans.'

Those are the six kinds of assertion. Now, how do you use them?

PREPARE YOURSELF MENTALLY

By now you will know how important we think your self-talk is, in all your feelings and behaviour, including assertion. A confrontation with someone else can blow up quickly, even if you knew it was coming, which isn't always possible.

You will feel more confident, and assert yourself more effectively, if appropriate self-talk has become something of a habit for you. It's a bit difficult to blow a whistle in the middle of a confrontation and announce you are taking a 10-minute think break.

Sometimes you may be able to do this. In our advice to couples, we suggest deliberately using time out from an escalating discussion to give them time to cool down and work out a constructive approach to the issue. You may be able to get agreement to take time out from someone who values your relationship, but not everyone you confront will feel like that and be willing to wait while you think things through.

Later, we will suggest some brief self-talk you can use to help you stay assertive during a confrontation, but right now we are suggesting you do some more extensive reviewing of your self-talk regarding assertion, aggression and submission. This is intended to help you develop assertive habits of mind.

DEVELOPING ASSERTIVE BELIEFS

On page 103 are the two major beliefs underlying responsible assertion. Review them again now. Genuine assertion isn't just a couple of tricks you use to get a bit more power over others. Although we have described different kinds of assertion, and below have a general strategy for being assertive, many of these procedures could be used aggressively, or even submissively. Genuine assertion is an interpersonal lifestyle that reflects a state of mind. The two major assertive beliefs can be spelled out in many ways. For example:

You have the right to be treated with respect. (Other people have the right to be treated with respect.)

You have the right to express your own feelings and opinions. (Other people have the right to express their own feelings and opinions.)

You have the right to be listened to and taken seriously. (Other people have the right to be listened to and taken seriously.)

You have the right to set your own priorities. (Other people have the right to set their own priorities.)

You have the right to say 'No' without feeling guilty. (Other people have the right to say 'No' without being considered mean.)

You have the right to ask for what you want. (Other people have the right to refuse your requests.)

You have the right to get what you paid for. (Other people have the right to get what they paid you for.)

You have the right to ask for information from others with more knowledge, including professionals like your psychologist or doctor. (Other people offering you information have the right to be listened to politely.)

You have the right to make your own mistakes. (Other people have the right to make their own mistakes, and to expect you to bear the consequences of your mistakes.)

You have the right to choose not to assert yourself. (Other people have the right to choose to assert themselves, or not, according to their own wishes.)

Practical exercise: Draw up your own Bill of Rights.
Think of situations in which it is, or could be, important for you to be assertive. For each situation, work out what rights you see yourself as having. Then work out the corresponding rights for the other person or people in that situation. Write them out. Use those above, if appropriate, or work out your own.

CHALLENGE YOUR SOCIALISATION MESSAGES

Socialisation is the process of learning how to behave, including think, in ways that are acceptable to the rest of our society. It occurs first at home, and then through school and other social institutions. Some socialisation is probably necessary for us to live together in a reasonably cohesive society, and not in anarchic, selfish chaos. But socialisation, because it teaches what has been acceptable, tends to be conservative, and inclined to favour what is thought to be the common good rather than any individual's wants. Again, some part of this is probably desirable, but it can be exaggerated, resulting in socialisation messages that discourage individual assertion.

There are many of these messages common in our culture. Each does have some sense to it, and that can make them deceptively appealing to someone trying to be sensible. But each one, taken to its extreme, will lead you to surrendering your personal rights.

Whenever you find yourself in doubt about whether you have the right to assert yourself, check your reasons for those doubts. If you find one or more of the following socialisation messages, you may find our discussion of them helpful in challenging their influence over you. They are:

'Don't be selfish.' Seeking your own goals and looking after yourself, regardless of the cost to others, you will recognise as aggression, one of the two non-assertive behaviours. We are not recommending that. But if you are not reasonably self-centred, and willing to look out for your own rights and wants, with due regard for others, then you are slipping into being submissive. We don't recommend that, either. Aim for the balance, not either extreme.

'Be modest and humble.' No one likes a loud-mouthed braggart, whose conversation consists only of a long list of his wonderful achievements, possessions, qualities, and so on. It's not hard to see the underlying lack of self-confidence. But if you don't have a realistic and reasonable appreciation of your good points, you will have great difficulty accepting close relationships with others because you won't understand or believe what they see in you.

'Always be understanding.' We believe there are always plausible reasons for people's actions, even if those reasons are sometimes hard to discover. So, in principle, you can always understand why someone does something. But that doesn't mean you have to accept it. However 'right' the other person's actions may be for her to do, that doesn't mean they have to be 'right' for you to receive.

'Don't be demanding.' Of course, you don't have the right to make unreasonable demands of other people; but you are perfectly entitled to make reasonable requests, just as others are entitled to refuse your requests. Even in situations where you are given some authority to ask others to do some things, requests will generally work better than demands.

'Don't hurt other people.' This is a noble, but impossible goal. Put two human beings on the same planet, and sooner or later they will probably tread on each other's toes, accidentally if not intentionally. Responsible assertion involves avoiding unnecessary hurt to others, but accepting that sometimes others may be hurt by even the most responsible assertion.

'**Win at all costs.**' Ours is a very competitive culture, and a great fuss is made about the importance of being a winner. It's a strange way of running a society, because it necessarily means there must be lots of losers. The next time you think this message, ask yourself what it is actually costing you, both as an individual, and as a member of a supposedly humane society. The most meaningful competition is one with yourself, to achieve as much as you can of your own potential, regardless of how that compares with others.

'**Don't let others get in your way.**' This variation on the preceding message urges you to ignore the rights and feelings of others, so that you can be a 'winner' again. You will recognise this as the basic rationale for being aggressive, and accepting it carries all the costs of aggression described earlier.

'**Don't be a coward. Stick up for yourself! Fight back!**' Our culture also makes a great fuss about courage, but sadly often confuses it with violent aggression, or sporadic outbursts of foolhardy behaviour in moments of crisis. We are more impressed by the quieter courage of assertion than fear-based outbursts of aggression, and by the courage of turning your back on a stupid confrontation rather than letting yourself be frightened into taking part.

Practical exercise: Check your own socialisation messages.
Which of the above socialisation messages do you think have influenced you? Are there others that you think have prevented you from being assertive?

If there are situations in which you would like to be more assertive, rather than aggressive or submissive, try to identify which socialisation messages may influence you there. Write them out, then write out a more balanced view of the situation, to prepare yourself for tackling it.

PRACTISE ASSERTIVE SELF-TALK
This means applying the coping statement from Chapter 2 to the situation of being assertive. It's fairly long, so you often won't have time to use it in full during a confrontation.

Instead use the shorter self-instructions described below, but they will have more effect for you if you have been practising this statement before. Write it out on a card so that you can carry it around to rehearse frequently until you really know it by heart. Stick to the version here; it's been carefully worked out.

'I expect to feel anxious when I assert myself, because most people do; I would feel disappointed if it doesn't work, and I might feel embarrassed or frightened if the other person overreacts; but I know I can cope with all those feelings, and the chance of them happening is not a good reason for me to surrender my rights. It's important to me to assert myself reasonably and responsibly, so I will think about the rights and feelings of all the people involved; but then I will assert myself, if I think it's appropriate.'

A STEP-BY-STEP STRATEGY FOR ASSERTION

After you have done the exercises above to prepare yourself mentally for being assertive, work out a short list of situations in which you would like to be more assertive. They need to be situations which are important to you and to which you have access. Keep the list reasonably short, say, five to ten situations.

Then rank them in order of expected difficulty for you. Put a '1' next to the situation you think would be least difficult for you to try, a '2' for the next most difficult, and so on. This is the order in which you will try them. Remember our general rule of changing things in small steps, so that each attempt is likely to succeed. Success encourages you to keep trying.

Before you tackle the first situation, imagine yourself applying the following strategy in that situation. Make sure you imagine yourself handling it well – imagined success promotes real success. Try to imagine how the other person or people in the situation will react, and work out how you will stick to being assertive, no matter what he or they do.

Step 1   Listen to the other person.

Tell yourself, 'I can listen to someone else's point of view without surrendering my own.' If you don't hear what she actually says, as distinct from what you may assume she is going to say, you may be asserting yourself for nothing, or over the wrong issue.

See if you can listen to the other person's unspoken message, too. What can you tell about his feelings from the tone and volume of his voice, regardless of what he may be saying? What about his facial expression, and the rest of his body language? If he has strong feelings which he is not expressing openly, you may need to reflect these.

Step 2   Think about the situation.

Tell yourself, 'I don't have to rush in. I'll take my time.'

Try to answer these three questions:

What are the rights of each of the people in this situation?

Are my rights really threatened here?

Is this a situation where it's genuinely important to me to assert myself?

Remember, you are trying to be responsibly assertive. If the situation isn't genuinely important to you, forget it. Use your relaxation skills to cope with any bad feelings and don't waste your energy on something trivial.

But, if you decide this is a situation where it's genuinely important to you to be assertive – and only you can decide that for yourself – go on to the next step.

Step 3   Work out how you see the situation.

You have already done this in part, by considering the rights of all of the people involved, and why you think your rights are importantly threatened here. Now go back to the description of the six kinds of assertion, and select the kind appropriate to this situation. This will take you a while at first.

Plan in your mind how you will apply that kind of assertion to this situation. Write a mental script of what you are going to say. Imagine how the other person will respond, and prepare your assertive reply.

At this point you can set one or both of two possible goals: first, to see yourself being assertive, and second, to change how the other person is behaving. You can **always** have the first goal, and it's the main reason for being assertive. Only set the second goal when it seems realistically possible. Aiming to change the behaviour of people who obviously aren't going to change just sets you up for disappointment.

Step 4   Assert yourself!

Enough preparation, enough thinking, now do it! Stick to your plan as well as you can. If the other person reacts in a way you didn't expect, or if you forget what you were going to say next, take your time to think out your next move. Say to yourself, 'Relax, I can take my time to think about what I want to say.'

Step 5   Use helpful self-talk.

As you need them, use the following self-instructions to help you stay assertive.

If the other person starts to get upset or angry, say to yourself, 'Stay calm; I don't have to get upset. If she wants to, that's her problem.'

If you start to get upset or angry, say to yourself, 'Relax, I'm in control.'

If either of you starts to wander off the topic or introduce some other issue, say to yourself, 'Stick to the issue; don't get side-tracked.' Then make that suggestion to the other person.

Step 6   Review the situation afterwards.

If you were successful at staying assertive, give yourself a pat on the back. Notice that success means only staying assertive, not necessarily changing the other person's behaviour. That's good if it was your goal and it happens, but it's not under your control. How the other person reacts is up to him. The only bit you can take responsibility for is your behaviour.

If you weren't successful this time – if you slipped back into being submissive, or lost your temper and became aggressive – too bad. Say to yourself, 'It is disappointing that I wasn't able to assert myself successfully that time, but

I can cope with that. Is there anything constructive I can learn for next time? I won't blow up one failure out of proportion. So what will I do now?'

Practical exercise: Try it out.
That's the basic strategy for being assertive in any situation. As soon as you have done enough imagined rehearsal for your first target situation, go and try it out. Flex the strategy, the words, and the self-talk appropriately, to suit the situation and your personal style. But try not to change anything in ways that will slip you into submission or aggression.

TWO SPECIAL CASES

Occasionally someone in an assertion group we are teaching will crack the tired old joke, 'But what happens if you try to assert yourself with someone who is also assertive?' Or the other version is, 'What if everyone in our organisation becomes assertive? Won't everything stop dead?' These jokes miss the essential point of assertion, respect for the rights and feelings of others.

A confrontation between two responsibly assertive people may be firm, but it will not be hostile or aggressive. They have a much better chance of negotiating a solution that suits them both reasonably well (see Chapter 6), than if they submissively swap unwanted solutions, or aggressively refuse to budge from their original positions.

The situations in which it can be difficult to maintain assertion are when you are confronted by someone who is being submissive or aggressive. So here are some suggestions for each.

Maintaining assertion in the face of submission

The risks here are that you may feel sorry for the submissive person, and back off in a way that is unfair to you, or you may find her submissiveness so frustrating that you become angry and aggressive. The best strategy is to use lots of 'I'-language assertion, telling the other person how his behaviour affects you, and requesting change if you want to. 'I'-language assertion is most appropriate since you are setting an example and giving an invitation to the other person to be assertive in return.

Maintaining assertion in the face of aggression
This is the situation most often feared by people becoming assertive, so it will be useful to have a number of strategies at your fingertips. Try these.

If the other person looks and sounds angry or upset, but isn't saying so, **reflect her feelings**. For example, 'You seem upset about this. I can see how this situation might make you feel like that, but I still see it this way.'

If the other person is trying to make you back down, use **empathic assertion**. Acknowledge what you see as his legitimate points, but keep repeating yours.

If the other person's argument rests on assumptions that you think are questionable, **point out her implicit assumptions**. For example, 'I can see your argument for a controlled use of kangaroo products makes economic sense, but you are assuming there is an over-population of kangaroos. I don't think that's true.'

If the other person's aggression is affecting you, use **'I'-language assertion**. For example, 'When you shout personal abuse at me like that, you are simply insulting me. I would prefer that we discussed this sensibly.'

CONSOLIDATION BREAK
If assertion is an important part of your stress-management programme, take time now to begin developing your assertion skills. Don't try to change too much at once. Go on to the next personally relevant part of the programme only when you think you have assertion under way.

5
IMPROVING COMMUNICATION

None of us lives or works in total isolation. We have to interact with other people some of the time. Even if you set out to be a hermit, you would undoubtedly find yourself having to tell other people to go away when they wanted to explore your cave.

In fact, humans are social animals, and mostly we want the company of others and feel bad without it (see Chapter 9 on loneliness). This gives a key role to communication, because it is through communication that we make contact with the other people in our lives.

Good communication can make our relationships and interactions with others rewarding and enjoyable. Bad communication, or a lack of communication, can make relationships unpleasant, interactions unrewarding, and diminish individual productivity. A lack of good communication is a common stressor.

A lack of good communication is a major factor in distressed relationships, such as marriages and parent-child relationships. If these are particular stressors for you, we recommend our manual, *Living and Loving Together*, also published by Viking O'Neil, although the principles we outline here apply to all relationships.

Since communication occurs between and amongst people, its lack or misuse not only causes individual dystress, but also particularly leads to negative effects in groups of people, such as organisations or corporations. We have been struck by the number of individual workers who have told us that one of the big problems in their respective organisations is a lack of communication.

You will note the strong possibility of double costs. Poor communications can be major stressors for the individuals involved, and thus contribute to their individual dystress problems. And the same poor communications can seriously reduce the productivity and effectiveness of the organisation to which those individuals belong. Perhaps one of the saddest examples of poor communication is the situation when a person is given a final cheque on Friday afternoon and told to clear his desk, or empty her locker. Often this sad event has been preceded by either no feedback to the unsatisfactory employee ('He should know what to do!'), or by vague and negative feedback ('You should pull your socks up! If you don't get your act together, you know what to expect!') Apart from the personally devastating effects on the ex-employee of being so suddenly devalued, the end result is a loss for everybody, a loss that may well have been avoided by clear, effective communication.

Many people find it hard to communicate clearly and honestly with others, especially if they want to communicate bad feelings. Partly, this results from simply never having the opportunity to learn good communication skills. It is no more logical to expect them to come 'naturally' than to expect to be born able to drive a car. Well, below we have set out the basic good communication skills.

But a lack of honest communication also often results from a confused wish not to hurt the other person. We'll encourage you to look critically at this goal, for two reasons. First, which is likely to hurt the other person more? Some critical but constructive feedback that helps him improve his performance and keep his job, or a sudden sacking? Second, when you try not to hurt the other person, is it really her you are protecting, or are you avoiding your own feelings of discomfort and embarrassment?

If you think a lack of good communication has been contributing to your dystress, you can begin changing that by identifying which of the common obstacles to communication have applied to you. Then you know what to aim at changing, when you try the good communication skills later.

COMMON OBSTACLES TO COMMUNICATION

Dr Robert Bolton is an American psychologist who heads an organisation similar to our own, providing consultation and training in improving human performance and relationships. He has proposed that there are three broad kinds of common obstacles to good communication.

These obstacles are responses which you may make when someone is trying to communicate with you and which have a high chance of blocking communication. They don't **always** block communication. But the more stress or tension in the interaction, the more likely it is that these obstacles will block communication. Here they are.

OBSTACLE NO. 1: JUDGING

This obstacle includes four responses: criticising, name-calling, diagnosing and praising. Yes, praising can be an obstacle to good communication! Let's consider each of these.

Criticising blocks communication when it becomes all the other person expects from you. Corrective feedback can help others improve their performance, but it is likely to be disregarded and avoided if it's all you have to offer.

Name-calling or labelling can block communication because of the negative connotations of the labels: 'loafer', 'whinger', 'intellectual', 'bully', 'snob'. Even apparently positive labels – 'dedicated', 'hard worker' – block you from appreciating the other person as an individual.

Diagnosing means to offer the other person (your) explanation of why he does what he does, to tell him you see his motives or personality at work. Many people will understandably resent this amateur psychological snooping.

Praising becomes an obstacle when it comes across to the other person as manipulative, even if it is still sincere. You aren't just saying, 'Well done!' but rather, 'Well done, now I want some more!'

OBSTACLE NO. 2: SENDING SOLUTIONS

This obstacle includes the responses of ordering, threatening, moralising, questioning and advising. Sending solutions in these ways can add to the other person's problems rather than reduce them and, even if you send a good solution, that can rob the other person of the chance to master the problem for himself.

Ordering means sending solutions coercively. It essentially says to the other person that she is inferior to you, which not surprisingly she may resent. Even if your order is apparently accepted, that resentment may later lead to sabotage. Ordering is based on the myth that you can control other people. We are pleased to say we don't know of any reliable method of doing this.

Threatening often accompanies ordering, and can give the illusion of control. If you threaten people with physical, emotional or material hurt, they may accept your orders while the threat is maintained, if it is important enough to them. They also learn to fear and not to trust you, and your 'control' disappears as soon as your threat slips, like when you back is turned.

Moralising involves preaching at the other person, usually with lots of 'shoulds' and 'oughts'. Again, you are essentially saying to the other person that he can't work out what's right for himself.

Questioning can block communication in two ways. Excessive questioning can come across as an interrogation, especially when the questions pursue answers you want, rather than what the other person would like to discuss.

Closed-end questions – those that restrict the answers available to the other person, such as 'Are you sorry that you did it?' – again take the conversation where you want to go, rather than where the other person may want to go. They imply that you already know the answer and the other person's answer is unimportant.

Advising can seem to the other person as if you devalue her by saying you don't think she can solve her problem for herself, and how stupid she must be because you can see a solution straight away. There is also a good risk that your advice, however much it may have been right for you in the past, will be wrong for this person now, because it is doubtful that you fully understand her problem.

OBSTACLE NO. 3: DODGING THE OTHER'S CONCERNS

This obstacle includes diverting, logical argument and reassurance. Essentially you are dodging the other person's real concerns, because you haven't noticed them, or don't see them as important, or are threatened by them.

Diverting means to take some unimportant point of the other person's statement as the jumping-off point for an almost irrelevant statement on something you find more interesting or comfortable.

Logical argument usually tries to focus on 'the facts' while ignoring the feelings in the situation. In problem situations the feelings are usually more important, at least at first. Work through the feelings together, and then you may be able to solve the problem.

Reassuring usually boils down to denying the other person's feelings, because you can't understand why he feels that way, or you feel obliged to try to lessen his bad feelings (because that lessens yours).

OBSTACLE NO. 4: 'I'VE SEEN THAT!'

There is one final obstacle. That's the response, after hearing about the other three obstacles, of saying, 'That's right! That's just what my wife/husband/boss/secretary has been doing all these years.'

If you only see these obstacles as applying to others, you will probably miss out on the most important possibility of reducing them, in your **own** communications.

It is equally unhelpful to be guilt-struck by discovering that you have been using some of these poor communication skills. So does everybody, and they aren't always blocks to communication. As we said before, they have a high risk of blocking communication, especially if used excessively and in tense situations.

Take a critical look at your communication style, and see if you need to reduce or eliminate any of them. If you do, pick one to work on at a time, moving on to another when you are satisfied with your progress.

If these obstacles are how not to communicate well, what should you do instead?

THE THREE BASIC COMMUNICATION SKILLS

We believe that three fairly simple skills provide the basis of good communication in relationships. Master these skills, and you have the basics of good communication for any of your relationships, at work, at home, with friends or acquaintances.

The degree of intimacy of what you share will vary, of course. You will probably share more intimate information with your spouse or a special friend than with a casual workmate. But the same processes will apply, so learning these skills can help improve all your relationships.

SKILL NO. 1: LEVELLING

Levelling means telling the other person clearly and non-defensively how you feel, or how you think about a particular issue, rather than trying to hide your feelings or misrepresent them. Notice we said, 'trying' to hide your true feelings.

You see, you actually have no choice about whether or not you share your feelings with those around you. **Most** of your emotional impact on another person is **non-verbal**. It is carried by your body language, and non-verbal cues in your voice, like tone and volume. Only a small part is carried by **what** you say.

Your only real choice, then, is not whether you will share your feelings, but how accurately you will share them. Because that's what the verbal part of your communication can provide: accuracy in communication.

Suppose you have had a really rotten day, several things have gone quite wrong, and you are feeling disappointed and miserable by the time you meet your friend for a drink after work. If you try to keep your feelings to yourself, your friend will pick up enough non-verbal clues from you to know that you are feeling bad. He will then **guess** how bad and why. In other words, because of a lack of communication from you, your friend will try to read your mind to establish the nature and cause of your feelings. This mind-reading seems to be a universal human behaviour: everybody seems to spend a lot of time guessing how everybody else thinks and feels.

The trouble is that researchers have found what you already guess to be true. People's mind-reading is often wrong! This is more likely the more strain there is in the relationship. So if you and your friend haven't been getting on too well lately, when he tries to guess about your feelings he is likely to exaggerate them – to assume you are feeling worse than you do – and to take them personally and assume that your bad feelings are directed towards him. He will probably act towards you in response to his guesses. You will suddenly wonder why he seems to respond so badly towards you. From that mutual misunderstanding, your relationship will probably deteriorate further, all for the lack of some simple communication.

There are broadly two ways of levelling, depending on the source of your feelings, outside or inside the relationship. The example we gave above about your mind-reading friend is a situation where your feelings – in this example, disappointment and misery – come from outside your relationship with that friend. Your feelings are not due to anything he has done, or not done. But because you haven't levelled with your friend, the original problem outside your relationship has intruded on your relationship. Because you didn't level, you left your friend no alternative but to mind-read; he exaggerated and took your bad feelings personally, and then reacted to his guesses.

You could have avoided all that by levelling, that is, by announcing your feelings. 'Gee, Charlie, I've had a rotten day at work. Everything went wrong, and I'm feeling lousy.' Immediately your friend knows exactly how you feel and that it has nothing to do with him or your relationship. He may already have done his incorrect mind-reading, but he doesn't have to rely on it for information about your feelings.

As we said above, just how intimate and personal the information is will depend on how close you feel to that person, but the principle remains the same: if you don't level with the other person about your feelings, you are expecting her to guess how and why you feel as you do, and there's a good chance she will guess worse than is true.

Ideally, whichever one of you brings a strong feeling to your relationship should always remember to level about it as soon as possible, thus reducing the risk of unnecessarily negative mind-reading. In the real world, you will sometimes forget, and many of the people around you may not even know about levelling. So if it looks to you that the other person is feeling something strongly, but he hasn't yet levelled, you can initiate better communication by inviting him to level. 'Gee, you look down, Clive. How was your day?' Of course, if your friend doesn't want to share his feelings, you should respect his wish for privacy, but at least you have indicated your willingness to communicate, if he wants to.

Similarly, if you have brought the strong feeling to the relationship but you have forgotten to level and your friend invites you to, recognise that he is being constructive, and make a levelling statement. If you were Clive, above, you might reply, 'Yeah, I am feeling pretty low. Nothing went right at work today, and I just can't get on with my boss.' Again, your friend knows exactly how you feel and that it has nothing to do with your relationship. Again, how much personal detail you give is up to you, but accept that you do not have a choice about whether you share your feelings, only about how accurately you share them.

The other major time for levelling is when your strong feeling comes from **inside** this relationship, and something that the other person has done, or not done, is affecting how you feel. Remember, you still only have a choice about how accurately you share your feelings, and if you try to hide them, you are setting up the other person to read your mind.

To level about feelings from inside a relationship, you should use an X-Y-Z statement, that is, 'When you do X in situation Y I feel Z.' For example, 'When you give me a load of urgent work to do five minutes before knock-off time, I feel angry.'

You will probably find it awkward trying to use X-Y-Z statements at first. Most people do. But X-Y-Z's avoid three of the common patterns of poor communication: kitchen-sinking, over-generalising, and character-assassination.

Kitchen-sinking means throwing everything into the conversation but the kitchen sink, so the original issue gets lost. Over-generalising means to accuse the other person of 'always' or 'never' doing something, so the fact that she did it this time gets lost in an argument about the truth of the generalisation. Character-assassination means to label the other person as having a faulty 'character' or 'personality' (note the obstacles above), which leaves you stuck with a faulty person who resents your labelling.

The advantages to the X-Y-Z formula are that it focuses on one, and only one, event at a time, so you have a fair chance of actually resolving that issue, and it focuses on the other person's behaviour, which he can choose to change, and not his character. For example:

'When you bring the car back with almost no petrol just before I have to go out, I feel very frustrated.'

You can vary the order of the X, Y and Z, but try to include all three items of information, and nothing else. For example:

'It really makes me angry when you haven't got your contracts ready on time, after you promised that you would.' (Z-X-Y)

'Since we are both stuck with the one phone, I find it annoying when you make such long calls.' (Y-Z-X)

The reason for leaving out most other pieces of information is that they are usually unnecessary and often examples of the common obstacles to communication described above. For example:

'When you talk for hours about your past achievements when we go out together, I feel put off because you are only doing it to prop up your weak ego.' (Adding the obstacle of diagnosing.)

Stick to the X-Y-Z formula. If you add some information about the effect of the other person's behaviour on you, as well as your feelings, you are making what you will recognise from the previous chapter, is an 'I'-language assertive statement. For example:

'When you bring back the truck too late for it to be serviced after you promised to be on time, you put all of my deliveries behind the next day and I feel really fed up.'

In this case, the information about the **effect** of the other person's behaviour may help to convince her to change it, but beware of thinking that you always have to justify your feelings. You don't; you are entitled to them, like everybody else. What you should be doing, for your own sake, is sharing them, but constructively by levelling.

Don't be confused by the natural overlap between communication and assertion. Clear communication is a good example of assertive behaviour, and assertion is mostly done through communicating. In this chapter we are concentrating on how you can effectively communicate your feelings. In the real world you will often be communicating and asserting yourself at the same time.

Practice

Take some time now to write out some levelling statements for situations that involve strong feelings for you. If they involve feelings from inside relationships, try to use the X-Y-Z formula.

Here are some tips to help you with levelling.

Watch your X's! When you tell the other person what he

did to affect your feelings, make sure you describe a behaviour that an independent observer could have seen, and not your interpretation of the other person's behaviour. For example, you begin levelling: 'When you contradict me in front of the boss...', because an independent observer could have seen the contradicting behaviour in the other person.

But you should not level, 'When you try to make a fool of me in front of the boss...', because that is your **interpretation** of what the other person did, not a description of her behaviour. Your interpretations of other people's behaviour are a part of **your** self-talk and, as such, are finally your own responsibility.

If your interpretations are wrong, you are only making yourself feel worse than is necessary. Even if your interpretation was right on any occasion, it is unlikely the other person will admit it, and you will just have a useless and unwinnable argument. Make your X's observable behaviours.

If you have trouble identifying your feelings even to know what you are going to level, go back to Chapter 2 and our suggestions for getting in touch with your feelings.

Similarly, if you have trouble levelling because you are too upset or angry to make a reasonably calm statement, first use the mental relaxation skills in that chapter to bring your feelings down. When you reach the step of asking yourself what constructive steps you can take to improve the situation, then prepare and make your levelling statement.

Watch your self-talk! Whenever communication breaks down or becomes very difficult, check your own self-talk: 'What am I saying to myself that is interfering with our communication?'

Here are some examples of unhelpful self-talk when you should be levelling:

'There's no point telling him how I feel; he doesn't care.'
'If I let her close to me again, she'll only hurt me again.'
'He ought to know how I feel. It's obvious. We've been through this before.'
'Here we go again.'

If you are having trouble levelling, check your self-talk. If you find you are thinking along the lines just above, deliberately replace that unhelpful self-talk with more helpful self-talk, like:

'I know I will feel uncomfortable or anxious when I level, but I can cope with that. If this relationship is going to be any good, we must communicate better, so I'll give it a try.'

'I would feel hurt if trying to get closer backfires, but I would survive that and if I don't take the chance we may never get any closer.'

'It is sad that we haven't communicated well in the past, but I can manage that, and it's no reason why we can't do it now.'

Get your complaints into perspective! The other side of the communication coin to levelling is editing. Editing means deciding which of your complaints are really important, and editing out the rest.

It's unlikely you will ever have such a perfect relationship with anyone that nothing she does ever irks you. In most relationships, the other person will annoy, disappoint and otherwise upset you from time to time. If you level about all of these events, you may drive the other person away by your unending complaining.

We are not suggesting you bottle up your feelings on important issues, only that you look at them as reasonably as you can. Let your feelings guide you; if your bad feelings are very strong, or if the issue is one which is likely to keep coming back, then you should probably level, because it is doubtful you will be able to hide your feelings.

On the other hand, if you believe the issue is really trivial, or unlikely ever to occur again, you may prefer to edit out your complaint for the sake of not giving too negative a flavour to the relationship.

One very important way of achieving balance in your feedback to others is to put as much effort into levelling about your good feelings as your bad feelings. We often don't handle compliments well, yet they can do wonders for a relationship.

Dodging the obstacle of giving only critical feedback, and avoiding the obstacle of giving manipulative praise, look for opportunities to tell people what they do that makes you feel good. That gives them a better chance of doing it more often. If you find this difficult, check your self-talk!

SKILL NO. 2: LISTENING

By listening we mean actively trying to hear what the other person **really** says, rather than assuming you know what he is going to say, or listening to yourself, or interrupting. Obviously, if you don't hear what the other person actually says, you don't have much chance of communicating well. Yet it is remarkable how badly many people listen, and instead fall into one of the three traps we just listed.

If you have been in a relationship any length of time, you may be tempted to assume that you already know how the other person thinks and feels. In other words, you can read her mind! To repeat, the more strain there is in the relationship, the more your mind-reading will be wrong.

If a discussion is becoming heated, people tend to focus their attention on preparing their next clever statements with which they intend to slay the opposition. So you are busy writing and reviewing your own script: listening to yourself, which makes it very difficult to listen to anyone else at the same time. We are not being sexist when we report that this observation seems to apply to men more than women. Part of the stereotyped image of successful masculinity is to win, all the time at everything. So men do tend to spend more time listening to themselves, and consequently less time listening to others.

If the conversation has become even more heated, and the other person is saying – or you believe is about to say – something with which you strongly disagree, then there is a temptation to interrupt. The trouble is, interrupting means you don't get to hear what they were really going to say and, even if your guess would have been right, your interruption just escalates the conflict.

There is an easy trick to active listening: pretend to be a tape recorder! No, you don't have to rotate your eyes at different speeds; we mean that you should always be able to play back, nearly word for word, what the other person just said to you. You won't repeat back to others everything that is said to you. That would obviously be clumsy and time-consuming, although sometimes a playback is helpful, as we'll explain shortly. What we are suggesting is that you set yourself the goal of always being **able** to playback what was said. To be able to do this, you will find you have to listen carefully.

We recommend you give an immediate playback under some circumstances: firstly, when you are practising these skills with someone to improve communication in that relationship; secondly, whenever you are not sure you heard the other person correctly; and thirdly, when the discussion is getting heated. As well as making sure that you did in fact hear the other person correctly, instant playback will help him to feel that you are trying to listen, and it slows down an escalating discussion, giving you both time to cool down a bit. For example:

'Gee, Stan, when you spend all of our budget by the middle of the week, I feel really frustrated and hopeless.'
'You said that when I spend all of our budget by the middle of the week, you feel frustrated and hopeless. Is that right?'

Or:

'It really depresses me when you sit around the place looking miserable but saying nothing.'
'I see, when I look miserable but don't say anything, that makes you depressed, huh?'

Once you think you are getting good at active listening, and you have caught the main drift of what the other person is saying, you can reflect her message back in your own words, rather than just parroting it back. This will feel more natural, but **beware** of changing the message.

Don't add your own editorial comments or explanations – you can level with them later – just paraphrase what you heard. And be careful to reflect as accurately as you can **both** the nature and the intensity of the other person's feelings. For example:

'I feel desperate about keeping up with the kids by the end of the day when I know you won't be home for another couple of hours.'

Reflect:

'You are feeling really bad about coping with the kids when I'm not home by the end of the day, are you?'

Not:

'You feel desperate about keeping up with the kids by the end of the day, but you know I can't get home earlier because I'm really working for all of us.'

And not:

'The kids getting you down a little, are they?'

Practice

You will need someone else to practise listening with. Take it in turns to make levelling statements to each other, and see how well you can play them back. Start out by trying to parrot word for word, and then try reflecting in your own words. Tell each other if you think the other person has missed or changed your message.

Here are some tips to help you at active listening.

Watch your **self-talk** again. Catch yourself especially if you are falling into the trap of using the other person's talking time to write your own next statement. Common examples of unhelpful self-talk when you should be listening are:

'What right has he to feel like that!'
'It's silly for her to feel like that!'
'I didn't mean it that way!'
'You're not going to get away with that!'

As for levelling, if you find you are having trouble listening, check your self-talk. If you find you are having thoughts like those above, replace them with more helpful self-talk, like:

'It's my turn to listen now. I can always level later if I want to. Now **listen**! What is she saying?'

Watch your **body talk** too. Remember how much of your impact on the other person is non-verbal. Try to have eye contact around half the time; if that makes you feel uncomfortable, use a coping self-statement. Face mostly towards him, and show you are interested in what he has to say.

Watch her body-talk, as well. Remember that not everybody has learned to level. If someone is saying something to you, but her non-verbal cues suggest she has a strong feeling she is not telling you about, invite her to. Don't rely on your mind-reading, but do ask. For example:

(Said in a low voice, with eyes down) 'I would like to take two weeks leave, beginning next week.'

Reflect and invite:

'I see, you'd like to start two weeks leave next week. You look unhappy, is there anything wrong that you'd like to discuss?'

As we said above, respect the other person's privacy, if that's what he wants. You have made your contribution to opening up communication by inviting him to level.

SKILL NO. 3: VALIDATING

Validating means to accept as true what the other person tells you about her feelings, rather than denying her feelings, or insisting that she feels as you would, or as you think she should.

When you think about it, it's hard to see how anyone could **not** validate someone else's feelings, because if that someone doesn't know how he feels, who does? Yet many people find it difficult to validate. This is because they keep confusing validating with giving in, seeing things the way the other person does, or understanding why the other person has the particular feelings in the levelling statement.

Validating is none of those things. Its basic formula is only: 'I understand and accept that's **how** you feel.'

Notice that it does **not** mean: 'I understand **why** you feel that way', nor 'Yes, I would (or do) feel the same.'

To validate the feelings that someone has shared with you in her levelling, say something along the lines of: 'Yes, I can see that's how you feel.' If it would be true, you could say something like: 'Yes, I understand why you feel like that.' But the minimum, and sufficient, validation is just to accept how the other person feels. For example, he levels to you:

'When you didn't bring back my chainsaw last weekend, after I told you I wanted to use it, I felt really let down.'

You reflect:

'I made you feel let down when I didn't bring back your chainsaw last weekend, like you asked, huh?'

And then you validate:

'Yeah, I can see that made you feel let down.'

If you wanted to then, you could offer an apology or an explanation, but the validation is more important, and be very careful that your explanation doesn't deny his feelings. For example, you might add:

'I had to visit my Dad in hospital and I just forgot about everything else, but I can see that it would still leave you feeling let down.'

Do **not** add:

'Well, I'm sorry, but I had to visit my sick father in hospital, so I don't see what you're getting so uptight about.'

What's difficult for you here is that your actions have made your friend feel bad in a way you didn't mean. In other words: your intent does not match the impact your actions have had.

INTENT VS IMPACT

You will have many experiences of a mismatch between what you intend and the impact you in fact have.

You see a friend walking down the street, and you are feeling good, so you say jokingly, 'Gee, Brenda, how about we sneak off to the Riviera tonight?'

What you don't know is that her husband has just left her and gone to live with someone else. Your remark, which you intended to be funny, makes her feel bad and she snaps at you then starts to cry.

Under circumstances like these there is a lot of pressure on you to be defensive and say something like: 'Hold it! I didn't mean to make you feel bad, so you shouldn't.' Which boils down to saying that other people are only allowed to have the feelings you want them to. Good luck!

So long as you didn't mean to make the other person feel bad, there is no need for you to be defensive when someone levels with you that you did make them feel bad. You may feel bad yourself, but you can handle that with a coping self-statement, and help the other person by sticking to your validation.

The basic formula for this is: 'Yes, I can see that's how I made you feel; I didn't mean it that way, but I see that it came across to you that way.' For example:

'Gosh, Brenda, I can see my remark would upset you under the circumstances; I didn't mean to upset you, but I can understand why I did.'

Validating, and clarifying your intent when it is apparent that you had quite a different impact from what you intended, will help the other person to feel understood and accepted by you, and also help them not to misunderstand you.

Some tips to help you validate: Yes, watch your **self-talk.** We have described above how common it is for people to have difficulty validating, because they confuse it with other actions. If you have trouble, look for self-talk like these:

'If I give in now, he will have it all his way.'
'**I** wouldn't feel like that under those circumstances.'
'It's **silly** for her to feel like that.'
'I didn't mean it **that** way!'

If you find you are having thoughts like those, when you should be validating, replace them with helpful self-talk:

'I can validate his point of view without surrendering mine.'
'We are two individuals who have the right to think and feel differently.'
'I don't have the right to tell other people how they should feel.'

BUT I DON'T SEE IT THAT WAY AT ALL!

Quite possibly. No matter how good a relationship you are looking at, it's doubtful that you will think and feel the same on all important issues all the time. And not necessary for a good relationship. What is necessary is your willingness to each accept the other's right to her own opinions and feelings. One of you may level to the other about a particular issue, while the second person listens and validates.

But then the second person may want to say, 'Now I'd like to level about that, because I see it differently.' Then it's up to the first person to listen and validate. You may exchange several rounds of levelling, listening and validating before you think you fully understand each other's point of view. At that point you may be able to say to each other: 'I see that's how you see it; it's not how I see it, but I accept it's how you see it.'

On many issues you can simply agree to differ, and your use of good communication skills has promoted closeness and understanding, while avoiding unnecessary arguments. But there will be some issues on which you cannot simply agree to differ.

For instance, you may have been communicating very effectively on how to rearrange the files in the office. You can both see and accept each other's proposal quite well, but you still don't agree on the best way to do the job. This means you are ready to do some problem solving (see Chapter 6).

These communication skills will eliminate some problems by allowing you to agree to differ, but they are not intended to **solve** problems. For that you will need specific problem-solving skills, as set out in the next chapter.

The strongly recommended rule of thumb is share your feelings **first**, and you may find the problem has disappeared. If not, you will at least be emotionally ready to co-operate on solving the problem, rather than fighting over it.

Practice

You are now ready to practise all three skills together, as you will normally use them. You can try some written practice alone, by imagining appropriate situations, but you will get more from a live practice with a willing friend or associate.

Take it in turns to level to each other, while the other person listens and validates. Give each other helpful feedback.

If you have the means, record some of your practice sessions and play them back later. It can be surprising, if not dismaying, to find out how you really sound, compared to what you thought you were doing. Use the tape to monitor **your own** performance, not your friend's.

If you practise communicating with someone important to you, like a close friend, or your spouse, or child, it's usually better to start on easy issues, so that you can concentrate on the skills without feelings getting too high. But don't leave out the hard issues; eventually cover them too.

FURTHER SELF-HELP

Dr Bob Montgomery and Lynette Evans, *Living and Loving Together* (published by Viking O'Neil), covers communication within the family.

R. Bolton, *People Skills* (published by Prentice-Hall), covers communication in general life and especially work settings.

CONSOLIDATION BREAK?

Communications skills are essentially practical skills. Take a reasonable amount of time now to consolidate them before going on.

6

SOLVING PROBLEMS AND MANAGING TIME

A common source of dystress for many people is the day-to-day task of managing the business of living, solving the problems that occur in everyone's lives and organising time efficiently.

Some dystressed people are inclined to spend hours mulling over their problems, contemplating various possible solutions, but never actually acting on one. You will recall from our discussion of relaxation in Chapter 2 that this tendency to rehearse your problems fruitlessly is a common reason for physical relaxation training to be useless, or even aggravating, if it isn't accompanied by mental relaxation. Mental relaxation should help you to prevent your current problems from intruding into your relaxation periods, but after you have finished relaxing, the problems are still there to be solved.

Another expression of the same phenomenon is the difficulty some people have in getting to sleep, or staying asleep, because they use bed as a place to worry about their current problems. In Chapter 7 we will give you some suggestions on how to protect your sleep from these intrusions, but the problems will still be there in the morning. So in this chapter we will outline some steps you can take to solve the problems in your life.

Problem solving is an important stress-management technique in another way, too. Another common source of dystress is conflict. In this case, two or more people are facing the same problem; they may have no shortage of possible solutions and may be keen to apply one. The trouble is, they can't agree on which one!

So instead there is argument, sometimes bitter and prolonged, guaranteeing a prolonged elevation of the protagonists' dystress levels. Sometimes, particularly in hierarchical organisations, such conflicts may be unspoken but still stress-inducing, or resolved by authoritarian coercion, which guarantees more stress and a low probability that the authoritarian decision will be effectively implemented.

The problem-solving process we will describe later is ideally suited for resolving such conflicts, for two reasons. It gives all participants maximum chance to be genuinely involved in choosing the final decision, and therefore being committed to its successful implementation. And it gives maximum opportunity for creative thinking, and therefore increases the likelihood of coming up with a really good solution.

Finally in this chapter, we will give you some advice on how to organise your time with reasonable efficiency, so that you are able to keep up with the demands of your life, assuming they are reasonable, and also have time for yourself, for relaxation, recreation and relationships.

A balanced life is the key to effective stress management, so making sure you have the time for all of the components of a balanced life is an essential stress-management technique. Some people jib at the 'artificiality' of planning time, especially for 'fun' or 'love'. 'Surely it should all happen spontaneously and naturally?'

Well, if you find you are spontaneously and naturally leading a balanced life, good luck to you. You don't need the time-organisation section of our programme. But if, like many of us, you find it a bit hard to fit everything in and you often feel you just can't keep up, or you have been sacrificing some important parts of that balanced life, then some time-organisation skills may be an important part of your stress-management programme.

HOW NOT TO SOLVE PROBLEMS

You may have decided you don't really need to learn about problem solving. We have often found, while conducting training courses in business or industry, that managers have already been introduced to a process similar to the one described below. If this is true for you, and you honestly believe that you are able to apply that procedure effectively, great!

But we will encourage you to do that evaluation thoughtfully. We have been struck by the number of times people have either been taught only parts of the whole problem-solving process, or don't carry it right through. They generate solutions, but don't have much success in actually implementing them. In the procedure described below, you will notice we pay specific attention to the actual implementation of a chosen solution. Even if you already know a fair bit about problem solving, you may strengthen that skill by reviewing the implementation steps.

Another example of inadequate problem-solving skills we have observed is where people have been taught the problem-solving procedure pretty much as we have it below but they have not been taught much else. Unless the participants in a group problem-solving exercise all have reasonable communication and assertion skills, there is a strong risk that people will bring to the exercise the same reticence to speak up that prevails outside the group.

There may be some benefit from the consultative aspects of the group process, but the possible benefits of combining the group members' creative capacities and achieving genuine agreement, and therefore commitment to the solution, will be reduced.

For example, if a senior executive has an aggressive interpersonal style, while one or two key staff members have adopted a submissive interpersonal style towards that executive, and none of them knows how to move towards being assertive (see Chapter 4), there is a strong risk that those two staff members will still be inclined to follow the aggressive executive's lead in a problem-solving session, rather than say what they really feel or think.

There will be an illusion of genuine problem solving, but not the real benefits that process has to offer. So, even if you think you are an old hand at problem solving, there may be further gains awaiting you from thinking about how problem-solving skills often need to be combined with communication and assertion skills.

Or you may think that you don't need to learn about

problem solving because you don't have any problems. Again, if a thoughtful review by you of that possibility convinces you that it's true, great! As an individual, you may genuinely feel you don't have any major problems, or that you do know how to solve them. As a member of an organisation (company, department, club or whatever), you may decide similarly, or at least that whatever conflicts occur are settled amicably and efficiently. If you think that is true, fine. Concentrate on other parts of the programme. But be careful that the apparent lack of problems or conflict doesn't result from your using one of the following **undesirable problem-solving techniques**.

WHAT THE BOSS SAYS, GOES

The 'boss' may be someone who actually occupies a formal position of authority, such as a manager, or foreman, or supervisor. Or the 'boss' may be someone who has come to assume a dominant role in a group, perhaps by being aggressive, while other members of the group tend to be submissive.

When a problem arises, the boss decides the solution, sometimes by just announcing it, or perhaps after some consultation, but even then it's clear just whose decision it is. This is, of course, a very traditional approach to problem solving, especially in business and industry, and many people are surprised that it should be questioned.

Bosses are often threatened by the apparent loss of their personal power in suggestions that problem solving should be shared. In Chapter 10 we will consider in more detail how illusory that power is; for now, we'll repeat the point above. Decisions imposed on people without their genuine participation are unlikely to receive whole-hearted support.

In very authoritarian systems, you may obtain compliance with such decisions by maintaining extensive, and expensive, surveillance. One of the side effects of this approach is to create resentment in those who did not participate in the decision, a resentment which may be expressed in attempts to sabotage implementation of the decision.

In Chapter 5 we outlined how giving orders, which is

effectively what we are talking about here, is a block to communication. In essence, the authoritarian approach boils down to one person saying to another or others, 'I am superior to you, and you are inferior to me, so we will now solve this problem in the way I decide.' Little wonder that it blocks communication and reduces co-operation in problem solving!

Some people will argue that their organisation has a particular need for 'discipline' and therefore an authoritarian decision-making structure, because of the peculiar nature of that organisation's activities, such as emergency services or the military. Their argument is that, in the crisis situations their organisations deal with, there isn't time for all this consultation and communication stuff. What is needed is strong leadership, swift decisions and obedience!

We agree, at least for genuine crisis situations. But, we would add, such organisations will obtain much better compliance with their leaders' orders if all members of the organisation have previously participated in deciding the procedures and principles to be followed in dealing with crises. Problem solving, as we outline it below, may not be possible in all problem situations. But if it can be done before the problem arises, we think you will still solve it better.

IT'S GETTING LATE.

Where people are trying to solve a problem, but lack good problem-solving (or communication or assertion) skills, the attempt often breaks down into going over the same ideas again and again. If you are tackling a personal problem, you may do all of this repetition inside your head. If two or more of you are involved, it is a repetitive discussion.

Eventually you think, 'It's getting late, I've got to do something. Oh well, I might as well do that.' Or someone in the group says, 'We've been arguing about this for three hours. I'm fed up. Let's try anything that stops this discussion.'

We have called this process 'decision by attrition' since it amounts to making a decision by wearing down people's resistance to other people's opinions. Unfortunately, it also wears down their interest and involvement. Fatigued and fed-up people are unlikely to make good choices, or to feel good about how the choice was finally made.

You will notice in the problem-solving procedure that we recommend you keep problem-solving sessions brief enough not to reach decision by attrition. Later, in the discussion on time organisation, you will see how using very brief bites of working on a problem can help you get unstuck.

LET'S COMPROMISE.

People in conflict are often advised to compromise, and a willingness to do so is often suggested to be a sign of 'reasonableness' or 'maturity'. Beware: compromise, as it is often practised, produces no-win solutions. That is, solutions that make no one feel she is winning and everyone feel he is losing.

Compromise properly means to settle a dispute by all parties conceding some part of their original views or goals. It does sound fair, doesn't it, with everybody giving up a bit. But that's its essential flaw: everybody gives up some of what they wanted. The assumption is that they will be satisfied with what's left of their original goal.

'Let's go to see movie X.'

'Well, I want to see movie Y.'

'OK, let's compromise. We'll go to half of movie X, and then to half of movie Y.'

Would you be satisfied with that solution? This example may seem silly, but that's what compromise often leads to, a solution that leaves everybody dissatisfied.

Some creative problem solving, rather than compromise, might have been, 'Well, let's go to movie X tonight, and then to movie Y tomorrow night.' Notice that this combines the two original suggestions.

Or, 'Well, let's go out to dinner together tonight, and then tomorrow, we can each go to our preferred movie.' 'Yeah, that suits me.' Notice that this is a different solution from either of the two original suggestions, but it makes both people happy.

Good problem solving should provide win-win solutions: all the people involved feel that they are winning. Achieving this naturally means people are committed to implementing the chosen solution.

BEWARE OF THE HIDDEN AGENDA.

An agenda, you will know, is just a list of the items to be considered at a meeting. It should really define everything that's going to be considered at that meeting and so everything that is directly relevant to discussions at the meeting.

A 'hidden agenda' refers to the situation where one or more of the people at a meeting has an issue or feeling which she sees as relevant to the group's discussions, but which she does not state openly. Because she sees it as important, it will influence the group's discussions but, because it is never stated, its influence may puzzle or frustrate the rest of the group.

For example, Charlie and George are both assistant supervisors. Charlie has been with the firm longer and thinks his seniority means he should be promoted before George. For his part, George thinks he works better and harder than old Charlie, so he should be promoted before Charlie is. Neither of them wants to admit to worrying about promotion, so they make a show of getting along with each other, although both are inclined to make occasional put-down remarks behind the other's back.

The department manager holds regular meetings of supervisory staff, to discuss productivity, wastage, and ideas for improving performance. Promotion is not on the agenda of these meetings, because the manager thinks that is his prerogative to decide.

In fact, both Charlie and George are experienced and able, and do have some good suggestions to make from time to time. But when Charlie makes a suggestion, George is likely to criticise it and, when George makes a suggestion, Charlie is likely to criticise it. Both men feel it is important to show the manager that he outperforms the other.

Sometimes their differences become heated and personal. This has the effect of embarrassing others at the meeting, and making them reluctant to say anything. Because they each expect the other to criticise their suggestions, Charlie and George have become reluctant to say anything unless they feel sure of themselves.

The meetings have gradually become less and less pleasant or productive, with people finding excuses not to attend. The manager cannot understand why his attempt to be 'democratic' isn't working, and is tempted to go back to the 'good old way' of making all the decisions himself.

You will have gathered that problem solving by this group is really in a mess. Some steps that could be taken to rectify this would be for the group to discuss the process of their meetings (see below) which would identify the pattern of interactions between Charlie and George, or for Charlie and George to communicate more openly about their feelings, or for the manager to share the problem of promotion with the group.

People don't exist in vacuums, and it is inevitable that they will bring to any meeting some concerns that are not on the agenda. This only becomes a problem when those concerns are felt strongly, are seen by their holders as relevant to the group's discussions, but are not stated openly.

Appropriate use of communication and assertion skills, coupled with the problem-solving technique of reviewing the group discussion process, should prevent hidden agendas from sabotaging your group's problem solving.

HOW TO SOLVE PROBLEMS

On page 156 you will find a brief checklist of the problem-solving procedure. You may find it a handy 'road-map' to refer to as we go through a detailed description of the whole process. It could also be helpful to write it out, for use as a personal prompt, or a guide to group members.

It consists of six major steps. It's a good idea to keep these steps separate, even to set aside a different time for each step, so that they don't get blurred into each other. This is an important element of the problem-solving procedure.

For both individual and group problem solving, taking time to complete each step properly means you will get the benefit of each step, particularly the creativity encouraged

HOW TO SOLVE PROBLEMS

This procedure can be used by one person, or by groups of two or more, such as a married couple or work team. Just adapt it appropriately. To get the benefits of the procedure, it's important to keep the steps separate. Even have different meetings for each step.

1 Define the problem.
Do this in terms of wants — what does each of the people affected want? — not solutions. Beginning with solutions bogs you down in each defending your own preferred solution.
If it's a big problem, you may need to break it down into sub-problems, and take them one at a time.

2 Brainstorm possible solutions.
Think of as many possible solutions as you can. The only goal at this stage is to come up with as long a list of possibilities as you can. No criticism or evaluation of suggestions is permitted. This frees up your creativity. To relieve tension, throw in some deliberately silly solutions.

3 Evaluate the possibilities.
Go down your list of possible solutions, noting next to each its pros and cons. What are the probable consequences of each? Each person in a group can rate each solution + ('I would be willing to try it') or − ('I wouldn't be willing to try it').

4 Select a solution.
Does one solution emerge as a common choice? Is there one that has clearly got more pluses? If you can't agree on which one to try, go back to step 2.

5 Plan the solution.
Who will do what, where, and by when? What resources are needed? How and by whom will they be obtained?

6 Implement the plan.
Follow it through, a step at a time. If it works, great. If it doesn't, find out why, and feed that information back in when you start back at whatever step you need to repeat.
In a group, it's a good idea to review the problem-solving process as well. It should be generating feelings of co-operation and involvement.

by the process. Conversely, it is important to set a reasonable time limit for each step or meeting, so that you don't fall into the trap of making decisions by attrition.

For group problem solving, particularly involving conflict-resolution, keeping the steps separate has major advantages. In a conflict situation, people are usually scared that a decision they don't want is going to be inflicted on them against their will, or a decision will be made before they have had a real chance to say their opinion.

From the checklist you will note that the choice of a solution doesn't occur until Step 4, and this has been preceded by three steps in which everybody is encouraged to offer their views. This postponement of the choice of a solution, coupled with repeated opportunities to participate in the procedure, takes the urgency out of 'a conflict situation and facilitates genuinely co-operative problem solving.

So, keep the steps of your problem solving separate. If working in a group, the chairman should tactfully prevent people from getting ahead of the present step. If you don't hold separate meetings for each step, make certain that everyone in the group is finished with the present step before going on to the next.

PREPARATION
If you are doing some individual problem solving, have you set aside enough, interruption-free time, say half an hour? Do you have any information you need for this problem? Something to write on?

If you are working in a group, do some of the group members need to learn about problem solving, or communication and assertion? If one or two of the group members are 'experts' who know the rules, while others have to be told what to do, you can wind up with a power imbalance which is resented by the novices. Do the others need to read Chapters 4, 5 and 6 of this manual? Would it be better to have an outside consultant guide the process for the group? This can be an important way of breaking down antagonism within groups with a history of conflict: the 'referee' is clearly neutral.

STEP 1 DEFINE THE PROBLEM.
This is a vital step since it defines the task, and yet it is often

skipped over hastily, to later regret. It is essential that you define the problem in terms of what each of the people involved **wants**, not in terms of possible solutions to the problem.

Many conflicts arise from people defining the problem as a clash between possible solutions, with each bitterly defending her proposed solution. No one listens to anyone else because each is frightened of not having his solution adopted. For example:

'I need the car in the morning.'
'Well, that's no good. I need it, too. I've got an appointment across town at half past nine.'
'Well, that's bad luck. I said I wanted it first.'
'Don't be childish! My appointment's important.'

And so on. Sound familiar? These two people are stuck, because each is defending the first solution he thought of, rather than discussing what each wants, transport to a certain place at a certain time. Redefining their problem in terms of wants would free them up to do some creative problem solving, perhaps even allowing a co-operative solution.

Some more examples:

'I would like to see the foreman in the packing section sacked,' could mean, 'I want our goods to go out reasonably packed and reasonably quickly.'
'I'm going to quit my stupid job,' could mean, 'I want my boss at least to listen to my suggestions so that I don't feel stuck with frustrating procedures that aren't necessary.'
'We'll have to sack half of our production staff the way things are going,' could mean, 'I want us to increase our profitability.'

Practical exercise: Write out a short list of your most important current problems, including your personal problems, or those you share with any other person or group in your life. For each problem, ask yourself, 'What do I really want from this situation?' and begin to define your problems in terms of your wants.

STEP 2   BRAINSTORM POSSIBLE SOLUTIONS.
This is the step that gets your creativity going, and gives you

your best chance of coming up with a really good solution. Look around your home or workplace. Chances are that more than half the' gadgets you can see were designed by brainstorming; it is now a well-established technique for solving problems in industry and manufacturing.

There are two rules for brainstorming if you want to get its full benefit: first, the sole aim is to think up as many solutions as possible, that is, quantity not quality; second, there must be no evaluation or criticism of any suggested solutions at this stage, even of your own.

Stick to these rules, for your personal problem solving, and your group's chairman should tactfully enforce them, too. By allowing your imagination free rein, you give yourself an opportunity to do some lateral thinking, to escape from the straitjackets of tradition or prejudice, and come up with novel and more effective solutions.

Even throw in obviously silly or funny solutions. They can act as springboards for effective solutions that you might otherwise not have thought of. And they can reduce tension in conflict situations.

In group problem solving, people may withhold quite good suggestions, because they fear how others will react. Look at Charlie and George, above. One person's suggestion, even if unworkable in itself, may prompt someone else's brilliant solution. But not if it's never offered because of fear of ridicule or criticism.

As solutions are brainstormed, they should be written down, either by yourself, or by someone the group appoints as recorder. In group problem solving, all members of the group should be able to see this list of possible solutions for the next step.

Practical exercise: Choose one or two of the personal problems on your list. Write a problem at the top of a blank page and brainstorm solutions to that problem below it. Do this for a couple of problems, to get the feel of brainstorming.

If you are working in a group, try some co-operative brainstorming. Remember, no criticism or evaluation yet.

STEP 3   EVALUATE THE POSSIBLE SOLUTIONS.
By now you should have a written list of all of the suggested

solutions, including those you see as funny or silly. Someone
else may see them as real alternatives. You may need to
rewrite the list, so that there is room next to each solution to
record the pros and cons of each.

Work through the solutions systematically, recording
next to each the advantages and disadvantages you can
imagine for each. In a group, this should be a co-operative
exercise, although the proposers of various solutions will
probably see more advantages to them than disadvantages.

In a group, after everyone has proposed all the pros and
cons they see for a particular solution, each person should
give a rating to that solution, of '+' or '−'. A plus rating
means, 'Yes, I would be willing to try this solution', while a
minus rating means, 'No, I would not be willing to try this
solution.'

Practical exercise: Now work through the solutions you have
brainstormed for your problems, noting the pros and cons of each.
If appropriate, rate each with a + or −.

STEP 4   CHOOSE A SOLUTION.
Often by this stage an appropriate solution has become
obvious; in a group, there may be consensus where before
there was conflict. If this is not immediately apparent, you
may need to count up the pluses, to see which solution has
majority support. But beware of quickly adopting a solution
with many minuses as well; some more problem solving may
be indicated.

It is not unusual to decide to combine two or more
suggested solutions in order to obtain a comprehensive
solution that does have unanimous support. If no obvious or
shared choice emerges, you will need to recycle the whole
process. Perhaps the problem was not accurately defined in
the first place, or perhaps you need some more brainstorming?

Sometimes problem solving bogs down because the
original problem was too big and complex, and a solution to
it becomes too complicated. Taking our earlier example of
wanting to raise profitability, this is usually affected by a
number of factors, including work efficiency, wastage, sales,

absenteeism, staff turnover, employer-employee relations, costs of materials, profit margins, marketing, and so on.

No single solution is likely to be sufficient to cope with the various contributions of all of these factors. Solving the problem of increased profitability is likely to be more successful if that problem is broken down into a number of smaller sub-problems, each taken one at a time.

This need to break complex problems down into sub-problems is not restricted to business. You may have decided that one of your personal problems is being overweight. When you look at it carefully, you may have recognised that you are overweight because you overeat and don't exercise. Then you realise that you overeat to cope with bad feelings, and these tend to occur both at work and at home. Clearly, no single simple solution, such as a diet, is going to solve your problem of overweight. Instead you need to do some brainstorming on each of the following sub-problems: regular exercise; sensible eating; reducing and coping with bad feelings at work; reducing and coping with bad feelings at home. The last two may even need to be broken down even further.

Time-consuming? Yes, but at least this approach means you are likely eventually to solve the problems in your life. Typical of dystressed people is the tendency to look at all of their problems at once, throw their hands up in the air, and say, 'That's too much ever to cope with. I give up.' Tackling your problems in manageable bites gets you moving.

It is, of course, possible that there may be some insoluble problems in your life, or some insoluble conflicts. There are limits on how much any one person, or procedure, can change. If you find, after carefully applying the whole of this procedure, that you have an insoluble problem, your only realistic goal is to reduce its impact on your stress level by using your total relaxation skills.

Practical exercise: Can you select solutions for your problems? If not, recycle the process.

STEP 5   PLAN TO IMPLEMENT YOUR SOLUTION.
This is the step so often missed, as we mentioned earlier, yet it's so obviously necessary. Make concrete plans as to exactly how your solution will be implemented.

In a group you may need to answer the following questions: Who will do what? Where? By when? What resources are needed? From where will they be obtained? By whom? How? And so on.

If your solution is to take effect, you need to plan exactly how that will happen. Otherwise it may stay just a good idea.

Practical exercise Take your own solutions one at a time and, for each, plan a step-by-step approach to making them work. Doing this sometimes throws up new problems. That's OK; recycle your problem-solving skills whenever you need.

STEP 6 IMPLEMENT YOUR PLAN.
Follow your plan through, one step at a time. If it works, congratulations! From you, as well as us. You have solved one of your problems, and shown yourself that you can tackle others, using the same basic approach.

If your solution doesn't work, accept your disappointment, using your mental relaxation skills if you need to. But see if you can find out why your solution didn't work.

Did you define the problem accurately? Do you need to try a different solution? Does the failure of this attempt give you new information about the problem, information which needs to be fed back into your problem-solving process?

In a group, it's a good idea also to review the problem-solving **process**, as well as its content. By process, we mean the interactions amongst the group members, and the related feelings. Again, remember the example of Charlie and George above. Any hidden agendas?

If the problem-solving procedure in a group is working well, it should generate feelings of group identity and closeness, and facilitate co-operation amongst the group members. This does not mean that everybody will simply agree all the time; that would be an unlikely situation, or more probably representative of a lack of communication or assertion.

But good group problem solving should be marked by a clear, non-defensive statement of different opinions, eventually resolved by a shared agreement. If you are not achieving this, you may again need to check the levels of communication and assertion skills, as well as problem solving. You may need to involve a consultant if you need further help.

On an individual level, you may well find your solutions require some of the other coping skills described in this manual, such as communication, assertion, relaxation, exercise, recreation, and so on. That's fine; you are beginning to see how to design your own, comprehensive stress-management programme.

TIME MANAGEMENT

Do you have some days when you feel you have achieved absolutely nothing, despite a great deal of running around and worrying? Or days when you feel you have more to do by the end of the day than you did at the start? Do you sometimes have trouble finding time for your relationships, recreation or relaxation?

If this only happens to you on some days and at some times, it's probably not a problem. Occasionally events

outside of our control do coincide in ways that frustrate the best laid plans, although a good time-management system has some flexibility built in, to allow for the unexpected.

But if you have these feelings on most days and much of the time, then you probably need to learn how to manage your time better. As we said earlier, don't be put off by the apparent artificiality of planning your activities. One of the major advantages of efficient time management is that it will give you more free time for whatever spontaneous activities take your fancy.

For example, if your time-management system saves you only ten minutes a day – and most people can save more than that – you will gain the equivalent of more than seven eight-hour days to spend on whatever activity you like, in just one year. Over your lifetime, you could gain one or two or more years worth of free time!

But time management offers you some other important advantages as well. Seeing yourself fitting in all of your important tasks, and having time for a balanced life of the kind you will design through your stress-management programme, are major steps in reducing your dystress level.

You will sometimes see time management described as time organisation, but in fact it boils down to organising yourself, your resources and your tasks in ways that result in your getting your tasks done reasonably quickly and successfully. We will now explain how you can plan your own time management system, then some suggestions on how to make it work, and finally give you some hints on saving time.

PLANNING YOUR TIME-MANAGEMENT SYSTEM

STEP 1 LIST YOUR TASKS AND ACTIVITIES.
Carefully list all the tasks and activities you want to do. This list should be as complete as possible, so it will include regular activities, such as recreations, exercise, social activities and regular jobs, and should also include any irregular but current tasks or problems, such as painting the house, preparing an annual budget, or buying your spouse's birthday gift.

Your list may start to get quite long, and probably should, unless you are leading a very simple life. Don't worry about this; it just means you are doing this step thoroughly. You will find it helpful to organise your various tasks into areas, such as job, domestic chores, exercise, recreations, family activities, special problems, and so on. The actual categories you use will depend on your lifestyle.

Practical exercise: List your tasks and activities, under the headings that are appropriate for you.

STEP 2   DRAW UP A TIMETABLE.
Using a large sheet of paper, draw up a timetable for a week, with days of the week across the top, and times down the left, like this:

	Mon.	Tues.	Wed.	Thur.	Fri.	Sat.	Sun.
7.00							
7.30							
8.00							

and so on. The times your timetable begins and ends will depend on when you usually get up and go to bed. You can also decide for yourself whether you need blocks of 60 or 30 minutes duration; depending on how fine you want to make your timetable.

Now write into your timetable the regular and essential activities on your list, as you do them already. For example, your job may have set starting and finishing times, or you may have regular times for some recreation, like a weekly tennis game.

STEP 3   DECIDE YOUR PRIORITIES.
Look at one area of your life at a time. Read through the tasks you have listed for that area and decide which is the most important. It might be one that you think is essential, or one whose completion would make a big difference to you, or one which needs to be done very soon. Give it a no. 1 ranking, and then look for no. 2, and so on.

If you really can't decide between a couple of items, toss a coin; it's not worth wasting time worrying about it. You will eventually tackle them all, anyway.

When you have ranked the items in one area in order of their priority, go on to another area until you have ranked all of the items on your list.

STEP 4   REVIEW YOUR TIMETABLE.

Now, in light of the priorities you have assigned to your various tasks and activities, go back over your present timetable. Is there some time allocated for all of your high priority activities, or are you missing some (like exercise, or recreation, or relationships)? Does the amount of time allocated to each area reasonably reflect its genuine importance in your life (or is something getting an unfair share, like your job, or a particular hobby)?

Rewrite your timetable as much as you need to achieve these two aims, of fitting in everything currently important, and of giving each its fair share of your time. As your current problems and priorities change, you will need to repeat this review. You might find it easier to schedule a regular review, each week or fortnight. How much is my timetable meeting my present needs?

As a part of planning and reviewing your timetable, try to adopt the following suggestions.

SOME TIME-MANAGEMENT STRATEGIES

If possible, arrange for **uninterrupted time** to work on your high priority tasks. Don't answer the telephone; ask your spouse to look after the kids; take whatever steps are necessary to protect that time.

Expect the unexpected. The world rarely goes just as we expect it to, so, if your timetable is too tight with no flexibility, you may often find it breaking down 'for reasons beyond your control'. But they're not; expect some things to go wrong, or at least differently, and have some flexible, unallocated time available to deal with the unexpected.

Keep records of important things, whether they are aspects of your job, like orders or purchases or plans or memos, or home management, such as bills, appointments and so on. Make sure your records cover everything important, and keep them up-to-date. Allow time to do this. Plan them so you can find information quickly.

Try to make at least a **start on new tasks** as soon as

possible, so that they don't seem to be building up into a great untouched heap. Plan time to start them. Having trouble getting started? Try Dr William Knaus's *Five Minute Plan*. This can be very helpful when the sheer size of a new task is putting you off starting: 'There's just so much, I'll never finish this, so what's the point in starting.' Instead, commit yourself to working on the project for only five minutes. At the end of that five minutes, see how you are going and how you feel. If you want to, commit yourself to another five minutes, then stop and review again. If five minutes seems too short and interrupts your work too much, use ten minutes, or even fifteen, but beware of making your initial commitment so long that it puts you off again. What you will often find, of course, is that once you have overcome your resistance to starting, the project gathers its own momentum and rolls along.

Have trouble deciding priorities, especially amongst a number of smaller tasks? 'So many things to do, where do I start?' As we said earlier, if a difference in priorities isn't clear, then it doesn't matter which task you start on, and it is very unproductive to spend too long agonising over your choice. Toss a coin, draw a slip of paper out of a hat, by whatever means, arbitrarily select a task, and get started on it. Knaus calls this the **bits and pieces technique**, and again recommends it as a way of getting started.

Have trouble remembering what has to be done? Then deliberately work out a **reminder system**. Write important dates or appointments on a calendar or in a diary; write yourself reminder notes and put them in your purse or wallet, or in strategic places around home or your workplace.

Tend to forget or skip the more boring and less interesting tasks? Use the **cross-out technique**: this involves writing yourself a list for today, including all the activities you have timetabled, and ranked in order of priority to you. Then work through the list, crossing out tasks as you complete them; stick to the list, except for genuinely exceptional circumstances. Many people find a daily cross-out list an essential way of organising their time on the job, and making sure that no part of it gets neglected.

Tend to avoid certain unrewarding tasks? **Reward**

yourself for tackling them. Remember in Chapter 2 we talked about the importance of your using self-reward to help strengthen your problem-solving behaviour, usually by giving yourself a pat on the back for genuine attempts. Take note of your successes, even if at the moment they are only small goals.

To help you tackle large but not very rewarding tasks, like losing weight, offer yourself tangible rewards, such as a new item of clothing, a record or cassette, and so on, as well as your own pat on the back.

More self-help? The instructions above should be sufficient for your needs, but if you are interested in more detail, try these two books:

People Skills by Robert Bolton (Prentice-Hall) is a good review of problem-solving and conflict-resolution.

Do It Now by William Knaus (Prentice-Hall) includes ideas on time management, and is specifically written for people with a tendency to procrastinate.

7

INSOMNIA

Difficulty in sleeping is commonly associated with dystress, and can become involved in a vicious cycle with your stress levels. The more dystressed you are, the more your sleep is disrupted; the worse you sleep, the more fatigued you are during the day, and the greater your dystress.

For some people, just solving their sleeping problem is enough to produce marked improvement across their whole lives. For many dystressed people, improving their sleep is a necessary part of an effective stress-management programme.

Sleeping problems are amazingly common. American research has found that one in ten people have frequent or severe sleep problems. One in four people seek relief from insomnia at some time in their lives. In the United States a multi-million dollar industry has grown up, selling alleged remedies for insomnia, most of them having limited value at best.

Unfortunately, the most common medical approach to insomnia is still some form of drug treatment. We say 'unfortunately' because it appears that most, if not all, of the drugs used actually make the sleeping problem worse. To understand why, you first need to understand a little about sleep.

WHAT IS SLEEP?
Although we all spend perhaps a third of our lives asleep, and generally sleep (or try to) every night, most of us don't really know much about sleep. Maybe that's because we sleep through it! (Sorry, couldn't resist that.)

Sleep is not a single, simple state consisting just of being relaxed and unconscious. In fact, there are five distinct stages of sleep. They can be distinguished from each other by the brain waves occurring during each. So, we had better explain a little about brainwaves.

Brainwaves are patterns of electrical activity which are detected on the outside of the brain, or really, usually on the outside of the head using special equipment. They are a rough indication of what the brain is doing. It is only rough, because it's a bit like listening through a small hole in the wall to a room full of people. You would only get an overall impression of what was going on.

Although they are only a general indication of brain activity, brainwaves have been found to be useful in finding out about brain functions during different states and conditions, including sleep. By recording them in sleeping people, scientists have identified the five different stages of sleep.

Stages 1 to 4 range from light to very deep sleep. People move back and forth through these stages during the night. Stage 4, the deepest sleep, occurs a couple of hours after falling asleep. But it was Stage 5 that was very interesting.

The scientists found that in this stage people had brain waves similar to those occurring when they were awake. At the same time, the sleepers' eyes could be seen moving about rapidly, under their closed eyelids, as though they were looking at something. Because of this, Stage 5 has been called Rapid Eye Movement (or REM) sleep.

If a sleeper was woken while in REM sleep, he or she would usually report that they were dreaming at the time, and they would be able to describe the dream quite vividly. This association between REM sleep and dreaming is now well-established, and it has led to other important information about sleep.

First, it was noticed that everybody will usually dream, during REM sleep, several times each night. We don't all remember our dreams equally well – some people can give you detailed descriptions of their dreams; others don't remember dreaming at all. But all the people studied in this now extensive research would usually have several bouts of

REM sleep a night, and would report dreaming if woken up during REM sleep.

Second, REM sleep is marked by extreme muscular relaxation, more so than in any other stage of sleep. This may be why it appears to contribute essential refreshment to the sleeper, although this isn't clear yet. What this characteristic of REM sleep did do was spark off an ingenious set of experiments with non-human animals.

Rats (and other non-human animals with brains) also have brainwaves, from which we can tell that they also have stages of sleep, including REM sleep. We can't ask them whether they have dreams but, by using this extreme relaxation during REM sleep, scientists were able to study how important it is.

A laboratory rat would be given a small platform to sleep on, suspended over some water – not enough to do the rat any harm, but enough to wake him up if he fell into it. Like people, the rats would have enough tension in their muscles to stay on the platform during the lighter stages of sleep. But once they reached REM sleep, they would relax completely, fall off into the water, and wake up.

In this way, the rats were able to get as much sleep as they wanted, but very little of it was REM sleep. They very soon showed obvious signs of distress, and did poorly at learning tasks.

Similar effects have been found in humans. If volunteer research subjects were woken up each time they began REM sleep, they soon showed obvious signs of dystress, even though they were allowed as much of the lighter stages of sleep as they wanted. They reported emotional upsets, with feelings of depression and irritability, and reduced ability to do thinking tasks.

When these volunteers were then allowed to sleep undisturbed, they showed a rebound effect. For several nights they would have increased amounts of REM sleep, with frequent dreams, but often marred by nightmares and disturbed, restless sleep.

Thus it appears that REM sleep, or the dreams occurring during it, serve an essential function for well-being. People deprived of REM sleep will develop marked signs of dystress; when allowed to catch up later, their sleep will be disturbed for some time. All this information becomes relevant when we consider the use of drugs to manage sleeping difficulties.

WHAT IS INSOMNIA?

Insomnia is not a single problem. It can occur in several forms, for a number of reasons. It will help you to decide whether, and which parts of this chapter will be helpful to you if you first decide whether you really have insomnia and, if so, for which reasons.

In principle, insomnia is a combination of 1 poor sleep with 2 daytime fatigue. Both elements need to be present to justify labelling the problem as insomnia. For example, some people don't sleep much, but feel fine. They don't have insomnia. Some depressed people will sleep nearly all the time, so they obviously don't have insomnia, but they will complain of being fatigued when they are awake. They need depression management.

Poor sleep may fall into one or more of four patterns. You may

- be unable to go to sleep within 30 minutes of trying;
- be awake and unable to sleep for more than 30 minutes during the night, including waking up very early and not being able to go back to sleep;
- sleep restlessly with many brief awakenings; or
- sleep for a nightly total of less than six and a half hours.

Daytime fatigue has one or more of the following characteristics. You may feel:

- physically tired;
- unable to concentrate;
- depressed;
- irritable;
- lethargic.

Insomnia is not dangerous, in the sense of being immediately life-threatening, but it is very unpleasant for the sufferer, and can interact in the vicious cycle described above with problems like stress or depression.

CAUSES OF SLEEP DISTURBANCE

We can identify six broad causes of sleeping difficulties, each requiring its own solution.

1 Stress, not surprisingly, is a common cause of insomnia. The dystressed person will often go to bed in such a state of tension and agitation that there is little chance of their going to sleep readily. They will often spend their waking time in bed, when they are trying to sleep, mulling over the problems of the day and worrying about the problems of tomorrow.

The more they mull and worry, the more agitated they become, and the less likely they are to sleep. Often they will add to the day's worries their growing concern about not being able to go to sleep. The more they worry about not sleeping, the less likely they are to sleep.

Obviously these people need a stress-management programme like that described in this book or at least the parts which are individually relevant! The steps for feeling better by thinking straighter, especially for coping with intrusive thoughts and stopping excessive worrying, will be helpful. We'll describe how later.

2 Some **physical problems** can disturb sleep. One such problem is called sleep apnea, which means that the sufferer literally stops breathing and then is jolted awake by his lack of oxygen and excessive carbon dioxide levels. This can be detected by an observer watching the sleeper to see if there are long pauses in his breathing just before he wakes each time.

Another physical problem has the technical name, nocturnal myoclonus, which simply means that the sufferer's muscles have occasional large twitches, which wake him up. Not surprisingly, this problem will often be detected by anyone sharing their bed with the sufferer. It can be associated with other problems, like Parkinson's disease.

These physical problems are beyond the bounds of the self-help approach described in this book. If they, or anything similar, are contributing to your sleeping difficulty, you should see your doctor.

3 Poor sleep habits are often involved in sleeping difficulties. Many body functions have natural rhythms or cycles, often repeating every 24 hours. For example, your body temperature does not really remain constant, but fluctuates steadily around the usual average, reaching a peak in mid-afternoon, and a trough in the early morning. These natural rhythms seem to be an important part of biological functioning and disturbing them can upset you in a number of ways. A well-known example of this is jet-lag, when you quickly change the external time of day compared to what your body 'thinks' it is. This can have such a disruptive effect on your functioning that many international pilots try to live as though they were always in their home time zone, even if this means sleeping in the middle of the day when away!

If you go to bed at widely differing times on different nights, or try to get up at widely differing times, your body has trouble adjusting its sleep and wakefulness cycles, so it will not feel sleepy when you would like it to.

A related problem is sleeping in, something that many people tell themselves is a luxury much to be desired. In fact, if you try to sleep much past your regular rising time, you will usually feel worse than if you got up then.

Similarly, if you have had a bad night's sleep, and you try to make up for this by napping during the day, don't be surprised if you don't need to sleep when you go to bed that night. We will make some suggestions for brushing up your sleeping habits below.

4 Using your bed for other activities can give it associations for you that make it difficult to use it for sleeping. One of the most common we have already mentioned, and that's using your bed as somewhere to worry, especially worrying about whether you will sleep. If you do this often, just going to bed can make you feel worried rather than restful.

We have been surprised by the number of couples we have seen who postpone discussion of relationship problems until they go to bed, sometimes just as the light is switched off. 'By the way, dear, there's something I've been meaning to talk to you about.'

Discussing problems is not a good way of relaxing. With both partners fatigued, such discussions run a fair risk of escalating into arguments, and arguing is an even worse way of relaxing. Elsewhere in this book we talk about the possibility of improving your key relationships as a part of effective stress management, and the chapters on changing your self-talk, improving communications and learning to solve problems are particularly relevant.

However, if relationship problems are a major contributor to your sleeping difficulty, or your dystress in general, you should consider our self-help manual for improving relationships (*Living and Loving Together*, also published by Viking O'Neil) or see a qualified clinical psychologist.

Some people use their beds as convenient places for arousing entertainment, such as watching television or reading books. It's a bit unrealistic to spend an hour or two getting thoroughly aroused by a good thriller, and then expect to be able to switch off instantly and go to sleep. Give yourself time to wind down, and the same advice applies to arousing or exciting activities.

Which brings up sex. Many people do most or all of their sexual relating in bed, and don't particularly want to change that. This need not be a problem, since successful sexual expression usually produces pleasant feelings of relaxation and tiredness. Sex can even be a good tension-reliever, although we wouldn't suggest you use it only for this.

If your sexual expression is unsuccessful and associated with increased feelings of tension, then we are back to our advice above about our self-help manual for improving relationships, or seeing a qualified clinical psychologist.

5 Eating or drinking can both contribute to sleeping difficulties, depending on what and how much. Eating very rich or spicy food can upset sleep for some people, not least because of the accompanying indigestion.

Popular drinks contain drugs which can affect sleep. Tea, coffee and some soft drinks contain caffeine, which is a brain stimulant. It is this stimulating property that makes the drinks popular and they are often drunk, and marketed, for the 'lift' they give.

In fact, some people become literally addicted to these drinks, although they may not be aware of it, because their consumption is so socially acceptable. They will say things like, 'I can't start the day without my cuppa', and show typical signs of drug withdrawal when their cuppa is unavailable. This problem has now been recognised as serious enough to deserve its own label, caffeinism. Because the caffeine addict is drinking large amounts of a brain stimulant each day, it is not surprising that he or she may have difficulty sleeping, as well as showing other undesirable side effects.

We have already suggested you monitor your caffeine consumption carefully. As a rule of thumb, four ordinary-sized caffeine drinks (tea, coffee, cola, or whatever) a day is enough. If you have a sleeping problem, avoid drinking these before you go to bed.

Alcohol is the other popular drug with a marked effect on sleep. Unlike caffeine, alcohol is a tranquilliser, although many people would not think so because of its effect of suppressing inhibitions when taken in small doses. At larger doses, which seem to be the social norm, its brain suppressing effects become more obvious, even leading to unconsciousness. So it can look as though alcohol is facilitating sleep and sadly it is used for just that purpose by a surprising number of insomnia sufferers. It is sad because alcohol, like the sleeping drugs we are about to consider, actually interferes with sleep and makes sleeping problems worse.

It does this in the same way as sleeping drugs do, so we will consider those next. The practical implication is that alcohol is **not** the answer for sleeping problems, any more than it is the answer for dystress.

6 Sleeping drugs may seem odd in a list of causes of sleeping disturbances, but considerable research and clinical experience suggest very firmly that this is where they belong. Needless to say, this would be disputed by the drug companies that sell them and some, but not all, of the doctors that prescribe them.

Despite growing criticism, they are still the most common form of treatment for insomnia. In the USA in one year, $60 million are spent on sleeping drugs over the counter, and this does not include the huge amount of sleeping drugs used in hospitals.

If you have had a sleeping problem for any time, or if you have consulted your doctor about one, the chances are you have tried or may still be taking a sleeping drug. So we will take a little time to explain why we believe they are not the answer for, but a cause of, sleeping problems.

The major problems with sleeping drugs is that, although they may increase the total amount of sleep you get, they change it. According to one eminent authority in the field, Dr Richard Bootzin, this is true of **all** sleeping drugs although, again, the drug companies would argue about this.

Certainly most, if not all, sleeping drugs deprive the user of Stages 3 and 4 and REM sleep, that is, of the heavier stages of sleep, including dreaming sleep. Well, in light of the research we described above, you can work out for yourself what effect this will have on the user of a sleeping drug.

Although the person may seem to have solved her insomnia problem because she spends more time asleep, her day-time fatigue will actually be made worse by the loss of deep sleep. This effect can understandably make the person believe she is sleeping worse than before, so she will increase the dose, which increases the side effects and raises the risk of accidental overdose.

If the poor sufferer gets fed up with sleeping drugs and suddenly throws them out, he will then have that rebound effect we described above, with many dreams, restless sleep and possibly nightmares. You will note that this is due to cutting out the drug which was, in fact, making the sleeping problem worse.

But the uninformed user doesn't know this and instead interprets the rebound effect as evidence for his needing to stay on the sleeping drug. This is understandable, particularly since the rebound effect can last several weeks in someone who has been using sleeping drugs for a long time.

Not only sleeping drugs have been used in attempts to treat insomnia. Sedatives, tranquillisers and anti-depressant drugs have all been used from time to time, sometimes in an honest attempt by the prescribing doctor to avoid the problems associated with sleeping drugs. The trouble with this is that many of these drugs also have negative side effects and they, along with the sleeping drugs, have the risk of being habit-forming. This is because of the process called tolerance, which occurs for many drugs, sometimes quite quickly. Initially, a fairly small dose will have the desired effect (and any unwanted side effects) but, as the body develops tolerance to the drug, you need to take even larger doses to get the same effect. Eventually the largest dose you can safely take may not help you sleep.

But the trap is that, although you are no longer obtaining any helpful effects from these large doses of the drug, your body has become accustomed to it. If you suddenly stop taking it, because it doesn't seem to be helping any more, you will probably suffer from withdrawal symptoms, such as the rebound effect, which can be very unpleasant and even dangerous.

Let us sum up our position on the use of drugs to treat sleeping problems. We are not automatically anti-drug. There may be some psychological problems where drug treatment is the best approach. Intelligent use of the appropriate drugs may also help someone cope with a temporary crisis, and even help them also to undertake a psychotherapy programme to prevent the recurrence of their problem.

But we are doubtful about using drugs as maintenance therapy for common living problems, such as stress, anxiety, depression and insomnia. Even for those patients who are genuinely helped by the drugs, and who do not suffer distressing side effects, the drug at best temporarily reduces the symptoms of the person's problems, without really doing anything to solve them.

For example, the most common form of drug treatment for depression uses a group of substances called the tricyclic anti-depressants. Only about two thirds of depressed patients get any benefit from these drugs, and most of these patients will relapse into further depression within a year of stopping the drug. When you take into account the high incidence of negative side effects associated with these drugs, you have to ask what these patients have really gained?

As far as sleeping drugs are concerned, the picture appears even blacker, because these substances seem actually to worsen the very problem they are supposed to be alleviating. Adding to this the high incidence of unwanted side effects and the risks of habituation and overdose, and we cannot justify recommending them to anybody under any circumstances.

You will have to make up your own mind. Psychological programmes for the management of insomnia, or stress or depression, certainly require much more effort on your part than popping a pill or two. On the other hand, they do not have the risks of unwanted physical side effects and they do offer the chance of really tackling the causes of your difficulties, giving a much more lasting solution.

One important practical implication flows from this discussion. If you have been using sleeping drugs (or anti-anxiety or anti-depressant drugs) for a while, you should not just stop taking them, or you run the risk of withdrawal symptoms including the rebound effect.

Ideally, you should discuss with the doctor who prescribed your drugs the fact that you are doing this programme and that you would like to be gradually eased off the drugs. Listen carefully to his or her advice as there may be some good medical reason why you should continue taking a particular drug.

But you are also entitled to recognise that your doctor may favour drug treatment because he or she has not been trained in any other approach, and may have been influenced by the very extensive advertising of the drug companies. You are entitled to disagree with his or her advice if you think it does not have sufficient evidence to support it. Don't be put off by attempts to pull rank or claim special authority. A good doctor can and will explain his or her advice.

If your doctor is unwilling to assist you in going off your drug(s), but agrees that there is no threat to your life in doing so, you can wean yourself off. The rule of thumb is to start reducing the dose as soon as you feel that you no longer need to depend on that drug.

This usually means that you are already having some success with this programme, or similar approaches, and you can see yourself coping better. Cut your daily dose in half, and see how you feel. If that produces too uncomfortable a withdrawal, go back up to three quarters.

Stay at the reduced dose for a week or two, then cut it in half
again.

Again, if you have severe withdrawal symptoms, put the
dose back up a little. The aim is to wean yourself off steadily,
but at a pace that allows your body time to adjust to being
without the drug. After sleeping drugs, you may still have
some rebound effect but at least you will know that is
temporary, and caused by the drug you are getting rid of, not
by your sleeping problem.

Another way of gradually reducing your own drug levels is
to disguise the amount of the drug you are taking in a 'drug
cocktail'. This helps get around the psychological
expectations of knowing that you have reduced the drug.
'Will I be able to go to sleep tonight because I am now down
to half my daily dose?' or 'Will I have any rebound effects
yet; I am down to quarter of my daily dose?' These
expectations themselves are enough to give you sleeping
problems.

Apart from using appropriate self-talk, described below
and in earlier chapters, you can disguise the amount of the
drug you are taking. Enlist the help of your partner, or
friend, or even ask your pharmacist if she would help.

Your helper takes control of the drugs you are taking from
now on. He should take your drug and divide the tablets into
groups, the first few groups should contain the number of
tablets you are taking at the moment, the next few groups
should contain less of the tablets and so on until there are no
tablets left.

For example, if you were taking two tablets a night, your
helper could have groups of tablets in this order:

2, 2, 2, 2, 1½, 1½, 1½,
1¼, 1¼, 1¼, 1, 1, 1, 1,
½, ½, ½, ½, ½, ¼, ¼,
¼, ¼, ¼, 0, 0, 0, 0.

Your helper should only reduce the amount of the drug
gradually, and should make the amount of the drug
reduction uneven, so that you can't guess how much you are
taking. In the above example, for instance the person would
take 2 tablets for four nights, then 1½ tablets for three
nights, then 1¼ tablets for three nights, 1 tablet for four
nights and so on.

Your helper then needs to find a way of disguising the drugs. If your pharmacist is involved he will probably be able to mix up a syrup for you; if not you can always crush the tablets in jam or honey or butter. You may find some other ingenious way of disguising the tablets. (**Do not** mix with alcohol.)

Then at the time you would normally take your drug, your helper now gives his prearranged dose to you in the disguised form. This is your 'drug cocktail'. Under no circumstances should you try to find out how much of the drug is in the mixture, otherwise you are defeating the purpose of it being disguised.

If you suffer any withdrawal effects you should let your helper know and she should raise the dose again and decrease it more gradually. Your helper needs to take your word for this and comply with your wishes. Many helpers are tempted to think 'Oh, he is only saying he feels bad; I won't increase the dose; I will trick him.' **Don't** do this; if the person taking the drugs says he would like to put the dose up again, do it and gradually reduce it again.

Once your helper has reduced your dose to 0, he should continue giving you your 'drug cocktail' for a couple of nights, with no drug in it. Your helper should only let you know that you are off the drugs once he is satisfied that you have slept well for at least three or four nights without any drugs.

This procedure can take quite a long time but is worth the trouble in the long run.

For further information on the 'drug cocktail' and weaning yourself off drugs, we recommend a book by Dr Connie Peck, *Chronic Pain*, published by Fontana.

So, if drugs are not the answer to insomnia, what is?

A BRIEF GUIDE TO SLEEPING BETTER

1 MONITOR YOUR SLEEPING.

Keep a diary of your sleeping and any difficulty in going to or staying asleep. Using the information above, try to work out the causes of your sleeping difficulty. Do you think your sleep is disturbed by one of the physical problems, like sleep apnea or muscular twitches, that need medical attention?

Have you got into bad sleeping habits, like irregular hours, or using your bed to watch TV, or as somewhere to worry? Are you drinking too much caffeine during the day, especially close to bedtime?

David had problems getting off to sleep, he usually stayed awake for one or two hours after going to bed. When he kept a record of his habits it looked like this:

Night	Time to bed	Activities in bed	Hours of sleep
Mon.	10.30 p.m.	Worried about day Read for a while Drank cup of coffee	5½
Tues.	10.00 p.m.	Felt exhausted Listened to music Worried about day	5
Wed.	12.20 p.m.	Drank cup of coffee Read	4
Thur.	9.30 p.m.	Worried about day Listened to music	5½

and so on, clearly David is making a number of mistakes, he has irregular sleeping hours; he drinks coffee before attempting to sleep; and he reads, worries and listens to music in bed.

Identifying the nature and possible causes of your sleeping problem will help you to choose which parts of this programme should help you.

2 CONTRACT WITH YOURSELF.

If you expect to find it difficult to stick to a good sleep programme, write yourself a contract as a motivational aid. This can be very helpful when your programme is going to require breaking old habits, or giving up some things you have enjoyed.

Here is a standard contract. Fill in the blank spaces to suit yourself: your rewards and penalties should be big enough to be a real incentive, but not so big that it isn't practical to enforce your contract on yourself. It can be helpful to write the contract out and put it up on a wall, say in your bedroom, as a reminder of what you are going to do to solve your sleeping problem.

I (*your name*) promise myself that, for each week that I stick to my good sleeping programme, I will reward myself with (*fill in your idea of a suitable reward, such as a record, or small piece of clothing, or cash towards a large reward later*).

Any week that I don't stick to my programme, my penalty will be (*fill in your idea of a suitable penalty, such as an unpleasant chore, or a cash gift to your least favourite charity*).

I recognise that this contract is a way of helping myself achieve a goal I have set myself so, if I break it, only I lose.

Signed (*you sign; it can be supportive to get your spouse or a friend to hold your contract*).

David's contract looked like this:

I promise myself that I will go to bed at 11.00 p.m. each night. Once in bed I will immediately switch off the light and concentrate on relaxing. If I do not sleep within 20 minutes I will get up, do something else until I am tired. I will repeat this until I am able to sleep.

I will reward myself with $5.00 each night I follow this procedure. If I stick to my programme for a week I will go out to a restaurant of my choosing.

Any night I don't stick to my programme I will not watch my favourite television show the next evening. If I do not stick to my programme at all during the week I have to clean the house by myself.

I recognise that this contract is to help me achieve my own goal, if I break it only I will lose.

Signed . . . . David

. . . . Helen (David's wife)

3 LEARN TO RELAX.

By now you will know that total relaxation is both mental and physical. This is nowhere more apparent than in insomnia-management. You may well be able to lie on your bed, reasonably relaxed in your body, but with your mind so tense and active that you have little chance of going to sleep. For this, you need mental relaxation, as it is described in Chapter 2.

Physical relaxation has been shown to be a very helpful component of better sleeping programmes, obviously because it helps you to drift off to sleep. It is also a practical component of sensible strategies for coping with not falling asleep readily. If you need to, go back to the physical relaxation section, and plan what you will do to learn good physical relaxation skills.

4 USE SENSIBLE SELF-TALK.

If you find yourself lying in bed, not able to go to sleep or go back to sleep as readily as you would like, don't start to fill your mind with upsetting thoughts about how bad your sleeping problem is or how rotten you are going to feel the next day. Do learn off by heart and then practise in your mind, the following sensible self-talk:

'It is disappointing that I am not easily able to sleep now, but I can cope with feeling disappointed. So, I won't pretend I'm not disappointed, but I also won't exaggerate my disappointment and arouse myself more by dwelling on negative thoughts.

Lying here relaxed is nearly as refreshing as being asleep. So, I will concentrate on relaxing myself physically, and then I will occupy my mind with pleasant and restful thoughts and images.'

Repeat this self-talk to yourself when you need it, and follow the instructions about relaxing yourself and concentrating on pleasant and restful thoughts.

5 ESTABLISH GOOD SLEEPING HABITS.

Try to go to bed and get up at around the same times each day, within reasonable limits, making sure these two times allow for a reasonable amount of sleep. Avoid frequent or marked changes to your sleeping times. If you are a shift worker, see if you can arrange not to change your shift times too often.

If it comes up to your regular bedtime, and you aren't at all sleepy, don't go to bed until you feel drowsy. Similarly, if you are in bed, and you haven't gone to sleep within 30 minutes (after using sensible self-talk and relaxation), get up and go to a different room. Do something relaxing, like reading, until you do feel drowsy.

A warm milk drink, with or without flavourings, can help you feel sleepy. Milk actually contains a chemical which naturally helps sleep.

Don't use your bed for arousing activities, like reading or watching horror stories, or eating and drinking. Avoid caffeine or alcohol drinks just before going to bed. (Smoking in bed is literally dangerous.)

If you have had trouble sleeping, don't 'make up' by sleeping in the next morning, or taking naps during the day. Get up at your regular time, and save your sleep needs for the next night.

These procedures can be very disruptive, but unfortunately, like all habits, bad sleep habits are difficult, at first, to change.

6 MANAGE DAYTIME FEELINGS.

If stress, tension, anxiety or anger during the day are setting you up for difficulty sleeping at night, use the relevant sections of this manual to learn how to manage those bad feelings better. You could start back at Chapter 2.

7 WEAN YOURSELF OFF DRUGS SLOWLY.

If you have been using sleeping drugs (or any other drugs), and you now want to stop using them, first discuss it with your doctor, as outlined above. Then reduce your use of the drugs gradually, to minimise any withdrawal discomfort. Don't be surprised if you get the rebound effect if you are cutting out sleeping drugs.

Recognise that, although the rebound effect is genuinely unpleasant, it is temporary and it results from the drugs, not your sleeping problem.

MORE DETAILED SELF-HELP

If sleeping problems are a major difficulty for you, and the good sleeping programme above is not detailed enough for you, either of the following self-help programmes may be more helpful:

How to sleep better: A drug-free program for overcoming insomnia by Thomas J. Coates and Carl E. Thoresen (published by Prentice-Hall).

Insomnia-Management, a cassette and workbook programme, by Dr Richard Bootzin (published by BMA Audiocassettes).

8

DEPRESSION – COPING WITH THE BLUES WITHOUT THE DRUGS

Depression is a common result of unresolved stress. If you often feel bad about much of your life and there doesn't seem to be any way of making things better, it is hardly surprising that you might become depressed.

Similarly depression can be a source of dystress in your life. The low feelings, lack of enjoyment, low activity levels and sense of hopelessness that characterise depression can be stressors themselves. There is a good deal of overlap and interaction between stress and depression. It is important, because of this overlap, to change both your stress reactions and your depressed moods. Otherwise you leave yourself vulnerable to becoming depressed, or feeling depressed again in the future.

Coping with stress is similar to coping with depression. The rest of this book could be used as a self-help guide for someone who feels depressed, although depression has a few added characteristics which we will discuss in this chapter.

If you think you have or may have depression, or if you're not sure, read on.

WHAT IS DEPRESSION?

We all feel low occasionally. As we have emphasised, some bad feelings are normal and are not a reason for concern. If you lost someone very dear to you, you would probably feel unhappy about that for a while. As before, we are only concerned here with bad feelings that are intense, long-lasting and interfering with your life.

A person suffering from clinically significant depression

will show one or more of the following characteristics:
- prolonged and strong feelings of depression, sadness, dejection, misery and so on;
- low activity levels: they just don't do much any more; problems in their relationships because of or contributing to their depression;
- feelings of guilt and a tendency to blame themselves for everything that's wrong;
- a tendency to see the world as making overwhelming demands on them and placing insurmountable problems in their path;
- a sense of hopelessness about the future: things are never going to get better;
- sleep disturbances, in either direction, either having difficulty sleeping, or spending lots of time sleeping;
- fatigue and a lack of enthusiasm or energy, even though they may be sleeping more than usual;
- eating disturbances, in either direction, either eating much less or much more than usual, often resulting in marked changes in body weight;
- a loss of interest in sex;
- and some depressed people will think about or even try suicide.

Not every depressed person shows all of these character-istics. We would usually say someone was depressed if they complained of the depressed feelings at the top of the list, accompanied by one or more of the other signs of depression. If you are not sure whether you have depression, or whether your depression is strong enough to need some attention, complete the self-assessment scale below.

HOW DEPRESSED AM I?

This is the Beck Depression Inventory, a standard measure of depression. If you are going to do the Inventory to measure your level of depression, you should do it **now**, before you read any further, so that your answers are not influenced by what we discuss later.

The self-help steps in this unit are intended mostly for people whose scores are between 5 and 15. If you scored less than 5, you don't seem to have a problem with depression. If this does not seem right to you – that is, you still think you do have a problem with depression – ask yourself if your score was artificially lowered because you are having a good run just now or because you are taking some drugs to lift your mood. If you decide that you do have, or have had, a problem with depression, even though you score less than 5, go ahead with this unit. It certainly can't do you any harm.

If you scored 16 or more, you may be feeling too bad to get far with self-help. By all means, give it a good try but, if you don't seem to be getting out of your depression, see a qualified clinical psychologist.

If you are seriously thinking of suicide, you should discuss that with a clinical psychologist, or some other counsellor. Self-help is unlikely to be sufficient; you will probably need to speak to someone and get some specific advice for your individual situation. We think that, under certain circum-stances, suicide may be a valid choice for a person to make. However, nearly all the people who attempt suicide unsuccessfully later say they are glad they weren't successful.

It would seem that choosing suicide is, according to many of the people who try it, often a mistake that reflects their problem with depression, rather than a careful weighing up

BECK DEPRESSION INVENTORY

Instructions

Each item consists of a group of statements describing possible feelings. Read each item right through, and then pick out the one statement in that group which best describes how you have been feeling lately, in the last day or so. Circle the number beside the statement you have chosen. If several statements in the group seem to apply equally well to you, circle each one.

Be sure to read all the statements in a group before making your choice.

Item A (Sadness)
0 I do not feel sad.
1 I feel blue or sad.
2 I am blue or sad all the time and I can't snap out of it.
2 I am so sad or unhappy that it is quite painful.
3 I am so sad or unhappy that I can't stand it.

Item B (Pessimism)
0 I am not particularly pessimistic or discouraged about the future.
1 I feel discouraged about the future.
2 I feel I have nothing to look forward to.
2 I feel that I won't ever get over my troubles.
3 I feel that the future is hopeless and that things cannot improve.

Item C (Sense of failure)
0 I do not feel like a failure.
1 I feel I have failed more than the average person.
2 I feel that I have accomplished very little that is worthwhile or that means anything.
2 As I look back on my life all I can see is a lot of failure.
3 I feel I am a complete failure as a person.

Item D (Dissatisfaction)
0 I am not particularly dissatisfied with my life.
1 I feel bored most of the time.
2 I don't enjoy things the way I used to.
2 I don't get satisfaction out of anything any more.
3 I am dissatisfied with everything.

Item E (Guilt)
0 I don't feel particularly guilty.
1 I feel bad or unworthy a good part of the time.

2 I feel quite guilty.
2 I feel bad or unworthy practically all of the time now.
3 I feel as though I am very bad or worthless.

Item F (Expectation of punishment)
0 I don't feel I am being punished.
1 I have a feeling that something bad may happen to me.
2 I feel I am being punished or will be punished.
2 I feel I deserve to be punished.
3 I want to be punished.

Item G (Self-dislike)
0 I don't feel disappointed in myself.
1 I am disappointed in myself.
2 I don't like myself.
2 I am disgusted with myself.
3 I hate myself.

Item H (Self-accusation)
0 I don't feel I am worse than anybody else.
1 I am critical of myself for my weaknesses or mistakes.
2 I blame myself for my faults.
3 I blame myself for everything that happens.

Item I (Suicidal ideas)
0 I don't have any thoughts of harming myself.
1 I have thoughts of harming myself, but I would not carry them out.
2 I feel I would be better off dead.
2 I feel my family would be better off if I were dead.
3 I have definite plans about committing suicide.
3 I would kill myself if I could.

Item J (Crying)
0 I don't cry any more than usual.
1 I cry more than I used to.
2 I cry all of the time now; I can't stop it.
3 I used to be able to cry but now I can't cry at all even though I want to.

Item K (Irritability)
0 I am no more irritated now than I ever am.
1 I get annoyed or irritated more easily than I used to.
2 I feel irritated all of the time.
3 I don't get irritated at all at things that used to irritate me.

Item L (Social withdrawal)

0   I have not lost interest in other people.
1   I am less interested in other people now than I used to be.
2   I have lost most of my interest in other people and have little feeling for them.
3   I have lost all of my interest in other people and don't care about them at all.

Item M (Indecisiveness)

0   I make decisions about as well as ever.
1   I try to put off making decisions.
2   I have great difficulty in making decisions.
3   I can't make any decisions at all anymore.

Item N (Body image change)

0   I don't feel I look any worse than I used to.
1   I am worried that I am looking old or unattractive.
2   I feel that there are permanent changes in my appearance and they make me look unattractive.
3   I feel that I am ugly or repulsive looking.

Item O (Work retardation)

0   I can work as well as before.
1   It takes extra effort to get started doing something.
1   I don't work as well as I used to.
2   I have to push myself very hard to do anything.
3   I can't do any work at all.

Item P (Insomnia)

0   I can sleep as well as usual.
1   I wake up more tired in the morning than I used to.
2   I wake up 2–3 hours earlier than usual and find it hard to get back to sleep.
3   I wake up early every day and can't get more than 5 hours sleep.

Item Q (Fatigability)

0   I don't get any more tired than usual.
1   I get tired more easily than I used to.
2   I get tired from doing nothing.
3   I get too tired to do anything.

Item R (Appetite)

0   My appetite is not worse than usual.
1   My appetite is not as good as it used to be.

2 My appetite is much worse now.
2 I am eating much more than I used to.
3 I have no appetite at all.
3 I eat compulsively all the time.

Item S (Weight loss)
0 I haven't lost much weight, if any, lately.
1 I have lost more than 2 kilos (or 5 pounds).
2 I have lost more than 5 kilos (or 10 pounds).
3 I have lost more than 7 kilos (or 1 stone).

Item T (Health concerns)
0 I am no more concerned about my health than usual.
1 I am concerned about aches and pains or upset stomach or constipation.
2 I am so concerned with how I feel physically or what I feel physically that it's hard to think of much else.
3 I am completely absorbed in how or what I feel physically.

Item U (Sex interest)
0 I have not noticed any recent change in my interest in sex.
1 I am less interested in sex than I used to be.
2 I am much less interested in sex now.
3 I have lost interest in sex completely.

Scoring
Add up the numbers you have circled to get your total score. If you have circled more than one number for an item, add **only** the highest number circled for that item. For example, if you circled both the 2 and the 3 for Item O because you thought they both applied to you, you now count only the 3. If you circled two 2s or 3s for any item, now count only one of those numbers. You can check your total against this table.

Degree of depression for Beck inventory scores

Score	Level of depression
0 to 4	None or minimal
5 to 7	Mild
8 to 15	Moderate
16 or over	Potentially serious

of the alternatives. The trouble with suicide is that, if it was a mistake for you but you attempt it successfully, it's a bit hard to undo that mistake. You owe it to yourself first to discuss the alternatives with someone trained to do that.

MEDICAL TREATMENTS OF DEPRESSION

The medical approach to depression, as adopted by most general practitioners and psychiatrists, involves drug treatment or electroconvulsive shock treatment (ECT) or both. We like to think that this is because most medicos have not had the chance to learn alternative approaches, because the track records of these two approaches are not great.

The idea behind using a physical intervention (anything you do externally to your body, such as taking drugs, or receiving electric shocks) to treat an emotional disorder (such as depression) is that the bad feelings are the result of some physiological malfunction (something wrong inside your body, i.e. your body is producing an extra chemical, or not producing a normal chemical). People who take this approach believe it's your brain chemistry that is out of order, not what is happening to you in your life, and what you need is to have your body chemistry changed by drugs or ECT.

There is no scientific evidence to support the idea that chemical changes in your body produce depression. Some people have been helped by drugs or ECT when they were depressed, although scientists working in this field really don't know why. At the same time many people experience bad side effects with these treatments.

Even if there were evidence to suggest that bad feelings were the result of chemical changes in the body, it would only raise a chicken-and-egg question: did you become depressed because your brain wasn't functioning normally, or is your brain not functioning normally because you are depressed?

We doubt if they'll ever answer that one. Mind you, the lack of a theoretical basis for medical treatments of depression wouldn't necessarily mean they were bad; if you could still show convincingly they were helpful, without undue side effects, you'd be glad to use them. But in both of these areas they fall down rather badly.

ELECTROCONVULSIVE SHOCK TREATMENT

ECT basically consists of applying electric shocks to the brain, via electrodes applied to the head. As the technique has been refined, it is now usually applied to only half of the brain at one time, and the patient is anaesthetised and drugged to relax his or her muscles. It is claimed by those who use it that the modern procedure has minimal side effects.

ECT is a good example of how psychiatry has stumbled along looking for answers without adequate research, and clutching at straws without sufficient justification. It was first developed as a treatment for schizophrenia, and was hailed as a great breakthrough in this application, with many 'cures' claimed. But more careful research showed that it was in fact no help at all for schizophrenia. Some of the doctors using it in this way formed the opinion that their depressed schizophrenic patients were less depressed after ECT, so it was then hailed as a great breakthrough in the treatment of depression. It is still widely used, although no one can accurately say how widely as there is no monitoring of its use in private psychiatric hospitals. By now, its negative side effects are very well known: loss of some memory from before treatment, confusion and interference with learning after treatment; brain damage, particularly bleeding, and occasionally death resulting from this.

The psychological side effects do lessen with time after treatment and, as mentioned above, it is claimed that the more modern application has less side effects. However, this claim has been disputed by some other experts.

Doctors who use ECT on their patients will usually acknowledge some risk of negative side effects, but claim its use is justified because it is effective when other treatments are not. We dispute both these points, beginning with the second. The simple truth is that ECT is typically used before and instead of a proper psychological treatment for depression. Whether this is because the doctors involved don't know how to provide psychological treatment, or prefer the cheapness and ease of ECT, is up to them to say.

The claim that ECT is an effective treatment of depression is very shaky indeed. Initial claims for this were based on simple clinical observations, which are just not scientifically acceptable. When better research was done, looking both at patients who received ECT and those who didn't, the strongest claim that could be made was that ECT seemed to speed recovery from depression, but was not necessary for recovery.

Even this claim is now disputed by a recent British study which found that depressed patients receiving ECT showed a slight advantage over those not receiving ECT, soon after treatment, but this advantage was small and temporary. Within a couple of months, the group not getting ECT was doing as well as the group that did get it. The researchers concluded that supportive hospitalisation, without ECT, was eventually as helpful for depressed patients as hospitalisation with ECT. And, of course, just hospitalisation does not have the risk of side effects that ECT does!

Australia does not have a proper legal procedure of informed consent, by which patients must be fully informed about the nature and side effects of a treatment being suggested to them, so that they can give genuinely informed consent to having that treatment, or refuse it if they prefer. If a doctor suggests to you that you should have ECT, we suggest you ask for a good explanation of why it is supposed to be helpful and not harmful to you. If you are not satisfied with the discussion, refuse the treatment, and ask to have your refusal recorded before treatment. Tell as many people as possible that you have refused. Later, if you are dissatisfied with the outcome, you will have evidence and witnesses that you refused to consent to ECT.

DRUG TREATMENT
Drug treatments for depression have a similar lack of evidence. Although a lot of research is done applying the chemicals involved to the brains, directly or indirectly, of non-human animals, even the results of this research are not easy to make sense of. Even a rat has a complicated brain.

And humans are not just giant rats with little tails. There is now plenty of evidence that human experience and emotions are not simply reflections of the underlying physiology (chemicals in the body). In fact there is some suggestion that the underlying body chemicals may change in response to thoughts and feelings, rather than the other way round. In truth there is very complex interaction between a person's physical and psychological make-up and one always influences the other in a complex way. It is more important, for our purposes, how we interpret our body's responses and thus how we feel.

The drug companies conduct a vast amount of research but it is ultimately based on what the effects of a drug seem to be, rather than on knowing how those effects occur. They start with a drug that is already supposed to have some beneficial effect, and they change its structure a little, looking for new substances with improved beneficial effects and reduced negative side effects. This approach would not be too bad if it did lead to effective and safe drugs. Again, sadly, this has really not been the case with the anti-depressive drugs. Despite their wide use – they are some of the most frequently prescribed drugs in Australia – their track record is poor.

The most commonly used anti-depressive drugs belong to a chemical group called the tricyclics. From 35 to 40 per cent of depressed patients treated with the tricyclics show no improvement at all. That is, only about two thirds of them do improve.

Of these two thirds, many refuse to continue their drug treatment, because they don't like the idea of taking drugs continuously, or because they develop negative side effects which the patients see as outweighing any benefit they get from the drugs. A standard medical reference book lists the possible side effects of these drugs as including:

- interference with blood pressure and heart beat
- confusion (especially in older people)
- hallucinations and delusions
- anxiety, restlessness and agitation
- insomnia and nightmares
- shaking
- dry mouth
- blurred vision
- nausea, vomiting, stomach cramps and diarrhoea
- skin rashes
- and, although the drugs are not supposed to be addictive,

if you suddenly stop taking them after using them for a while, you may get nausea, headaches, malaise and convulsions.

Nearly enough to make you feel depressed, isn't it! More seriously, we emphasise that not all users of these drugs get any of these side effects, and some users do find them helpful with their depression.

Even then, the help may be short-lived. Of those who are helped by the anti-depressant drugs and who continue taking them until their depression has lifted, up to 50 per cent will relapse into depression again within a year of stopping the drugs. This is possibly because, when a person 'cures' his or her depression by taking a drug, the cure is seen as being due to the drug, and not as due to anything the person has done.

Drug users do not see themselves as having increased their coping skills or worked out better strategies for handling problems so, when things go wrong again, they are just as vulnerable to depression as they were before.

As we have said earlier, we are not simply anti-drug. If you find an anti-depressant drug genuinely helpful with your depression, and you do not suffer from unreasonable side effects, then by all means use it. But we would encourage you to use it as a temporary crisis measure while you strengthen your coping skills by picking the ones you need from this book or by seeing a clinical psychologist.

An American research study, conducted by medical doctors, not psychologists, compared drug treatment and psychological treatment (of the kind outlined below) for depression. Both groups improved, but the psychotherapy group showed a greater degree of improvement, more of them improved (79 versus 23 per cent), fewer of them dropped out of treatment (1 versus 8 per cent), and fewer of them needed to come back for more treatment (16 versus 68 per cent).

You can see that on every major factor, the psychological treatment was superior to the drug treatment, and it has one other major advantage. When applied properly by an appropriately trained psychotherapist, the psychological programme begins to get results in the first interview.

Anti-depressant drugs take a week or more before they have any effect.

A PSYCHOLOGICAL APPROACH TO DEPRESSION

WHAT CAUSES DEPRESSION?

We believe that depression usually results from an interaction between adverse circumstances in the person's life, and how the person copes with them. In other words, some of the causes lie outside the person, and some within, and they interact to produce the depression.

This is contrary to traditional psychiatric thinking, which tended to see depression as either externally caused or internally caused, including so-called 'psychotic depression', where the depression is part of a more general 'mental illness'. We don't find such ideas realistic or helpful, and will not consider them further. We will say, however, if your depression is only one of several major problems or difficulties in your life, then you will probably find self-help difficult and you may be better off going to see a clinical psychologist.

The adverse life circumstances are of two kinds:

1 Your life does not give you many rewards. This may have been true for some time because you are not very skilful at getting what you want from life. For example, you may lack social skills and confidence, and therefore have trouble making rewarding relationships. Or it may be a recent state, resulting from some change in your circumstances. For example, you may have lost your job, or have moved a long way and left behind rewarding friendships and activities.

In any case, you will recall that one of the symptoms of depression is a low activity level: depressed people often don't do much. Because of this, there is less chance for them to get any rewards from life. The lower they feel, the less they do, so the lower they feel, and so on. This vicious cycle is a common part of depression.

2 Your life has become very punishing. Things are going wrong that you don't seem to be able to cope with, and they

don't look like ever getting any better. For example, a boring and monotonous job, or a distressed marriage, or a failing financial situation, can all contribute to depression.

Because of their low activity levels, depressed people may not have many current rewards to counterbalance life's punishments, so these loom even larger. Again, a lack of effective living skills may prevent them from dealing adequately with their sources of punishment, and the sense of hopelessness common in depression may lead to their not even trying.

In addition to the weak or absent living skills mentioned above, depressed people show two common weaknesses in their internal coping skills:

3 You automatically think negatively. Depressed people tend to have a negative view of themselves, of the world and of the future. The depressed view of yourself includes a tendency to criticise yourself unfairly and to blame yourself for everything wrong in your life. The negative view of the world includes selectively attending to what is wrong – your problems, mistakes and failures – and ignoring what is right – your enjoyments, successes and achievements. The negative view of the future consists of believing that not only is your life in a mess now, but it's **always** going to be like that.

This negative thinking is automatic in that it has become a habit. We often find depressed people are initially surprised when we point out how often they are taking a negative point of view, but that's the trouble with habits. They become so practised that they occur automatically, with little conscious awareness. Because you aren't aware of how totally negative your thinking has become, you accept your thoughts as true and reasonable, and then understandably feel depressed. These unrealistic mental habits raise the fourth common cause of depression.

4 You have irrational beliefs about yourself and the rest of the world. We have previously described, in Chapter 2, how irrational beliefs underlie unrealistic and exaggerated self-talk, and thus result in exaggeratedly bad feelings.

Depression is, of course, one example of a bad feeling and the principles we described in Chapter 2 about the causes, and management, of bad feelings apply equally well to depression. All you need to do is to add a couple of extra steps to cope with the specific causes of depression discussed above.

Typically a depressed person has a style of thinking that prevents them from dealing constructively with problems, so that when they have a problem in their life, they often make it worse, rather than solving it.

One of us saw an attractive woman in her mid-thirties who was complaining about depression recently. She stands out as an example because on meeting her most people would find it hard to believe that she would really have anything to worry about. She was good-looking, had a well-paid job, dressed well and appeared reasonably confident.

The main problem in her life was a failing marriage, in fact it had been bad for a number of years and, although she had the financial resources to leave the relationship, she had stayed, enduring a very unhappy situation. Her husband was often out late, never let her know when he was coming home, he was cross and angry at home, their sex life didn't exist and she suspected he was having an affair.

This situation unfortunately isn't unusual but Margaret was unusually depressed about it. She had reached the stage where she was having trouble getting out of bed for the day, she was able to push herself to go to work but on weekends she was spending more and more time in bed. When she was in bed she just daydreamed or tried to sleep. She was becoming less efficient at her work and found her two small children's demands impossible to meet.

She spent a lot of her time by herself thinking about what a terrible person she was, how she couldn't make a good marriage, how bad she was at her job, how terrible she was as a mother pushing her children away from her, she would never be a success at anything and so on.

Margaret's depressed behaviour put more strain on the relationship and drove her husband even further away from her, which in turn made her feel more depressed.

It was important to help Margaret change her exaggerated,

negative thinking about herself and her situation because her thinking style made her behave in ways that caused the initial problem, the bad marriage, to become worse. At the same time Margaret was encouraged to do something about her marriage.

The point of using Margaret as an example is that many people face difficult problems or a bad marriage, but people with a tendency to think in negative, irrational or exaggerated ways, which is characteristic of someone who feels depressed, often make their problem worse and then feel more depressed about it.

Some people, with this style of thinking, will even become depressed when there is no obvious problem; they will spend their time worrying about all sorts of what appear to others to be mundane problems.

You can probably see from these examples that we believe depression is the result of a style of thinking that makes the person vulnerable when they have to face a normal living problem. We do not believe that this style of thinking is the result of a chemical in the brain, we believe this style of thinking is the result of inappropriate learning. Therefore the way to change that learning is to change your habit of thinking unrealistically, at the same time making the environment supportive of a new style of thinking.

It was necessary for Margaret to change her thinking about herself (I am someone who can cope and handle my problems), as well as changing her marriage situation, otherwise she was at risk of changing her thinking but having nothing positive in her environment to support it.

Changing your behaviour is important because it enables you to support your new coping style of thinking. For example, you are stressed from overwork and overworry, which results in you feeling depressed because all you do is work, sleep and eat and, even when you do try some recreation, you feel bad because you still worry. To change your depressed feelings you would need to cope with your stress, change your style of thinking **and** increase the pleasure and recreation in your life.

Some people say to us in defence of thinking negatively, 'What if my thoughts are realistic?' 'What if I really am a poor mixer and find it very difficult to talk to people?' It is true that some situations are difficult or genuinely unpleasant but thinking negatively about them does not change the situation, nor does it help you change your behaviour.

Tom was in a very poor way when he saw us. He was untidy in appearance, stooped when he walked, avoided all eye contact and mumbled so low in response to a question that often he had to be asked to repeat himself a number of times. When he did raise his eyes he became embarrassed and often blushed scarlet.

Tom was depressed; he found it hard to meet people. When he did mix with teenagers his own age, they ignored him or made fun of him.

It would seem to most people that Tom had every reason to feel depressed and some of his negative thinking may appear realistic. Such as, 'I can never make friends', 'People don't like me', 'I get too embarrassed to talk to people'. Tom was asked to challenge some of the exaggerations in his thinking; at the same time he was encouraged to think in a more coping style. 'I do feel bad about my lack of social skills but I can handle those feelings. Now what constructive steps can I take to change my poor social skills?'

Tom was then helped to change his appearance and improve his social skills.

To help yourself change your depressed feelings you will need accurately to diagnose what bad feelings are happening in your life, why they are happening (is there something you can change, or get help to change?, do you need to increase your pleasure?), and in what ways is your thinking unrealistic or negative.

Accurate diagnosis is important to pinpoint reasons for depression. Even though we have outlined a formula for why people become depressed, as you can see from the examples this formula results in different answers for individuals. The next section outlines how you can pinpoint your problems.

SELF-HELP FOR DEPRESSION

1 Begin a depression diary. A small, spiral-backed notebook is best, starting a new page for each day. Record your level of depression on a 7-point scale, where 1 = no depression at all,

and 7 = as depressed as you could possibly be. Make a careful note of the situations which seem to trigger increased depression: where were you, what were you doing, with whom, and what were you thinking? This record should help you identify both the internal and external causes of your depression. For example:

Monday
9.30 a.m. depression = 5/7 Sitting at my desk looking at the day's work, thinking: 'I just can't cope anymore. I'll never get this done.'
4.30 p.m. depression = 5/7 After finishing day at work, thinking: 'What a dreadful day, I was very busy yet seemed to achieve nothing. Now I am tired for no reason.'
Tuesday
10.00 a.m. depression = 4/7 At work again, thinking: 'The week grinds on, I don't know how I am going to stay in this job but I need the money.'
8.00 p.m. depression = 6/7 At home wife nagging about me getting home late, thinking: 'I get it at work now I am getting it at home. Why does this happen to me? Everything goes wrong.'

2 Keep a record of your main activities each day. This step can be combined with the previous one, by recording the main activities of your day as they occur, and rating your mood level during each, at the same time. Remember to include your thoughts if you are combining these diaries.

Example of separate diary (you can combine both diaries by adding a record of your thoughts to this diary):
Monday
Work   depression = 5/7
Dinner   depression = 3/7
Watch TV   depression = 2/7
Tuesday
same as above
Wednesday
Work   depression = 4/7
Game of golf   depression = 2/7 to 4/7
Dinner with friends   depression = 6/7

We realise it may sometimes be difficult or awkward to keep

a record like this as you go but if you want an accurate diagnosis of your reasons for being depressed this is the only way. You may be very busy, or you may feel embarrassed about someone else seeing what you're doing. But be careful about trying to write it from memory later: the negative bias in depressed people's thinking tends to affect their memories as well. You may unconsciously omit or underplay the good parts of your day.

3 Rate each major activity for pleasure and mastery. If you derived any pleasure from the activity, put a P for pleasure next to it in your diary. If you did something well, put an M for mastery next to it in your diary.

Saturday

Played tennis	Depression = 3/7	Rated P & M (played a good game).
Dinner	Depression = 2/7	Rated P.

Sunday

Read paper, sat around	Depression = 4/7	
Kids screaming	Depression = 5/7	

Again beware of the negative bias that may be present in your view of your activities. We have had depressed people not put M's next to quite complex tasks because they think, 'Anyone can do that if I can.' Any task requiring any skill – however easy it has become for you – rates an M. You may have cooked a batch of scones that worked out well, that definitely rates an M. You may have handled difficulties at work well, that rates an M. Try to become more objective about your own behaviour. Ask yourself: 'If someone else did that, would I think it was good?' or 'If someone else did that, would I criticise them?' If you answered 'Yes', then 'No', put an M next to that task.

When you do rate anything with an M or P, follow that up by saying something good to yourself, or even to someone else. 'Gee, I enjoyed that game of tennis. I haven't played like that for a long time.'

4 Would it help if you learned to relax physically, if you haven't already done so? As we said before, relaxation

training alone is pretty useless, but it can contribute to the success of broader approaches, like this one. Being able to relax physically can be a useful, short-term approach to reducing bad feelings, especially tension. If this would help, go back to Chapter 2.

5 Plan to increase the rewards in your life. Most of us are looking for rewards of two kinds: we want to enjoy ourselves (P), and we want to feel we are making some worthwhile achievements (M). Gaps in either of these areas can contribute to depression.

If you have only a few M's and P's in your diary, you need to look at ways of increasing enjoyment and achievement. Or you may do lots of fun things – for example, if you are a housewife who plays tennis with friends, goes to social outings, and so on – and yet feels depressed because you see what you are doing as trivial, however much fun it is at the time. This can be especially so for housewives because often their work is devalued and trivialised by their husbands because it isn't paid.

Or you may be achieving a great deal, and doing very well at important tasks, but applying yourself so much to them that you have no time for recreation and fun, either alone, or with spouse or family or friends. We believe recreation is an essential part of a balanced and healthy life, as we have discussed elsewhere.

Use your activities record from above to identify what rewards you need to increase. Do you need more activities that give you pleasure? Or a sense of meaningful achievement? Or both?

If there are big gaps in your life in these areas, plan to fill them gradually. You are more likely to succeed, and therefore stick at, a plan that goes in small steps. For example, to increase enjoyment you might first set out only to discover what activities are open to you, via the newspapers' lists of coming events. Having done that, and given yourself an appropriate pat on the back, your next goal is to find out the details of one or two activities that look interesting. Then go along to those activities.

If you have been feeling depressed lately, you will probably find it hard to decide whether an activity would be enjoyable or not. Don't spend your time trying to find inspiration to enjoy the activity, just go out and do it. Keep pushing yourself to do things you think sound vaguely interesting. Your feelings will only begin to change once you are less depressed, but in the meantime you need to make yourself do something (otherwise you will remain in the old vicious circle).

Or if you feel you lack meaningful activities, you might first set out to investigate what jobs, paid and volunteer, or what training courses are open to you. Having done that, and given yourself an appropriate pat on the back, your next goal is to find out the details of one or two that look interesting. Then find out how to enrol or apply, and do it.

Once again remember that you will not feel 100 per cent certain that it is what you want to do. Try it anyway; you can always change later if it doesn't suit you.

Return to Chapter 2 and review coping self-statements if you need to give yourself a push to do things and review Chapter 3's discussion on contracting with yourself. You can apply contracts to help yourself change any behaviour.

Contract

I agree to plan three activities a week from my list of possible pleasurable activities.
Reward: I can sleep in Sunday morning.
Penalty: I wash the dishes every night of the next week.
If I can stick to my contract for three months I will reward myself by going out to dinner at an expensive restaurant.

Signed . . . .

As you progress down either of these paths, you may need to support your attempts to change with some of the skills described elsewhere in this programme, such as assertion, or communication or problem solving.

6 Plan to reduce the punishment in your life by facing up to and solving your problems, wherever possible. Begin by listing what you see as the main problems facing you now. Notice the emphasis on now: a bad event that happened to

you two years ago is not a problem now, even if you think it began your current depression. On the other hand, your tendency to keep thinking about that event, and then feel bad, could well be a current problem.

When you have your list, go through it and cross off any problems that are genuinely outside your control. For example, there is little you can individually do about the state of the economy. For some problems, you may need to set very limited individual goals: for example, the most you can do individually about a failing marriage is suggest to your partner that you work together on it (see our book, *Living and Loving Together*). Similarly, the most you can individually do about a company or factory that is run in people-crushing ways is suggest that it could be run better (see Chapter 10). There is no value in setting yourself unrealistic goals.

Next, rank your problems in order of ease and accessibility. That is, you should start on a problem that will be reasonably easy to solve, although still important to you, and that you can begin to tackle straight away. Starting on something very difficult or on a problem where you won't see results for a long time can be discouraging. Seeing yourself succeed is encouraging, and you are more likely to keep trying.

Plan a strategy to solve your first problem. Break it down into small steps, especially if it is a large problem, and take them one at a time. Identify what resources you need for each step. Do you need to master any of the skills described elsewhere in this book, like assertion, communication or problem solving itself? Do you need help of any kind from someone? If so, what, and how do you plan to get it?

It's usually better to concentrate on one problem at a time, at least until it's well under way. Spreading your efforts too thinly could result in your overloading yourself - not a good idea in a stress-management programme - or getting too little visible progress and so losing heart.

Expect to make mistakes and fail sometimes. Everybody does. Cope with these events realistically (see Chapter 2). Refresh and recycle the problem-solving steps (see Chapter 6), as you need to.

7 Challenge your automatically negative thoughts and replace them with more realistic ones. The detailed steps for doing this are already set out in Chapter 2, so we won't repeat them here. We will emphasise that learning to cope with downturns in your mood by thinking straighter is a key part of effective depression management.

Use your depression diary from above. Look through the thoughts you have recorded as associated with downturns in mood. Now tackle them with the steps for feeling better by thinking straighter, as outlined in Chapter 2. Work out a coping self-statement you could use in those situations in the future. Identify the irrational beliefs underlying your depression, and practise the matching rational ideas, so that you gradually come to look at those situations more realistically. Plan a constructive response, where possible.

8 Expect to relapse. Everybody does. People following this psychological approach to treating depression will sometimes get a marked improvement in their mood very quickly. Sometimes this fools them into stopping therapy too soon. Most depressed people will have one or more downturns in mood even though they are making good progress overall.

Of course, everybody has their bad days. As we said at the beginning, occasional feelings of depression are quite normal and not necessarily a problem. The trouble is that someone who has been badly depressed can be scared by these normal downturns, and may think: 'Oh no, I'm back where I started from! I'll never get rid of my depression.' And so on, talking themselves ever deeper into depression again.

The trick is not to aim never to relapse because nearly everyone will, but to aim to cope with occasional relapses realistically. Instead of using self-talk like that above, which turns a relapse into a collapse, say to yourself: 'Well, that's too bad. It is disappointing to slip back a bit, but I knew it was likely to happen sometime and I can cope with it. What will I do right now to get my mood moving up again?'

Then find and act on an answer to that last question. Again, set a realistic first goal. You may only walk around the block, but at least you are moving again. Draw on all of the procedures described throughout this book, to get yourself headed up again.

9 Take thoughts of suicide seriously, especially if you have previously tried suicide. As we said earlier, take suicide as one of your options, but recognise that you are quite likely to see it as a mistake when you are feeling better. Explore the other alternatives to solving your depression systematically, and get appropriate help if you don't think self-help is enough.

And that's a good general point to conclude our discussion of depression. Self-help is not for everybody, and can be especially hard to try when you are feeling low. At least make the effort to contact a clinical psychologist.

9

ENDING THE DYSTRESS OF LONELINESS

In Chapter 1 we pointed out that a person's relationships are quite often amongst his stressors, because of difficulties in those relationships. In the Introduction, we especially drew attention to how often a troubled marriage is part of people's personal dystress.

There we said that improving your troubled marriage, if you have one, would be an essential part of an effective stress-management programme, but that this was too large a topic to cover in this book. Instead, we recommend our self-help manual for improving relationships, *Living and Loving Together*, also published by Penguin Books. In that book we have also described procedures for improving relationships with your children.

If you feel that a significant part of your dystress arises from troubled relationships with friends, workmates, your boss, your employees, or members of your family other than your spouse or children, then we recommend you draw on the skills described in Chapters 2, 4, 5 and 6, as appropriate, to plan and carry out a constructive approach to those relationships.

In this chapter we will outline steps you can take to cope with the dystress arising from a **lack** of relationships, rather than from problems in existing relationships. It is possible to have both sources of dystress: sometimes we see a person who is staying in a very dystressing relationship because she doesn't have any others and, more importantly, doubts that she could find any. This chapter will help such a person challenge that irrational reason for staying in a bad relationship.

But quite often we have found one of the factors in a person's stress problem is a complete lack of any intimate relationships or friendships. Put simply, a part of his dystress is loneliness.

Psychologists have only recently come to recognise loneliness as a problem, in its own right. Previously, it has tended to be seen as a symptom of other problems, which ought to be the target of therapy. The assumption was that, if you treated these other problems, then the loneliness would disappear.

This tendency to ignore or discount loneliness has probably been exacerbated by the stigma attached to loneliness in our society. Because of the heavy emphasis on attractiveness, especially in advertising, as being a sign of success, it is often assumed that anyone who is lonely must therefore be unattractive and so a 'failure'.

We hope that by now you will recognise how irrational this argument is (check it against the table on page 58 in Chapter 2). But of course that doesn't stop it from being popular in our society.

This neglect of loneliness as a psychological problem is unfortunate. There is now good evidence that it is associated with a number of other, quite serious problems, such as depression, suicide and some heart disease. We believe that it is reasonable and useful to see loneliness as a problem in its own right, even if it is associated and interacting with other problems. So this chapter is intended to set out a constructive approach to dealing with the problem of loneliness.

WHAT IS LONELINESS?

Dr Jeffrey Young, at the University of Pennsylvania, has led the focus onto loneliness as a psychological problem, and we have drawn on his work in preparing this chapter. He defines loneliness as the unpleasant feeling that comes from a lack of satisfactory social relationships.

You will note that there are two key elements in this definition, and both are important. Firstly, there are bad feelings, and secondly, these arise from lacking relationships.

Being alone does not necessarily cause bad feelings. Indeed, sometimes being alone can feel quite good. We often like a breather from other people, a chance to relax and reflect. You can call these good feelings solitude, to distinguish them from the bad feelings of loneliness.

Obviously yet curiously, both solitude and loneliness arise from being alone. How does the one experience produce such different feelings? By now you will naturally know the answer. The clue lies in our description of solitude above, as a chance to relax and **reflect**. Yep, back to good old self-talk.

It is the nature of your reflections, the content of your self-talk, while you are alone that largely determines whether you will feel loneliness or solitude.

TURNING LONELINESS INTO SOLITUDE

Loneliness, like all other bad feelings, can occur to you as the quite reasonable consequence of your present life situation. In this case, you accept it as a bad feeling that you can cope with, and you plan constructive steps to change your life situation. This you will recognise as just a specific example of the application of mental relaxation.

If you think you may be feeling unnecessarily lonely, or

exaggerating your loneliness, you should first go back to Chapter 2 and revise the steps in mental relaxation, to apply them to the situations leading to your loneliness. Your coping self statement would look something like this.

'I sometimes feel bad that I have no close relationships with other people, but I can cope with these bad feelings. I do not need to exaggerate my bad feelings (by thinking irrationally about the situation), nor do I need to deny my bad feelings (by telling myself I shouldn't feel like this). I can take constructive steps to do something about my loneliness.'

When you get to Step 6 of the mental relaxation procedure, you will be looking for the irrational beliefs underlying your exaggerated loneliness. Common ones identified by lonely people are **1** (expecting everybody you meet to like you), **4** (believing it is dreadful that you are alone and lonely), and **5** (there's nothing you can do about it). They also often use **6** and **7** to talk themselves out of trying to make friends.

As well as these irrational beliefs and any others you identify as part of your loneliness problem, we encourage you to challenge the popular myth in our society that all healthy adults are in intimate relationships all of the time.

In a sense, this is a particular example of irrational belief no. 4 – 'It is absolutely dreadful that I am alone at present' – but it is such a popular myth in our society that we thought we should draw it to your attention.

Advertising, popular literature, songs, films and television all place such emphasis on the pursuit and possession of a living partner as the major goal of at least your personal life, and the absence of a living partner as proof that you have 'failed' as a whole person, that it is not surprising that so many people accept this myth.

Yet a myth it is. We agree that living in one or more good relationships can enrich your life and be a source of pleasure. So can owning your own yacht. Few people are queuing up to jump off the bridge because they haven't bought their own yacht. But many people are conned into believing it is the end of the world if they aren't coupled up with a suitable partner.

Making and keeping some good friendships and intimate relationships are excellent goals for you to set, if you want to. But they are not essential to your well-being or success, certainly not all of the time.

It is increasingly clear that some people enjoy quite successful lives without being coupled for much or even most of the time. In this area of life, as in others, different people want and are satisfied with different goals. The mistake is to assume that all people ought to want and enjoy the same living arrangements, seen in our society as living in long-term couples.

If you are presently spending much of your time alone, we encourage you to decide for yourself whether this is really not what you want, rather than just accepting the popular myth that being alone means there must be something wrong with you.

Dr Young talks about three kinds of loneliness: transient, situational and chronic.

Transient loneliness consists of the everyday, brief feelings of loneliness that occur occasionally to most of us. These are obviously not a problem, unless you talk yourself into seeing them as such. If you have, use your mental relaxation to talk yourself out again!

Situational loneliness involves people who have previously had good, successful relationships but who have now lost them as a result of a change in their living situation. Such changes can be moving home, separation or divorce, or losing relationships through death, particularly in old age.

If you think your loneliness problem represents situational loneliness, again you should be using your mental relaxation procedure to cope with the bad feelings and, when you reach the point in your coping self-statement and rational idea practice of planning constructive steps, you can adopt two possible strategies.

First, if you have made successful relationships before, can you use the same techniques to do it again? Just because your life situation has changed does not necessarily mean your old relationship-making skills won't work any more. Give them a try. Use your mental relaxation to help you cope with any anxiety in trying again.

Or second, if you can't remember what you did before, or it no longer seems appropriate, you can use the strategies we will describe below for ending chronic loneliness.

Chronic loneliness is the kind occurring in people who have never been able to establish successful relationships, or at least not for some years. Usually this means they have been lonely over at least two major life stages, such as adolescence and young adulthood.

If you think loneliness is a problem for you, and you apply your mental relaxation procedure with a special emphasis on challenging the myth that everybody has to be in relationships all of the time, and you still think you really have a loneliness problem that you should be doing something constructive about, you can measure it with the test on page 217. You should complete this now.

To get your total loneliness score, just add up all of the numbers you have circled. If you circled more than one number for any item, add only the higher number to your total. As with some of our other tests, we cannot give you population figures to compare yourself against, although obviously the higher you score the bigger your loneliness problem.

The value of this test is once again as a measure of your progress. Every few weeks, as you work on your loneliness problem, take the test again. Good progress will be shown by gradually lower scores.

You can also get another useful piece of information from your answers to this test. Look at the answers you chose for items 4, 7, 8 and 11. If you circled mostly higher numbers for most of these items, that suggests that you don't have many relationships at all. If that is correct, you will need to start at the beginning of the steps below, with **initiating** relationships.

If you chose mostly zeroes for these items, then you probably have a number of casual relationships, and your loneliness comes from a difficulty in **deepening** relationships. This would be shown by higher scores on items 1, 3, 6, 7, 10, 13 and 14. If you can begin relationships but not make them more intimate, skip over the early steps on making relationships and go straight to the ones on deepening

LONELINESS SCALE

Read each group of statements carefully. Then pick out the one statement in each group that best describes you. Circle the number beside the statement you picked. If several statements in the group seem to apply equally, circle each one. Be sure to read all the statements in each group before making your choice.

Group 1
0 When I want to do something for enjoyment, I can usually find someone to join me.
1 Sometimes I end up doing things alone even though I'd like to have someone join me.
2 It often bothers me that there is no one I can go out and do things with.
3 I'm extremely disturbed that there is no one I can go out and do things with.

Group 2
0 I have a close group of friends nearby that I feel part of.
1 I'm not sure that I really belong to any close group of friends nearby.
2 It often bothers me that I don't feel part of any close group of friends nearby.
3 I'm extremely disturbed that I don't have a close group of friends.

Group 3
0 I almost always have someone to be with when I do not want to be alone.
1 I am sometimes alone when I would prefer to be with other people.
2 It bothers me that I am often alone when I would prefer to be with other people.
3 I'm extremely disturbed that I am alone so often.

Group 4
0 I have a lot in common with other people I know.
1 I wish my values and interests, and those of other people I know, were more similar.
2 It often bothers me that I'm different from other people I know.
3 I'm extremely disturbed that I'm so different from other people.

Group 5
0 I feel that I generally fit in with people around me.
1 I sometimes feel that I don't fit in with the people around me.
2 I am often bothered that I feel isolated from the people around me.
3 I'm extremely disturbed by how isolated I feel from other people.

Group 6
0   There is someone nearby who really understands me.
1   I'm not sure there's anyone nearby who really understands me.
2   It often bothers me that no one nearby really understands me.
3   I'm extremely disturbed that no one really understands me.

Group 7
0   I have someone nearby who is really interested in hearing about my private feelings.
1   I'm not sure that anyone nearby is really interested in hearing about my private feelings.
2   It often bothers me that no one nearby is really interested in hearing about my private feelings.
3   I'm extremely disturbed that no one is really interested in hearing about my private feelings.

Group 8
0   I can usually talk freely to close friends about my thoughts and feelings.
1   I have some difficulty talking to close friends about my thoughts and feelings.
2   It often bothers me that I can't seem to communicate my thoughts and feelings to anyone.
3   I'm extremely disturbed that my thoughts and feelings are so bottled up inside.

Group 9
0   I have someone nearby I can really depend on when I need help and support.
1   I'm not sure there's anyone nearby I can really depend on when I need help and support.
2   It often bothers me that there is no one nearby I can really depend on when I need help and support.
3   I'm extremely disturbed that there is no one I can depend on when I need help and support.

Group 10
0   There is someone nearby who really cares about me.
1   I'm not sure there's anyone nearby who really cares about me.
2   It often bothers me that there is no one nearby who really cares about me.
3   I'm extremely disturbed that no one really cares about me.

Group 11
0   The important people in my life have not let me down.
1   Sometimes I feel disappointed at someone I thought I could trust.
2   I often think about the important people in my life I trusted who have let me down.
3   I can't trust anyone anymore.

Group 12

0   There is someone nearby who really needs me.

1   I'm not sure anyone nearby really needs me.

2   It often bothers me that there is no one nearby who really needs me.

3   I'm extremely disturbed that no one really needs me.

Group 13

0   I have a partner I love who loves me.

1   I'm not sure I have a partner nearby I love who also loves me.

2   It often bothers me that I do not have a partner nearby I love who loves me.

3   I'm extremely disturbed that I do not have a partner I love who loves me.

Group 14

0   I have a satisfying sexual relationship with someone now on a regular basis.

1   I sometimes wish that I had a satisfying sexual relationship on a regular basis.

2   It often bothers me that I do not have a satisfying sexual relationship with anyone.

3   I am extremely disturbed that I do not have a satisfying sexual relationship with anyone.

Group 15

0   I rarely think about particular times in my life when my relationships seemed better.

1   I sometimes wish my relationships now could be more like they were at another time in my life.

2   I am often bothered by how unsatisfactory my relationships now are compared with another time in my life.

3   I am extremely disturbed by how poor my relationships now are compared with another time in my life.

Group 16

0   I rarely wish that my relationships could be more like other people's.

1   I sometimes wish that I could have relationships that satisfied me the way other people's relationships seem to satisfy them.

2   I often compare the satisfaction other people seem to get from their relationships with my own lack of satisfaction.

3   I cannot stop comparing the satisfaction other people get from their relationships with my own lack of satisfaction.

Group 17

0   I am confident about the way I relate to men and women.

1   I sometimes question whether there is something wrong with the way I relate to men or women.

2   I often criticise myself for faults that seem to turn men or women off.

3   I'm extremely disturbed that I am so undesirable to other people.

Group 18

0 I am confident that I will have close, satisfying relationships in the future.

1 I sometimes question whether I will have close, satisfying relationships in the future.

2 I am often pessimistic about my chances of having close, satisfying relationships in the future.

3 I feel hopeless about ever having close, satisfying relationships.

Group 19

0 I haven't felt lonely during the past week (including today).

1 I've sometimes felt lonely during the past week (including today).

2 I've often felt lonely during the past week (including today).

3 I could barely stand the loneliness during the past week (including today).

relationships. But be careful not to leave out something that might really be helpful to you.

One final point on identifying loneliness problems. If you still are not sure that you have a loneliness problem, check the rest of your lifestyle. The unpleasant feelings of loneliness are often expressed as anxiety (especially in social situations), depression or insomnia, or are masked by bad feeling management techniques like smoking, over-drinking, over-eating, and drug abuse or dependence.

If one or more of these events is occurring in your life, analyse it carefully to see if a part of the problem is loneliness (see Chapters 2, 7, or 8).

INITIATING RELATIONSHIPS

1 PLAN ACTIVITIES

The first step in solving your loneliness problem is for you to plan a gradual increase in your activities for pleasure. You may already be quite busy with work, but these are to be activities for pleasure. If you think you haven't time for this, go back and refresh exploding the luxury myth in Chapter 2.

Lonely people are often also depressed, and inclined to spend most of their free time alone, doing nothing, as we described in Chapter 8. A depressed mood is not going to help you meet possible new friends, and nor is hiding in the broom cupboard. You need to plan a gradual but deliberate increase in your activity level, as described in the last chapter. Initially these may be activities you do alone. If you have really slowed down, then anything that gets you moving will do. Look for activities that involve vigorous movement, or that get you out of the house.

Eventually you will need activities that give you a chance to meet other people. What can you think of? Are there hobbies, sports, recreations or interests you have enjoyed in the past? Or do you need to find some new ones? If so, go back to Chapter 3, and work through the steps set out there for finding new recreations.

Make use of resources like newspapers, adult education groups, sporting clubs, and so on, but now you are especially looking for activities through which you might meet new friends. If your goals include sexual relationships, look for an activity that will allow you to meet people of the appropriate sex.

Make up a short list of possible activities, and begin to build up your activities **in small steps**, as we have emphasised before. Begin with the easiest activity. Start by getting information about it, and then planning to join it, and then going to your first session of it, and so on.

It is a good idea to begin by participating in hobby, sport, learning or craft type activities, rather than falling into the trap of trying to meet someone at a local 'pick-up' place. Many people find discos, large parties or pubs an unsatisfactory way of meeting people with whom they can develop friendships. You will probably find it easier to get to know people if you have something in common. If you have no sports or other interests, return to Chapter 3 and begin to develop some recreation skills.

Then set yourself the goal of introducing yourself to, or starting a conversation with, at least one person each time you go to that activity. You can always talk about the activity you are participating in. A good way of beginning a conversation might be to ask the other person about the activity. Enjoy the activity for its own sake, but look for opportunities to extend your relationship-making skills gradually. If you eventually decide that you don't really like the activity, or it genuinely offers you little chance of making new friendships, leave it and start another one on your list.

Karen had felt very lonely for two years after her divorce. She had rarely gone out and was becoming more and more of a recluse. This, of course, resulted in her feeling depressed most of the time. Until finally she decided she had to do something about her life.

She began by attending a course on motor mechanics. She thought this would be helpful for two reasons: she had always been interested in cars, and she thought she might meet some men with whom she could begin new friendships.

Karen was nervous the first night she attended the course but she made herself speak to a few people. By the end of the two hours she was enjoying herself tremendously.

The course became the highlight of her week. Karen met up with another woman who was also doing the course and they began having coffee together, at Karen's suggestion, after the course had finished.

The course lasted for eight weeks. During this time Karen became very friendly with Jane and Jane's friend Bill, and after the eight weeks she continued to see Jane and Bill. Through them she met a number of new people, including some male friends.

Sounds difficult? Feeling anxious at even the thought of starting? Then you are almost certainly talking nonsense to yourself.

2 WATCH YOUR SELF-TALK

Initiating relationships is a good opportunity to use your mental relaxation skills to help you cope with fears and anxieties that have previously stopped you from making friends. The unrealistic and unhelpful self-talk in this situation tends to fall into four main classes.

First, there are variations on the theme, 'I can't get into a new relationship because my last one ended'. This is usually taken as 'evidence' for some basic and unchangeable fault in the lonely person. 'I can't communicate properly', or 'I'm sexually boring'. Another common variation is 'I'll never be able to trust anyone again'.

If this self-talk applies to you, you should know relationships very rarely fail because of faults or problems in **one** of the partners. A relationship is an interaction between two people, and both contribute to how well, or badly, that interaction goes. Your mistakes would naturally have contributed to any decline in the relationship, so would your partner's.

It is also important that you recognise that mistakes can be corrected. If you really do have difficulty communicating, do something about it (see Chapter 5). If you really are sexually boring, do something about it (see our book, *Living and Loving Together*, for a start). No one is stuck with mistakes.

And finally, question the underlying assumption that somewhere, chiselled in granite, is the divine decree that your last relationship was the one you were meant to be in, for ever. People go into relationships for a variety of reasons, many of which are not so sound. Even a relationship which was right for you at one stage of your life, may no longer be so, as you and your partner develop in different directions.

Whether or not you trust another person to be close to you is your choice, not something outside your control. If your last relationship ended hurtfully, you will naturally feel anxious starting another one. Use your mental relaxation skills.

Secondly, there is unhelpful self-talk along the lines of, 'None of the people I meet are serious about relationships'. This is a good example of one of Beck's popular thinking errors (see page 58 in Chapter 2), the tendency to see things in black or white terms. Here it becomes, 'The only worthwhile friendship is a totally committed and deep relationship for a lifetime; the only real friend is one who shares all of your interests and values and is permanently available when you want her'.

If you set such unrealistically high standards for your friendships you will cut yourself off from many less intense but none the less rewarding friendships, one or two of which may even have eventually grown into the special relationship you are seeking.

In fact, relationships are as variable as the people who make them. Some people will be only briefly in your life, others for much longer. Some will share a great deal with you, others much less. All can contribute to the rewards in your life. Raise your expectations of a new relationship gradually and realistically as it grows, and you will neither miss out on what it has to offer, nor set yourself up to be hurt unnecessarily..

Malcolm, who was only 26, considered himself to be very lonely because he had no long-term intimate relationship with someone of the opposite sex. Yet he had a number of good friendships and more casual relationships with women of varying ages. Malcolm undervalued all of these relationships by telling himself that 'The only "real" relationship for me is marriage with a woman I love'.

Malcolm was asked to challenge this irrational idea. Apart from undervaluing all his present relationships, when he met a girl whom he might like to go out with, he began immediately to assess her as a possible marriage partner and when she didn't measure up he rejected her – often before he went out with her, or sometimes before he even spoke with her.

He was defeating himself by having such an unrealistic view of relationships.

Third, there is the self-talk of self-put down, 'No one could really like **me**, because I am ugly, dull, boring, etc.' This unhelpful self-talk raises two possibilities: it's wrong or it's right.

People will sometimes devalue themselves for no good reason. Ask yourself, 'What is the real world evidence for my being ugly, dull, boring or whatever? Have I ever had any friends, who found me attractive, interesting, likeable, and so on?' Sometimes people accept devaluing remarks or actions made to them by just one other person as being total, unchangeable truth. Go back and refresh rational idea no. 1!

But it is possible that you are doing something that puts off potential friends. Two common possibilities are how you look and how you act. Start with how you look, by giving yourself an inspection in a large mirror. We are **not** suggesting you buy into the myths of the fashion and cosmetics industries, but there may be some reasonable steps you can take to make your appearance more attractive.

If you look like a ragbag out for a walk, with an advanced fear of soap and water, you are considerably narrowing down your possible friendship market. We have often found that people who dress in aggressively outlandish ways are trying to cover up a lack of confidence. You now have better ways of dealing with that problem.

Now, take a look at how you act in social situations. The common, off-putting behaviours are trying too hard to make a good impression, trying to share too intimate information about yourself too soon, being too passive, making lots of self-devaluing remarks, and keeping people at an emotional distance by being sarcastic, cynical or aloof.

If you think you fall into any of these anti-relationship traps, try to write yourself another script. Watch people whom you regard as socially successful for ideas. You don't want to imitate them slavishly, but you can adapt their successful strategies to your own personal style. If you find this area important to you, and you cannot master it from a book or watching others, you may benefit from some social skills training from a qualified clinical psychologist.

The fourth and final piece of common anti-relationship self-talk is the expectation, 'If I try to make friends, I will only be rejected and that will hurt'. This is often associated with the expectation of doing something stupid or embarrassing, or with a tendency to observe yourself obsessively acting unsuccessfully in social situations. 'See, look how little I have to say; that proves I can't say anything.'

Notice the red herring in all of this. What the socially anxious person is **really** scared of is the anxiety of trying to make friends, because that anxiety happens every time. In fact, it is relatively unusual to be actually rejected by someone, although that does hurt when it happens.

You can replace all the above unhelpful self-talk with a coping self-statement:

'I expect to feel anxious when I try to make new friends, and I would feel hurt if one of them rejected me, but I know I can cope with feeling anxious or hurt, and the chance of being occasionally hurt is not a good reason to stay always lonely. It's important to me to end my loneliness and to make new relationships, so **now** I'll give it a try.'

If unhelpful self-talk has been a major obstacle to your

making friends, you should use this coping self-statement as we have suggested in Chapter 2, by writing it on a small card that you can carry about with you.

3 TALK ABOUT YOURSELF

This might sound as if we're suggesting you become a bore, but we're not. We don't intend that you should try to dominate every social conversation with a lengthy account of your achievements, possessions and qualities. That kind of talk about yourself you will recognise as one of the common off-putting behaviours mentioned above.

What we are recommending you try is self-disclosure. This means telling your potential friend something about yourself that you would not normally share with just anyone. You may talk about some problem or difficulty in your life and your feelings associated with that. But self-disclosure doesn't have to be only about bad things: you might share some private, good feelings, as well.

The key is the intimate nature of the information that you share. You are telling your potential friend that you see him as someone special compared to the general population, because you are trusting him with this information that you would not share with casual acquaintances. But go slowly.

Dr Arnold Lazarus, an American psychologist, has said people are like onions, made up of layer upon layer. The outermost layer you share with anyone: name, address and so on. The next layer contains information about you that is a bit more intimate and private, that you would share with a more restricted number of people. Your innermost layer contains thoughts and feelings you may only share with one very special friend, if anyone at all.

Peel your onion slowly, in developing your relationships. Jumping too fast down the layers is another off-putting behaviour, because the other person won't be ready to match you yet. She may see you as coming on too strong and back off as a result.

Do give the other person the chance to respond. Listen (see Chapter 5). If he wants to develop your relationship further, he will have listened to your self-disclosure, and respond with one of his own. If he doesn't, then he is telling you that he doesn't want to make your relationship any more intimate. That will probably be disappointing to you, but it's not a good reason to throw away a good, casual friendship. Just keep it casual.

It's usually easiest to start self-disclosure in a relationship with someone of the same sex, so that there is no pressure on either of you to see the relationship as necessarily becoming sexual or long-term. (Unless you prefer homosexual relationships, in which case you will probably find it easier to start self-disclosing with a friend of the opposite sex, for the same reasons.)

People are often scared of self-disclosure, because they expect the other person to think less of them for having a 'problem', or 'fear', or 'weakness'. You can dispel this myth easily. How have you felt when someone disclosed something about herself to you? Typically people receiving a self-disclosure say they feel understanding and caring for the other person, not dislike or rejection.

Beware of mind reading! People are forever guessing how other people think and feel. It's not just we psychologists who read minds, it's everybody. Mind-reading does seem to be a universal behaviour and, in that sense, unavoidable. The trick is not to rely on it too much.

In *Living and Loving Together* we spend some time outlining how destructive mind-reading can be, especially in the absence of clear communication. What research has found is that the more strain there is in a relationship, the more unrealistically negative the partners' mind-reading becomes. Each will assume the other feels and intends worse than is really true.

In the early, more anxious stages of developing relationships you could fall into a similar trap. It is not unusual for shy people to exaggerate and overreact to any disagreement, slight, injustice or criticism. Their unrealistic self-talk leads to unnecessarily bad feelings, which they end by ending the relationship. There goes the baby with the bathwater again.

If this happens to you, first use your mental relaxation skills to cope with the bad feelings, and then use your communication skills to share them constructively with your friend. That would be a very appropriate form of self-disclosure, giving your friend a real chance to respond constructively. Of course, he is more likely to do so if you are assertive, not aggressive.

MAKING RELATIONSHIPS MORE INTIMATE

So far, we have made suggestions to help you begin new friendships, most of which will be casual, lasting for varying periods, and possibly centred around some shared interest, like a recreation or club. Towards the end, we began the process of making some of those casual relationships into more intimate friendships by using the technique of self-disclosure.

How much of yourself you disclose in any relationship will depend on your feelings towards that person, and how much she wants to share a more intimate relationship with you. Let your friendships develop as far as each wants to.

Eventually, most of us seem to want to find a small number of relatively close and intimate relationships, usually including one special relationship for dating, or living together, or getting married. As we have emphasised above, there is no psychological law that says you have to get coupled, despite social pressure to do so, but if it is a goal of yours, here are some more suggestions.

4 TAKE YOUR TIME

Don't be in a hurry. If you are really looking for a relationship into which you intend to put a lot of time and effort, and from which you hope to obtain large emotional rewards, take the time to find one with a real chance of working out. Be content with more casual relationships at first, and only try to deepen one that really looks promising.

Let's make the not unreasonable guess that one in thirty potential intimate partners would be suitable for a relationship with you. This means that, on average, you will need to meet thirty possible partners, at least casually, in order to bump into your one real prospect.

Some of the lonely people we see in therapy will correctly say they have no trouble making casual acquaintances, but are fed up with that and want a more intimate relationship. So they respond to being fed up by withdrawing from their casual social activities and moping about at home! We doubt that the postman will deliver your new intimate partner for you. Get out and mix. It wards off depression, as well.

5 PRACTICAL STEPS
FOR GETTING TO KNOW SOMEONE

If you have met someone with whom you would like to develop a more intimate relationship, we suggest these following steps. We have emphasised the importance of taking things slowly, so we have included these steps to give you some idea of the speed at which you should develop a new relationship. Time after time we have seen people who are having difficulty getting into relationships make the mistake, often due to their own anxiety, of rushing 'full steam ahead' into a new relationship and end up by scaring the other person off. They then feel bad about themselves and even more anxious next time they attempt a new relationship, and so on around the vicious circle.

Step A   How to ask the other person out.   No matter how anxious you feel inside (you will need your self-talk to cope with this feeling), if you appear reasonably calm and casual the other person is likely to respond positively to your confident manner. Nothing scares someone off faster than a shaky, uncertain approach. On the other hand **don't** come across with a salesman-type positive approach. Aim for a quiet, relaxed manner.

It may seem silly and you will probably feel silly doing it but practise how you are going to act when you are asking someone out and watch yourself in the mirror. Observe your hands, face, body posture for signs of tension and practise changing so that you look more relaxed. For example, unclench your fists, leave your arms by your side, have a relaxed, casual smile, keep your voice tone fairly even and on the quiet side.

Step B   What to say.   Reviewing the communication and assertion chapters will be helpful at this stage.

Practise making an assertive, clear request: **don't** ask an open-ended question:
'What are you doing Saturday?'

Instead make your request specific; ask the person to an actual event; give him the time and day;

'Would you like to play a game of tennis on Sunday?'
You may like to lead into your request by briefly asking about the weather, work or the person's health, but do not waffle on and on in an attempt to hide your anxiety.

Step C Where to go? On your first date we suggest you choose a casual social event. Ideally the event should include an activity, and be during the day with other people present.

You will find this type of situation easier for a number of reasons. First, a woman is more likely to accept if the invitation is of a casual nature, rather than a more intimate situation. Secondly, the strain of maintaining a conversation together is reduced because there are other people present. Thirdly, you are not relying on conversation as the only source of entertainment. Fourthly, you will have plenty of chances to interact together but you can also interact with other people, which reduces the strain on the new relationship.

The sort of events you may ask a man to could be: a barbecue with friends, a sports match, a sporting event, the beach, a work get-together, a meeting, a concert with other people, a new restaurant you and a group of friends are going to try.

Not all of these events would be during the day but at first it will probably be easier if other people are present.

Step D How do you continue the relationship?
After your first date, try and find opportunities to meet with, or talk to the person on the phone. Make these contacts relatively brief; once again this is to avoid too much strain on the relationship too early. Concentrate on being friendly and relaxed during these brief conversations.

Actual time is hard to judge but don't rush into making another date too quickly; leave it at least a week. On the other hand, don't wait for a month or more. In the meantime keep up your brief contacts with the person, maybe arrange to meet them for a coffee, or drink once or twice, and concentrate on developing other social contacts or personal interests for yourself.

Your second and third dates could be an invitation to lunch. By this time you will have seen the person under a number of casual situations and should feel more comfortable with the idea of spending an hour over lunch chatting.

In between dates keep up friendly contact with this person, maintain other social contacts and your personal interests.

As the relationship becomes more involved, you can increase the intimacy of the date, e.g. dinner alone in an intimate restaurant. At the same time you will need to be using the other skills mentioned in this chapter.

You may feel dismayed looking at the steps we have outlined above. Many people we see who would like an intimate relationship, often imagine themselves closely involved with someone, but they forget about the steps in between and the time those steps involve. It is possible to be complete strangers and have a sexual relationship in one night, but for most people that rarely leads to intimacy or long-term involvement. You will need to go through the gradual steps of developing a relationship.

6 WATCH YOUR SELF-TALK AGAIN

The same unrealistic thoughts that discourage people from looking for friends can scare them off looking for intimates. It does hurt to get close to someone, and then to be treated unkindly or to lose that relationship. Use the coping self-statement above to prevent the fear of this infrequent event from interfering unduly with your life.

In addition to the common unhelpful self-talk listed in section 2 above, two other ideas may intrude into deepening relationships, and need to be met with your mental relaxation skills.

First, some lonely people fear that becoming involved in an intimate relationship will rob them of their freedom and privacy. This fear is more common in people who have by and large made a success of a single life in many ways, even though they are also unpleasantly lonely sometimes. They are used to a fair degree of independence in their lifestyle and fear losing this.

You will recognise this self-talk as an example of irrational belief no. 6: if something might go wrong in the future, I should worry like hell about it now.

Of course, being in a long-term, intimate relationship, especially living together or being married, does mean that you choose to give up some of your privacy and independence. Those of us in successful long-term relationships can assure you the pay-offs far outweigh the costs.

As rational idea no. 6 suggests, you can prepare constructively for possible future problems. For now, brushing up your assertion, problem-solving and communication skills will prepare you very well for developing a successful and even-handed relationship. When it gets serious, we strongly recommend *Living and Loving Together*. A gram of prevention is worth a kilo of cure.

Second, lonely people into self-devaluing self-talk will often start to add expectations of being a sexual failure, as the possibility of a sexual relationship looms larger. Men may convince themselves that they won't last long enough, or won't be able to satisfy her, while women are rehearsing the belief that they will be sexually boring, and both sexes can believe they will make fools of themselves.

We do see people in therapy who are able to develop quite successful relationships right up to the point of becoming openly sexual, and then balk. Their self-deflating self-talk centres very largely on their expectations of sexual failure. Because this is a common obstacle to making relationships more intimate, we will deal with it in some detail.

7 PREPARE FOR SEXUAL RELATIONSHIPS

It is not unusual for chronically lonely people to have little or no sexual experience, except possibly for masturbation. The fear of making a fool of yourself in bed is understandably high, especially for the older person who may be expected to be sexually experienced, and for the man who believes he is supposed to be the expert who already knows how to turn on any woman.

People suffering from situational loneliness may also unreasonably devalue themselves sexually because of their experience of a previous, unsuccessful sexual relationship. It is not unusual for the partners in a failing marriage to blame their sexual dissatisfaction on alleged faults in each other. You may angrily deny the accusation to your partner's face, but secretly worry about its possible truth.

Well, sexual expression is a practical skill, requiring adequate and accurate knowledge, and personal comfort with your own sexual identity. Then, with good communication and gentle assertion, you can build and keep a good sexual relationship with your partner. All of these requisites you can work on.

You can start on your sexual knowledge by looking through the popular sex myths on page 234. Don't ask yourself whether you simply believe these myths; rather as yourself how much you have been or might be influenced by them. At the end of the sex myths we have put forward our definition of what we think makes a good sexual relationship. For now, think about what it means for you.

If you believe you are generally sexually uninformed, we recommend the book *Human Sexuality* by Leonore Tiefer (published by Nelson). More comprehensive although much more expensive is *The Sex Atlas* by Erwin Haeberle (Seabury Press). Skip the funny books for so-called advanced lovers, at least until your sexual relationship is well-established and needing some idle amusement.

The best practical, self-help guide for developing a sexual relationship, and possibly avoiding or solving the common, minor sexual problems, is *Treat Yourself to a Better Sex Life* by Harvey Gochros and Joel Fisher (published by Prentice-Hall). It includes practical exercises to help a man or a woman explore and accept his or her own sexuality, and then to share that with each other. We strongly recommend it for developing your practical sexual expression skills, alone and then together.

If you are edging your way towards your first sexual relationship, our firm advice is to discuss that with your partner, especially if you think this may be his first sexual relationship, too. As we have explained above, an honest sharing of your anxiety about beginning sex is most likely

SEX MYTHS

Myth 1
'Intercourse is the 'adult', 'best', 'most important part of sex.'

Myth 2
'Men take the initiative in sex.'

Myth 3
'The man is responsible for his partner's satisfaction as well as his own.'

Myth 4
'Women are less interested in sex than men. They are slower to become sexually aroused and need more stimulation.'

Myth 5
'A man's penis is the best part of his body for stimulating his partner.'

Myth 6
'A woman's vagina is the best part of her body for receiving sexual stimulation.'

Myth 7
'All good sex ends in orgasm. In really good sex, both partners have orgasm at the same time.'

Myth 8
'Sex ends at fifty.'

In place of these myths, we suggest an alternative view of sex which we think is more realistically based. We suggest that a good sexual relationship is one in which both partners have orgasms most of the time, somehow or other. It doesn't matter what sexual techniques they use, so long as they are comfortable and acceptable for both partners. There are so many ways of expressing and sharing your sexuality that there is no need to over-emphasise any one sexual technique (such as intercourse), nor any need for either partner to put up with a sexual technique he or she doesn't really like. And it doesn't matter which partner may sometimes not have orgasm, so long as they are both content that they have orgasms as often as they want.

to be met by understanding and closeness from your partner.

If you are both beginners, then we recommend you read and discuss the sex myths together. Ideally, go on and read and discuss one or more of the recommended books. Yes, you will feel embarrassed – but you know how to cope with that – and it will be a lot less embarrassing than fumbling in the dark. And, we would add, unwanted pregnancies never enhance relationships.

Reading and discussing the sex myths or a good sexual education book kills two birds with the one stone. One, you systematically share accurate information about sex and remove popular misinformation; and two, you gradually replace embarrassment with good, clear communication, even about potentially awkward matters. And that's a good way to end your loneliness problems.

CONSOLIDATION BREAK

Do you need one now? If loneliness has been a major stressor for you, and you are going to need to apply our suggestions above, that will almost certainly take some time and effort. Don't neglect the parts of your stress-management programme that you have already begun, but be wary about adding any new goals or steps until you have your programme for finding and deepening relationships well in hand. This does not mean you have to stop at this point until you are married – obviously the process of making relationships takes time, and you won't be doing that to the exclusion of all else – just don't overload yourself with too many new tasks at any one time.

10
JOB REDESIGN

In a sense, this chapter is a ring-in, because what it describes isn't really suitable for self-help. But job redesign represents such a major possibility for stress-management for so many people that we did not feel we could leave it out of a book on that topic.

Many of the stress-management skills described elsewhere in this book will help you cope better with a stressful job. But notice that the implicit goal is to **cope**, not to **thrive**, because changing how you cope hasn't changed how stressful your job is. Often coping with a stressful job is the only realistic goal a person can set, at least in the short run, because no individual worker can bring about the kind of changes necessary to make most jobs less stressful, and economic conditions may make it difficult to leave a stressful job. In any case, the next one may well be no better.

So our goal in this chapter is to alert you to long-term possibilities for making your work less stressful. You may occupy some executive position where you work, and recognise that what we are proposing is very much in your interests, and in the interests of your corporation or whatever. Or you may be a worker, at middle-management or workface level, and recognise that the way your job is designed makes it a source of stress for you. Some of the most successful European job redesign projects have begun at the initiative of one or two people. The following information may help you convince others who work with you that job redesign is in everybody's interests.

WORK AND STRESS

Despite the usual jokes, work is not necessarily a source of dystress. In fact, as we discussed in the last chapter, **not** having worthwhile work to do is a common cause of depression. So why does there seem to be so much stress associated with work today?

Before the industrial revolution, most people did work with a considerable variety in it. Many people were almost self-sufficient, living on what they themselves produced. Of course, there was recognisable specialisation: you might be a farmhand, or a sailor, or a cobbler. But even these jobs meant a mixture of tasks. The extreme specialisation in jobs that is almost the norm today is a relatively new way of organising work.

As machines were invented and developed to do work which was previously done by hand, new jobs to tend the machines were created. As workplaces grew larger, the social relationships and co-operation which had been part of the traditional, smaller workplace, such as a tradesman's shop, were lost. In their place grew the division between employer and employees that now characterises much of modern industrial relations.

Many employers adopted the still too popular view that, on the one hand, a machine costs a lot of money and represents a major capital investment, while an employee, on the other, should cost as little as possible and does not represent much investment. He or she could always be discarded and replaced, if faulty.

The two sides adopted predictable views of each other. To the employees, employers were mean, selfish, greedy exploiters of labour, only interested in making maximum personal profits, regardless of how that affected others, especially their workers. To the employers, employees were lazy, selfish, dishonest and careless, out to get as much out of the boss as possible, while putting in as little effort as possible. They needed to be strictly controlled to get any work out of them, and to prevent them from doing the wrong thing. The outcome has been so-called scientific management, on the one hand, and dogmatic trade unionism, on the other.

The notion of scientific management is most associated
with Professor Frederick Taylor, whose book on the topic
was published in 1911. His approach regarded the worker as
an extension or servant of the machine. Jobs were designed
to meet the needs of the machine because this was the
'logical' way to get maximum productivity. For people who

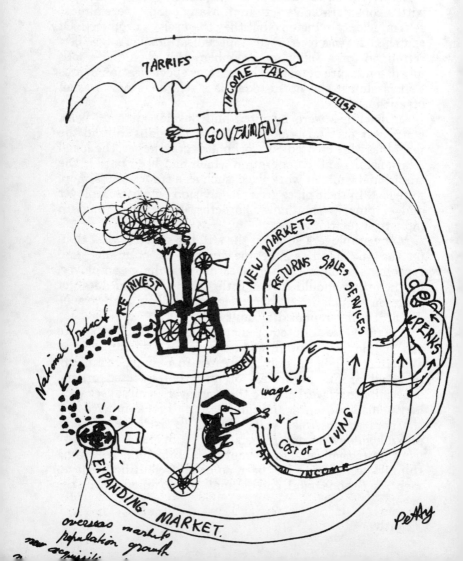

claimed to be 'scientific' and 'efficient' in their approach to work design, this was a remarkably silly idea.

It may have involved careful study of the characteristics of machines, but it ignored the characteristics of the human beings who were supposed to operate the machines. People are not, and don't like being regarded as, simple extensions or servants of their machines.

TRADITIONAL WORK DESIGN

The scientific management approach to work design has ten basic principles, all of which are intended to maximise the efficiency of the workers and to improve productivity. In fact, each has predictable effects on the workers, effects which are counter-productive. Let's consider them:

1 External design control means that engineers or managers design how the work will be done because they are the experts. The effect is to reduce for the workers any sense of worthwhile participation in their jobs. Instructions from the experts on how to do the job become no more than the boss telling the workers what to do.

2 Specialisation means that the flow of work is broken down into the smallest possible steps, and the smallest possible number of these is grouped into a job to reduce training needs and costs. The effect on the worker is to create boredom which is a major stressor.

3 Technological dominance means that the work is designed to meet the needs of the technology and the physical layout of the workplace, so as to get the most out of these costly investments. The effect on the worker is to create a feeling of alienation, and to lower his self-esteem as it is made obvious that workers are valued less than the machines.

4 Repetition means that the activities within a job are made as simple and repetitive as possible, again to reduce training needs. The effect on the worker is to reduce creativity, and to contribute to boredom and apathy.

5 Deskilling means that the skills needed for each job are reduced as much as possible, following from **2** and **4** above, again to reduce or even eliminate training needs. The effect on the worker is to stifle any desire to learn more about her work, and to add to boredom and apathy.

6 Equalised, distributed workloads mean that the various tasks making up the whole production process are shared across individual jobs so that every worker has a similar workload, because after all that's only fair. The effect on the worker is to take away any sense of responsibility for the whole process, or its finished product.

7 Work measurement then becomes necessary to see that each worker is producing his share of the workload determined in **6**. If the workload is not measured, the workers can't be trusted to deliver it. The effect on the worker is to put artificial limits on his performance since there is no point doing more than the set workload, and further to increase alienation because it just shows the boss doesn't trust you.

8 Individual financial incentives are used to induce employees to work harder, because money is believed to be the only reason they work at all. This reinforces the workers' belief that the only reward they will get from their jobs will be more money, and to create a competitive atmosphere while reducing social support amongst them.

9 Minimal social interaction amongst the workers is necessary so that they are not distracted from their work and do not waste valuable worktime in idle conversations with each other. The effect on the workers is to reduce social support in the workplace further and increase social alienation.

10 Close supervision is naturally necessary to co-ordinate the whole process and to control the individual worker's activities since none of them now takes responsibility for the whole process nor can they be trusted to work properly without supervision. This can either create dependency on the supervisors and take away the workers' initiative, responsibility and self-esteem; or it can create resentment against the supervisors and acts of rebellion, such as avoiding work.

Where a workforce has increasing educational levels and rising expectations the application of traditional scientific managements has, to paraphrase one of the leading

Australian exponents in this field, Professor Dexter Dunphy, predictable effects. It reduces commitment, creativity, responsibility and social support, and creates either dependency or rebellion. It lowers employees' self-esteem and so, we add, increases their dystress.

JOB TYPE, STRESS AND RECREATION

There is now little doubt about our addition of dystress to Dunphy's list of the undesirable effects of old-fashioned job design. Professor Bertill Gardell, one of the leading Scandinavian researchers in this field, has suggested that you can divide jobs into four classes, depending on how much control the worker has over his activities, and on how low or high are the demands of the job. The classification looks like this:

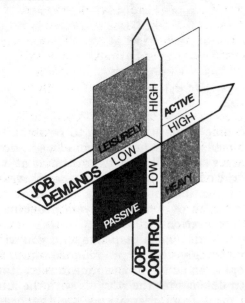

CLASSIFICATION OF FOUR MAJOR JOB TYPES

According to Gardell, as you move from high to low worker control, and from low to high demands – from 'leisurely' towards 'heavy' jobs – you get jobs with increasing strain. As you would expect now, this is accompanied by increasing physical illness and psychological problems, including stress.

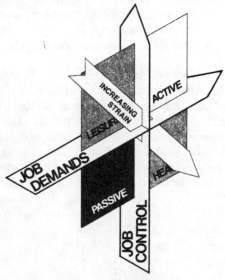

RELATIONSHIP BETWEEN JOB TYPE AND SYMPTOMS

But, some people argue, there have to be some boring, dirty, heavy or menial tasks, and someone has to do them. After all, you don't spend all your waking hours at work. If your job is a bad one, you can make up for it with good recreations and relationships. It's an argument that is implied by the action of some employers providing their employees with recreation facilities.

In principle, this idea looks plausible, and you will have noticed that we strongly suggest you manage your stress, in part, by developing an active programme of recreation and exercise. The trouble is that the workers with the jobs that would benefit most from recreations are the ones who participate least.

As you move from high to low worker control, and from high to low job demands - from 'active' towards 'passive' jobs - you get decreasing participation in leisure and political activity. As you may have already noticed yourself, the people most likely to be actively involved in sports,

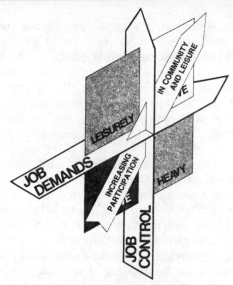

**RELATIONSHIP BETWEEN JOB TYPE
AND SOCIAL PARTICIPATION**

community affairs, recreations and so on, are the ones in 'active' jobs with a lot of control over their work and interesting, challenging jobs.

Of course there is the usual chicken-and-egg question: do workers in stressful jobs wind up with little recreation because of the effects of their work? Or do workers of a particular 'type' wind up with both the stressful jobs and little recreation? In practice, it doesn't matter. The clear point is that, without some special intervention, like redesigning their work or giving them stress-management courses, or both, many workers will remain victims of stressful lifestyles.

All of this raises an obvious question: if most jobs are so bad for the people who do them, why do we keep designing jobs that way?

WHY TRADITIONAL JOB DESIGN PERSISTS

There are six basic reasons for the continuation of attempts to apply the old job design principles.

First, a fresh attempt to apply them, perhaps in one of their newer, disguised forms, such as organisation and methods study or efficiency study, can produce temporary increases in productivity. So can painting the walls, changing the light bulbs, or almost anything, as has been demonstrated in a famous series of experiments, which found the Hawthorn effect. Changing almost anything in a workplace can temporarily improve productivity. Perhaps it's because everyone expects it to, or because of the increased attention. But whatever the reason, the Hawthorn effect wears off.

Second, the experts, like engineers and managers of various kinds, who are responsible for present job design, have an obvious interest in presenting their expertise as effective. Like all of us, they would like to believe they know what they are doing and that they do it reasonably well. So they are under some natural pressure to ignore or disregard any negative consequences of their decisions, or to blame them on someone or something else, like the workers' laziness or stupidity.

Third, in the old approach managers appear to have control, which they believe is their right as owners or experts, and essential if they are to run things properly. In practice, attempts to exert this control are often very counter-productive. Even attempting to sack a worker can lead to a strike under some circumstances, while other heavy-handed attempts at control of workers only inspire employees to look for new ways of defeating the rules or sabotaging the system.

Fourth, the old approach actually produces behaviour in the employees which fits the employers' traditional views of them: employers treat their employees like overgrown or untrustworthy kids, and then complain when they act like that.

Fifth, to return to the other half of the industrial relations gulf we mentioned earlier, trades unions are often major obstacles to any significant development in job design. Sometimes the membership of a trade union is defined in terms of a traditionally designed and recognised job, a definition which is entrenched in industrial awards which the union guards very jealously. Suggestions that jobs, and therefore union membership, be redesigned are not welcomed.

The rigidity of traditional job designers is matched by the suspicion of some union officials over any attempt to improve productivity. The fact that the process is also intended to improve the workers' well-being is obviously a smokescreen put up by the boss to hide his real motives.

And sixth, alternatives to traditional job design are not well known, in two senses. Many people, employers and employees, have never heard any of the above criticism of traditional job design nor of the existence of other approaches. And, we have found, many of the people with some introduction to the area have not really understood it at all, and are really only perpetuating old practices in new guises. So, what is job redesign?

REDESIGNING JOBS

A detailed description of the process of job redesign is set out in Professor Dexter Dunphy's book, *Organisational Change by Choice* (published by McGraw-Hill). This is a technical textbook intended for professionals working in the area, not lightweight reading. We will give only an outline of the process because, as we said at the beginning, we don't think job redesign is for self-help. An exceptional employer with a strong interest in this topic, starting a new business, preferably with employees who have never worked anywhere else, may be able to implement a job redesign process without outside help.

In our companion self-help book on relationship enhancement, *Living and Loving Together,* we emphasise that couples with a history of conflict often have trouble attempting self-help for their relationship because the self-help programme becomes just something more to fight about. So in the workplace where employer and employee don't really trust each other's motives.

As we see it, real job redesign becomes a never-ending process of improvement of jobs and productivity and, once it is established, genuine co-operation is the order of the day and outside consultants are no longer needed. But getting it launched seems to be much easier if you do use appropriate consultants. The consultants can act as neutral mediators to facilitate overcoming established mistrust and suspicion, and they make an important training contribution to help people master new skills needed for the job redesign process, such as co-operative problem solving. That is, they contribute skills identified as helpful by the participants, not content. That is supplied by the participants, because that is their expertise.

Job redesign proceeds through a series of meetings intended to gain the involvement and support of management, workers, unions and any other critical groups, and through a series of practical research projects to determine how the work is presently done, where redesign is needed, what new approaches to try, and how they work.

We strongly believe the essential ingredient in successful job redesign is participation. All those in the workplace – whether it's a factory, a bank, a school, or whatever – must believe they have meaningful involvement in deciding what is changed, and how. This taps into the wealth of often ignored practical knowledge and ideas in the workforce, and begins the development of greater commitment to and involvement in the work.

In some approaches to job redesign, the common interest in the success of the workplace is emphasised by agreeing to share equally between the workplace (say, a company) and its workers any increase in productivity resulting from the redesign process. Of course, this common interest already exists, in as much as everybody loses their jobs if the workplace fails completely.

Job redesign, especially where increased productivity is shared in this way, should change the motivational forces that operated under old job design. Now absenteeism, waste, accidents, sloppy and slow work affect everybody, as does poor management.

Job redesign is not a theoretical, academic exercise, even if it has not been tried much yet in Australia. To date, there have been over 500 studies involving different approaches to redesigning jobs in real workplaces. The results of these practical tests have been:

- A few failures: job redesign is not a panacea nor yet a guaranteed success. Of course, we are learning from the failures, making success more likely in the future.
- Significant improvements in work satisfaction, associated with reduced dystress.

- Decreased staff turnover and absenteeism representing decreased training costs for the employer and reduced illness, and thus stress, in employees.
- Significant increases in productivity, in both quantity and quality.
- An increase in the number of work problems being solved.
- Improved industrial relations (from which we all win).
- Increased work efficiency, and lower wastage and costs.

Not all of these results were obtained in each application, but the people-improving and dystress-reducing effects seem to be constant.

Acknowledgements

The authors and publisher wish to thank the following for permission to reproduce copyright material:

Alan Foley Pty Ltd for the cartoon on page 188; Bruce Petty for the cartoon on page 238 from *Petty's Australia and how it works* (Penguin, 1976); and United Feature Syndicate, Inc. for the cartoons on pages 2, 55, 84, 111, 129, 163, 170 and 212.

Dr Aaron T. Beck for the Beck Depression Inventory on pages 190 *et seq.* (Further information about this scale and/or permission to use the scale may be obtained from the Center for Cognitive Therapy, Room 602, 133 South 36th Street, Philadelphia, PA 19104, USA.) ● Dr S.D. Hollon for permission to use the Automatic Thoughts Questionnaire on page 33 from S.D. Hollon and T.C. Kendall, 'Cognitive Self-Statements in Depression: Development of an Automatic Thoughts Questionnaire', *Cognitive Therapy and Research*, 1980. ● Drs L.H. Miller and A.D. Smith of the Boston Medical Center for the Miller-Smith Lifestyle Inventory on pages 37-9. ● Professor R.W. Novaco of the Psychology Department of the University of California for Novaco's Dimensions of Anger Reactions Scale reproduced on page 37. ● Pergamon Press Ltd for the Holmes-Rahe Survey of Recent Experiences on pages 31-2, reprinted from the *Journal of Psychosomatic Research*, Vol. 11, 1967. ● Charles D. Spielberger, PhD, Professor of Psychology and Director of the Center for Research in Behavioral Medicine and Community Psychology at the University of South Florida for the Spielberger State-Trait Anxiety Inventory on pages 35-6 from his book, *Understanding Stress and Anxiety* (Nelson, 1979). ● Dr Jeffrey Young of the University of Pennsylvania for the Loneliness scale reproduced on pages 217 *et seq.*